Computer Vision and Image P

Computer Vision and Image Processing

Tim Morris

Department of Computation
UMIST

First published 2004 by
PALGRAVE MACMILLAN
Houndmills, Basingstoke, Hampshire RG21 6XS and
175 Fifth Avenue, New York, N. Y. 10010
Companies and representatives throughout the world

PALGRAVE MACMILLAN is the global academic imprint of the Palgrave
Macmillan division of St. Martin's Press, LLC and of Palgrave Macmillan Ltd.
Macmillan® is a registered trademark in the United States, United Kingdom
and other countries. Palgrave is a registered trademark in the European
Union and other countries.

ISBN 0–333–99451–5

This book is printed on paper suitable for recycling and made from fully
managed and sustained forest sources.

A catalogue record for this book is available from the British Library.

10   9   8   7   6   5   4   3   2   1
13 12 11 10 09 08 07 06 05 04

Printed in China

To Karen, Joshua and Hannah

Contents

Preface

Although the first images were coded for digital transmission in the 1920s, computer vision and image processing are subjects that originated in the mid-1960s. At that time, computers that were able to do significant processing within realistic time-scales began to be developed, and the Space Race was starting to generate large numbers of digital images that needed processing. Since that time, improvements in hardware cost and power have given researchers and practitioners the ability to implement an extremely wide range of image processing/computer vision applications and make them widely accessible. Although we may not realise it, computer vision does have an impact on our daily lives.

Today, image processing and computer vision are subjects that have reached a level of maturity. Much has been discovered regarding how images are processed to achieve various goals, but much still remains to be discovered. We could say that the foundations have been laid and the house is now being built. It is the aim of this text to present the foundational material of this subject and equip students to explore the rest of the building site.

The text is based on a course that has been taught at UMIST for several years. I would like to thank all of the students that have passed through it for their helpful comments and my postgraduate students for their help in software development. David Young, Dave Mort, Dave Britch and Osama Elshehri deserve special mention.

A website is associated with the text, containing software for processing images (written in Java) and video sequences (written in C/C++). Also included are copies of the images presented in the text and the transparencies used in the lectures. The website may be found at http://www.palgrave.com/resources.

1
Introduction

1.1 What are image processing and computer vision?

Many definitions for 'image processing' and 'computer vision' have been proposed, but it is usually accepted that image processing involves manipulating a digital image to generate a second image that differs in some respects from the first, whereas computer vision involves extracting numerical or symbolic information from images; see Figure 1.1.

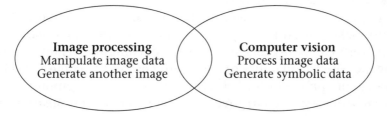

Image processing
Manipulate image data
Generate another image

Computer vision
Process image data
Generate symbolic data

Figure 1.1 Definitions of image processing and computer vision.

For example, a weather station might capture an image of rainfall intensity using the appropriate radar sensor. Each pixel in this image has a value that is proportional to the amount of rain falling in the corresponding area. This is usually presented by converting the data to a colour image (image processing). The image might also be interpreted to recognise areas of higher than average rainfall and potential flood risk (computer vision).

It is important to realise that alternative definitions exist: these are young disciplines, and there is as yet incomplete agreement over the subjects' boundaries. Indeed, the boundary is least distinct between image processing and computer vision, hence the large overlap in Figure 1.1.

In this text, we are going to examine the methods by which digital images are processed to extract useful information.

1.2 Historical overview

Although image processing and computer vision are relatively new subjects, the first digital image was created in the 1920s when photographs were converted to a numerical format for transmission by Morse code across the Atlantic by telegraph. In this process, the photograph was divided into small areas that were assigned a numerical code that depended on the distribution of brightnesses in them. The code was transmitted and the photograph reconstructed using specially designed printing blocks. This was a time-consuming process – each photograph would take several hours to code, transmit and print. However, the alternative was to send the photograph across the ocean by steamship, which could take over a week.

The process of coding, transmitting by telephone and printing photographs did not change conceptually for some 50 years, but the time taken to complete the process became shorter as the hardware that was used became more sophisticated.

Major advances in image processing began to be made in the 1960s. The US and Russian space programmes began to generate large amounts of image data that needed to have artefacts removed and to be enhanced for viewing. Simultaneously, advances in the technology meant that computers became powerful enough to store images and to process them within realistic time frames and to display the images.

Since then, we have seen the cost and availability of computer hardware change to make powerful computers available to the mass market – sufficiently powerful for many image processing or computer vision applications. With the increased availability of computing power has come a vast increase in the range of applications of image processing and computer vision systems. From being restricted to government, university or industrial laboratories, these systems have emerged into everyday life; we see their output in our entertainment and news, in medical imaging devices, in scientific research, in exploration and in many other activities.

1.3 Sample applications

Three simple applications of vision systems will be described. These have been selected on the basis of their familiarity with everyday situations.

1.3.1 Optical character recognition

Systems that recognise characters in an image have been in existence for many years. Their applications include simple interpretation of printed text, reading postcodes on envelopes, recognising signatures on cheques and reading car registration plates. In these systems, we may identify three levels of difficulty:

- Recognising printed text
- Recognising hand printed text
- Recognising cursively written text

Printed text is characterised by its quality and regularity. Any printed character will have a consistent appearance and it can therefore be recognised by comparison with a prototype. Figure 1.2 illustrates the process. A page of text was scanned (a) and the area surrounding one character (b) was copied into the prototype. The output image is the measure of similarity between the prototype and the different parts of the input image. Figure 1.2(d) shows a profile along the line indicated in (c): it is apparent that the largest response occurs where the prototype and image actually match, but large responses are also seen at locations where there are partial matches. A real character recognition system would require a prototype for every object that is to be

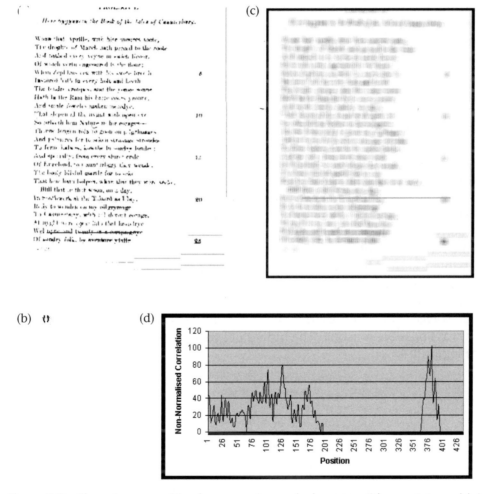

Figure 1.2 Character recognition by comparing each character with a prototype. (a) A scanned page of text; (b) a prototype for the character '0' derived from this image; (c) output of the comparison: the darker the pixel, the better the match between the scanned image and the prototype; (d) magnitude of the result along the line indicated in (c).

Figure 1.3   Samples of one handwritten character written by one person over a period of time.

recognised: each character (lower and upper case) and each punctuation mark. A set of prototypes is required for each font and font size. Any practical system will require a huge number of prototypes if it is to use this technique. Fortunately, other techniques are available.

Hand printed text is of a lower quality and is less regular. Hand printed text would need to be recognised by systems used for automatic sorting of the post (letters are sorted using the postcode) or by systems that read forms filled in by hand. Figure 1.3 shows samples of a letter written by one person over a period of time. Due to the irregularity of the character, we cannot recognise it by comparison with a template. Instead, we must use the structural characteristics to identify the letter. For example, the upper-case letter 'A' is composed of a horizontal stroke in the middle of the character and two diagonal strokes flaring outwards from the top central portion of the character. In fact, every character can be broken down to a set of strokes. If we are able to process the character image and identify those strokes, then we will be able to recognise the character.

The other major problem associated with recognising hand printed text is actually separating each character from its neighbours: adjacent characters can overlap each other and can therefore be difficult to separate; it is also possible for the strokes of an individual character to be separated and to appear as two separate characters.

Recognition of handwritten (cursive) text is a problem that has not yet been solved. The text is so irregular that templates cannot be used; neither is it always possible to isolate the individual strokes that make up a character – see Figure 1.4.

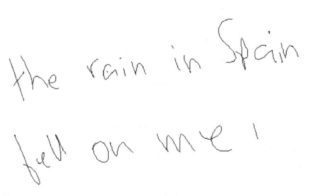

Figure 1.4   A sample of handwritten (cursive) text.

1.3.2 Biometry

Biometry is the science of identifying people from their physical characteristics. In the context of image processing and computer vision, this will imply recognition using images of the physical characteristics. Recognising individuals from images of their fingerprints is a problem that has been investigated for many years, as has recognition using the individual's face. One characteristic that has received attention recently is the iris. The striations on the iris are unique to each individual and are therefore ideally suited as a means of identification, for example to control access or for personal banking. Figure 1.5 illustrates an overview of the system.

An iris scanner will firstly identify the subject's eyes in a head and shoulders image. The iris region is then identified and resampled, converting the annular region into a rectangular one. Different lighting conditions will cause the pupil to dilate or contract, hence changing the size of the iris, so the resampling will ensure that the radial dimension is sampled with a constant number of samples, irrespective of its size. The iris region is then numerically transformed and represented by a small number of coefficients. These coefficients have been shown to be unique to each individual.

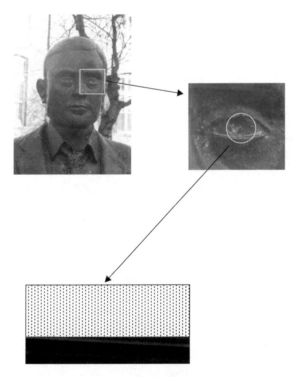

Figure 1.5 Processing stages of the iris recognition system. The eye is identified in the head and shoulders image and resampled to give a size-independent representation of the iris.

1.3.3 Aerial photography

Aerial photography finds many applications: mapping, land use analysis, land use change, entertainment etc. Although images may be captured from altitudes ranging from a few hundred metres to a few hundred kilometres, they are all treated in a similar fashion to generate the view that is seen when looking vertically towards the ground.

When an image is captured, we must record the exact location and attitude of the camera – that is, where the camera is situated relative to a fixed datum and what direction it is pointing in. The captured image will be distorted if the camera is not orientated vertically, since that would capture an oblique view of the ground; see Figure 1.6. The image will also be distorted, to a greater or lesser degree, by the camera's optical system: a short focal length lens, having a wide field of view, will distort objects such that those towards the periphery of the image appear to be larger than they actually are (other altitude-related distortions are also apparent).

Figure 1.6 Aerial photography. Images must be captured with the camera pointing vertically downwards to avoid distorted images.

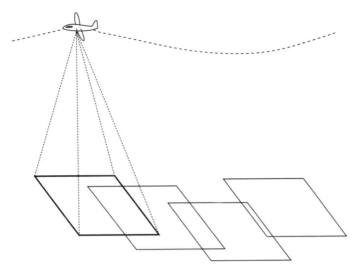

Figure 1.7 Building a mosaic image from a set of aerial photographs.

If, as is often the case, we wish to assemble a number of images into a larger mosaic, we must either ensure that the camera is moved along a level, straight path and images are taken at regular intervals, or we must record the exact positions of the camera as images are captured and subsequently modify the image data. The latter alternative effectively resamples the data to compute the image that would be captured if the camera had been moved along a level and straight path; see Figure 1.7. The images will also be corrected for any optical distortions.

1.4 Routemap to the book

A computer vision system will include some or all of the components shown in Figure 1.8, in the order demonstrated. In this text we shall discuss the properties of image capture devices, but will not examine any specific device. The starting point is a captured digital image. Chapter 2 deals with **image representation**: what do we require of an image capture device in order to have suitable data for the task at hand? Chapters 3–7 deal with the components of the vision system presented in Figure 1.8.

Enhancement is any operation that is applied to the data to remove the degradations that might have been introduced by the capture process: optical degradations mentioned above, the effect of camera movement or any loss of clarity caused by atmospheric conditions or lighting. Figure 1.9 presents some examples.

Feature extraction operations aim to identify structures in the image that are useful for recognising the objects being analysed. They might include the

Captured data

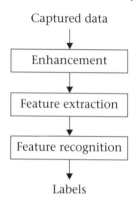

Enhancement

Feature extraction

Feature recognition

Labels

Figure 1.8 Overview of a computer vision system.

(a)

(b)

(c)

Figure 1.9 Examples of degradations to be removed by enhancement. (a) A poorly focused image; (b) a motion blurred image; (c) an underexposed image.

Figure 1.10 Examples of feature extraction.

pixels that constitute an area, or the straight boundaries between regions (Figure 1.10).

Feature recognition processes will use the features just extracted to assign a label to the image or to parts of the image by comparing the features against those derived from previously labelled objects.

Chapter 8 describes the architectures that have been suggested for computer vision systems. The flow diagram of Figure 1.8 might suggest that each step must be completed before the following one can be started, and that we cannot return to a step if the process subsequently fails. This is not a desirable property of any vision system; this chapter discusses the methods of implementing intelligent control.

Chapter 9 discusses the methods that have been proposed for tracking moving objects. We are primarily concerned with tracking these objects in real time, i.e. using live data. This imposes a hard constraint on the processing; we examine methods by which the constraint may be met.

Finally, Chapter 10 addresses the problem of image coding. Any moderately sized image will use a large amount of storage resource if it is not compressed in some way. The chapter examines solutions to the problem.

1.5 Bibliography

Gonzalez and Woods (2002) present a detailed historical review of the development of the subject. Additionally, Castleman (1996), Haralick and Shapiro

(1992), Jain *et al.* (1995), Schalkoff (1989) and Forsyth and Ponce (2003) provide a more advanced coverage of the topics covered in this text.

A number of websites and newsgroups have useful information. Probably the most important is the Computer Vision homepage at `http://www-2. cs.cmu.edu/afs/cs/project/cil/ftp/html/vision.html`, which has links to most computer vision research groups worldwide, research reports and demonstration software.

Three useful newsgroups are also active: `sci.image.processing`, `comp.ai. vision` and `sci.med.vision`.

Supporting material for this text is available on the web at `http:// www.co.umist.ac.uk/~dtm/IP4.html`.

1.6 Exercises

1.1   Suggest everyday problems that an image processing system could sensibly solve. Outline the tasks that the system would be required to perform. What difficulties would the system encounter? Are non-vision system solutions better?

1.2   Describe in outline an image processing system you have encountered. Identify the separate components of the system.

2
Image representation

This chapter presents material that is necessary to understand how a digital image is stored and represented: specifically the number of pixels that can or should be used to represent the image, and the number of shades of grey or number of colours that can or should be used. We also consider camera calibration, which is important when we must relate image coordinates to a location in the real world. Finally, we examine the parallels between computer vision systems and the human visual system.

After reading this chapter, you should be able to specify the image resolution required for a vision system to achieve a specific task. You should also understand how image and world coordinates are related – this will be used in later chapters that discuss methods of determining the shape of objects. Finally, you should appreciate the similarities and differences between human and computer vision systems.

2.1 Introduction

Many authors suggest that parallels exist between computer vision systems and the human visual system. There is no doubt that there are similarities, but there are also subtle differences. The human visual system is examined in this chapter, since an understanding of the human visual system can help in appreciating how computer vision systems might be designed. In particular, an examination of how humans solve visual problems can be beneficial when designing algorithms for processing visual data.

The real starting point of our examination of computer vision systems is with a captured digital image that is ready for processing. The reason for this is that images are captured using a multitude of devices and it is therefore not practicable to discuss them all. However, the processing of images cannot be considered without also considering the capture of the data: the data that is captured will determine what information can be extracted from it. If the image has so small a resolution that objects cannot be seen clearly, then this will obviously limit the amount of information that can be gleaned from it. An early part of this chapter discusses some of the image capture modalities;

the remainder of the book assumes that camera-based systems are used for capture: either still or video cameras.

Of primary importance in the design of any computer vision system is a consideration of the requirements of image capture without reference to how the data is collected. That is, we must consider spatial and brightness (or colour) resolutions and relate these to what are required of a particular task in order to capture images that contain the information required to solve the given problem. We also consider factors that limit the resolution that can be achieved by a specific image capture system.

We shall examine how captured data is represented. Monochrome image data is invariably represented using one storage unit per pixel, whether this storage unit is an eight bit value or greater. Colour image data, following the old tristimulus theory, is represented using a triplet of storage units for each pixel. However, the triplet may be organised in a variety of ways. These are discussed and analysed. Reasons for preferring one representation over any others are presented.

Camera calibration is discussed. This is the process by which relationships are established between image coordinates and a coordinate system tied to the real world. The process involves two steps, one relating the location and orientation of the camera to the world coordinate frame, and the second relating image coordinates to coordinates in a frame tied to the camera, which is essentially the process of correcting the image data for the defects introduced by the camera's optical system.

2.2 The human visual system

The human visual system provides a useful analogy with computer vision systems and is therefore a good starting point in our discussion of them. Often, when designing a computer vision system, the fact that a human can solve a visual problem is the only indication that the problem is indeed soluble.

The visual world is perceived because light reflected from surfaces in it is focused onto light-sensitive cells in the eye. These convert the light energy to electrical signals that are transmitted to the brain and there interpreted as the objects we 'see'. Figure 2.1 illustrates schematically the gross anatomy of the eye and will be used to explain this mechanism. The eye contains structures whose purposes are first to regulate the amount of light entering it and then to focus rays of light from objects at varying ranges onto the retina. Finally, the retina itself encodes the nerve pattern into nerve signals.

Light reflected from a surface in the scene being viewed is focused onto the retina in a two-stage process. The curved outer surface of the eyeball provides the primary focusing, but the variable focusing that is required to enable us to see objects at different ranges is achieved by changing the refractive power of the eye's lens, a process known as accommodation.

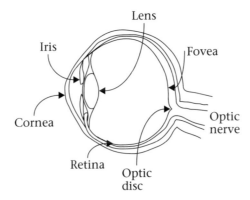

Figure 2.1 Schematic diagram of the cross-section through a human eye.

The iris regulates the amount of light entering the eye. In dark conditions, more light is needed to enable us to see clearly and consequently the iris dilates. The iris contracts in bright conditions, so admitting less light. However, the iris diameter changes only by a factor of four and its area therefore changes by a factor of 16, which is much less than the range of brightness levels over which we can comfortably see. The changing iris size provides fine control over the eye's adaptation; the major control is achieved by the retina itself changing its sensitivity – in bright conditions the retina is actually less sensitive to light. This is analogous to the case of a photographic camera: exposure control is achieved by choosing film of varying sensitivity and by altering the aperture of the lens.

Anatomical studies reveal that the retina contains some hundreds of millions of light-sensitive cells, whereas the optic nerve that transmits information from the eye to the brain has only some hundreds of thousands of individual nerve fibres. A significant amount of data reduction must therefore occur in the retina. It is suggested that the retina sends difference signals onwards to the brain to achieve the data reduction.

Spatial and temporal differences are computed. Spatial differences are simply the differences in the image data between nearby regions of an image; the computer vision analogy is edge detection. Temporal differences are the differences between the same region in temporally adjacent images. The latter effect can by observed by staring fixedly at a static scene without blinking or moving the eyes. Gradually the scene will fade to grey as the temporal differences fall to zero. Any movement, in the scene or the eyes, will result in the scene being regenerated.

When we view a scene, three factors influence the quality of the perceived data: the angular resolution of the eyes, the colour sensitivity and the brightness sensitivity. These in turn are determined by the eye's physiology: principally the number and distribution over the retina of light-sensitive cells and how these cells react to light of different brightness and wavelength.

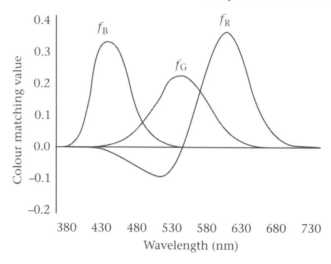

Figure 2.2   Sensitivity curves of 'red', 'green' and 'blue' receptors.

The retina consists of two types of light-sensitive cell, called rods and cones because of their shapes. The rods are generally sensitive to the intensity of the light striking them and therefore give a monochromatic response. They are also more sensitive in lower light levels than the cones; hence we are unable to see colours at night. The cones are differentially sensitive to light of varying wavelength. Figure 2.2 is a sketch graph of the three types of cones' reactivity to light. It is apparent that there are cones that are more sensitive in the red, green and blue regions of the spectrum, and that each type of cone is relatively insensate to light outside of its specialised wavelength range. Although it is incorrect to say so, we often suggest that the cones are red-, green- or blue-sensitive. The rods and cones are distributed across the retina as shown in Figure 2.3. The colour-sensitive cones are more densely packed on or near the optic axis and are largely absent from the remainder of the retina. It is not surprising that the processing power of the brain's visual centres is largely devoted to data received from this region. A consequence of this is that our peripheral vision is almost monochrome. Conversely, the rods are most highly concentrated in an annulus surrounding the eye's optical axis and are distributed more evenly over the rest of the retinal surface. The rod's distribution has two consequences: our spatial resolution in the peripheral visual regions is very poor (so an object must be large or fast-moving to be seen); and since the rods have their highest concentration just off-axis, we can see dimly illuminated objects most clearly by viewing them slightly askance.

The maximum concentration of light cells is in the foveal region on the eye's optic axis. The cells in this region are exclusively colour-sensitive cones, there may be approximately 2000 cones in a region that is

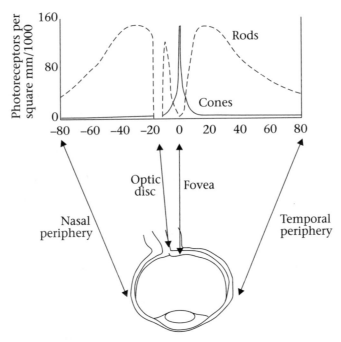

Figure 2.3   Distribution of rods and cones over the retina.

approximately 100 μm across. The sizes of the cones vary slightly – the smallest are 1 μm across and subtend an angle of 20 seconds of arc. This figure suggests a size for the smallest discernible object of 0.2 mm at a range of 1 m. In fact our visual acuity can be better than this because we make use of information from more than a single rod or cone in creating our understanding of the world.

Physiological studies have shown that at any one brightness adaptation, only about 40 shades of brightness may be distinguished. If you were to fixate on a single spot in an image, you would distinguish just those 40 shades. We are able to differentiate much more than this number as we scan over an image by using the differential information; in a sense our brightness adaptation alters as we scan over the image.

Colour vision is a more complex phenomenon. Newton suggested that there were seven colours of light that generated white when mixed. On that basis it would have been sensible to suggest cells sensitive to all seven colours. However, Thomas Young in 1801 proposed that there were in fact three identifiably different colour receptors. The basis of Young's theory was the observation that most colours could be matched by mixing different proportions of a red, a green and a blue primary source. These ideas are still in use – in fact they form the origin of the colour representation models to be discussed below.

2.3 Image capture

Images may be captured using a wide range of instruments, ranging from radio telescopes imaging the far reaches of the universe to electron microscopes investigating the smallest scale phenomena. More familiar will be, for example, the images collected by weather satellites and displayed daily during weather forecasts. Despite the range of data capture modalities, the majority of computer vision applications capture images generated by video cameras.

Whilst there are innumerable data capture methods, they all share the property of being able to transform some type of energy into a visible form. For example, a radio telescope will measure the intensities of radio waves received from various orientations in the sky and assemble an image; an ultrasound scanner will measure the intensity of the sound pulse reflected from structures within a body, and again the data will be assembled into an image.

An illuminated object is illustrated schematically in Figure 2.4. Light energy from a source falls on the object. A proportion of that light is reflected and some may fall on the light transducer (e.g. the detector). It should be noted that this is a generalised scenario; self-illuminated objects exist that do not require a source of illumination. The detector could be a video camera, a radio telescope or whatever instrument is used to convert energy into an image.

If a video camera is used for image conversion, it will transform the illuminated scene into an electrical signal. An analogue video camera will output a standard PAL or NTSC signal; a digital camera will output digitised data. The analogue signal must then be converted into a digital format. A frame

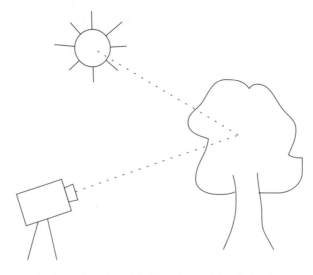

Figure 2.4 Image capture. An object is illuminated by light from an energy source. Reflected light may fall on a detector and be captured.

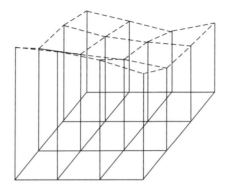

Figure 2.5 Rectangular sampling grid.

grabbing card that is mounted in the computer usually accomplishes this task. It will place the digitised image in the computer's memory or memory situated on the card ready to be transferred to the computer.

Whatever type of detector is used to capture the image data, it will transform a continuous brightness function into a discretely sampled image. For convenience, the sampling is usually performed on a rectangular grid; that is, the samples are equally separated in two orthogonal directions (Figure 2.5), but other alternatives have been used. The number of samples and the spatial separations of the samples are considered below.

We are now able to describe a simple model that explains image formation. The following discussion is restricted to monochrome (black and white) images, but is readily extended to explain colour image formation. An image is formed by the capture of radiant energy that has been reflected from surfaces that are viewed. We may therefore define upper and lower bounds for the values that the reflected energy, $f(i, j)$, can take:

$$0 \leq f(x,y) < \infty \qquad\qquad (2.1)$$

Clearly the value will be zero if no energy is reflected, and the amount of energy reflected must also be finite.

The amount of reflected energy is determined by two functions: the amount of light falling on a scene and the reflectivity of the various surfaces in the scene. The two functions are known as the illumination, $i(x, y)$, and reflectance, $r(x, y)$, components; they combine to give:

$$f(x,y) = i(x,y)r(x,y) \qquad\qquad (2.2)$$

The illumination function can theoretically take values between zero and infinity. In practice, the upper bound is set by the maximum ambient illumination, whether this is a well lit room indoors, a sunlit scene or a night-time scene.

The reflectivity function can take values within the range zero (complete absorption of incident energy) to one (complete reflection of incident energy). In practice, the complete range is not realised. Black velvet has a reflection coefficient of about 0.01 and snow a coefficient of approximately 0.95.

Thus the brightness values, l, in a scene can take values in the range:

$$i_{min}(x,y)r_{min}(x,y) \le l \le i_{max}(x,y)r_{max}(x,y) \qquad (2.3)$$

When an image of this scene is captured, it is usual practice to clamp the minimum value to zero and the maximum value to whatever maximum is allowed by the resolution of the hardware, typically 255. A value of zero will equate to black and 255 to white. Intervening values will equate to shades of grey of varying intensity. This range of values is termed the grey scale.

2.4 Image quality measurements

Any system that measures a physical property can only do so to a finite accuracy, which is determined in part by the property being measured and in part by the measuring equipment. For example, when measuring distances, an appropriate scale is used. One would not use a metre rule to determine the separation between two cities or the thickness of a piece of paper. Indeed, even if the metre rule was being used to measure an appropriate distance, such as the width of a doorway, the measurement that is obtained could still be erroneous – is the metre rule accurate? Can I read the distance accurately?

These problems are equally applicable to image data. Imaging devices focus radiant energy from specific orientations onto a photosensitive detector. The quantity of energy that is absorbed by the detector in a specified time is measured digitally. The measurements are assembled into an image. All of these processes are subject to inaccuracies in one form or another and the net effect is that the image we derive is not strictly accurate – there is some measurement uncertainty that must be associated with each pixel value. The uncertainty is usually quantified by measuring the system's signal to noise ratio. In this section we shall discuss some of the causes of the loss of image quality and the measurement of image quality.

2.4.1 Sources of degradation

A major cause of loss of quality in the image has been alluded to: noise in the electronics that converts radiant energy to an electrical signal. This is the easiest degradation to measure and is usually quoted by camera manufacturers. However, it is not the sole source of degradation: the camera's lenses

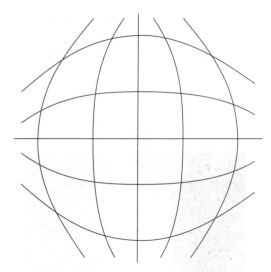

Figure 2.6 Image of a rectangular grid captured using a short focal length lens (schematic).

also distort the image and the detector itself may not respond as we would like it to. Several sources of degradation may be identified.

Geometric distortion is a problem with all lenses. It arises because the best focus of the scene in front of the lens is in fact on a spherical surface behind it. In practice it is not possible to fabricate detectors of this shape, so the image is projected onto a planar detector, with an associated distortion of the image (recall the problem of drawing a map of the world). The distortions become more severe as we use lenses with progressively shorter focal lengths to give wider angles of view. Figure 2.6 illustrates the effect of imaging a rectangular grid: the distortions are apparent around the periphery of the image.

Scattering occurs when rays of light reflected by the surface to be viewed are further dispersed by material in the optical path between the surface and the detector. Fog is the obvious example; it gives rise to a common name for this phenomenon: fogging.

The refractive index of the glass or plastic from which a lens is constructed is a function of the wavelength (colour) of the light being refracted. This is demonstrated by passing a ray of white light through a prism, splitting the white light into the constituent colours. The consequence of this for an optical system that should focus light onto a fixed point is serious: it cannot be done. The effect of this is that white objects will have a coloured fringe and sharp boundaries are blurred.

Blooming is the effect that is seen when a bright point source is imaged. The image is blurred slightly due to two causes: the camera's optical system will blur the image slightly and neighbouring cells in the detector will respond to the received impulse; see Figure 2.7.

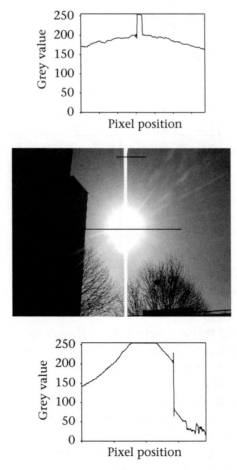

Figure 2.7 Blooming and saturation. The image contains a highly overexposed region. Pixels within this region have the maximum possible grey value, shown in the lower profile. The upper profile shows an exposure artefact.

In all of our discussions, we have assumed that the sensitivity of the detector is uniform, i.e. all cells of the detector will respond equally to the same impulse. This is often not the case. The uniformity of a detector may be determined by capturing an image of a uniform scene (as described below). For accurate work, it may be necessary to derive a calibration function for each pixel.

Overflow or clipping of a signal occurs whenever the signal is of excessive amplitude. In such cases the signal might be clipped to the maximum value or it might overflow, resulting in the values being much smaller than they should. Overflow is not normally a problem with the solid state detectors currently used, but automatic exposure does cause a loss of image detail in under-illuminated regions, as shown in Figures 2.7 and 2.8.

Figure 2.8 Underexposure. Large regions of the image are underexposed due to the bright light source just out of view at the top of the image.

2.4.2 Signal to noise ratio

Noise in an imaging system is defined as any deviation of the signal from its expected value. It may be observed as speckle in the image where one would expect to see areas of uniform colour or brightness, and many other effects.

Two types of speckle effect are seen; one is more common than the other. The less commonly observed type is called salt and pepper noise. Its effect is to randomly introduce pixels of pure black and pure white into the image. The more commonly seen type of noise is termed Gaussian noise; its amplitude distribution is described by a Gaussian or normal distribution. Gaussian noise is commonly observed in all systems, and arises due to randomness superimposed on the signal being captured or processed.

Gaussian noise is described by the Gaussian or normal distribution (Figure 2.9). The noise will usually have zero mean and finite amplitude. The consequence of the image being corrupted in this way is that any pixel will have a value that differs from the expected one: it is equally likely to be increased or decreased and by an amount that is random but whose maximum is related to the deviation (width) of the distribution.

Video camera manufacturers will often quote their devices' signal to noise ratios. Whilst this is a useful quantity to know, it ignores half of the imaging

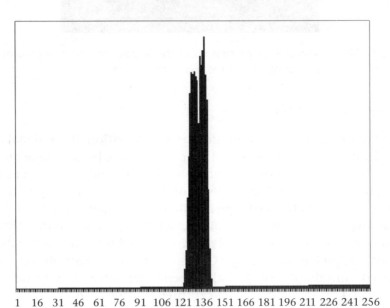

1   16 31 46 61 76 91 106 121 136 151 166 181 196 211 226 241 256

Figure 2.9   Gaussian noise distribution.

system: the conversion of the video signal to an analogue format. It is more useful to measure the signal to noise ratio of the image capture system. Imaging a completely uniform scene and measuring the variation in the image data can achieve this.

Finding a completely uniform scene is not the difficult problem it might seem. A uniformly painted wall or a piece of card are suitable 'scenes', provided that they are illuminated uniformly, or we may direct the camera at the sky, provided it is a uniform colour. It is also useful to defocus the camera viewing the scene slightly, as this has the effect of reducing the influence of any non-uniformity in the scene. Having captured the image, we may measure the amount of noise in it by computing the image histogram (defined more rigorously in the following chapter). The histogram describes the frequency with which each grey level or each colour occurs in the image. The standard deviation of the histogram may be used as a measure of the noise amplitude. Figure 2.10 shows a uniform image captured using a low-quality webcam and the image's histogram.

A single measurement of the noise amplitude is not instructive, as it does not inform us of the influence of the noise on our data. This extra information

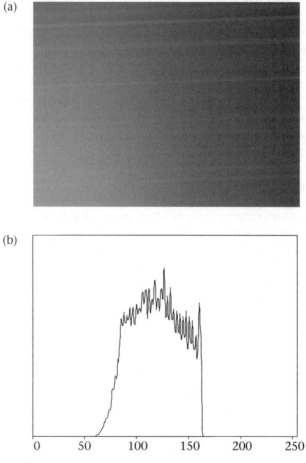

Figure 2.10 (a) Uniform image captured from a low-quality webcam; (b) the histogram of this image.

can be determined by comparing the noise amplitude just measured against the amplitude of the noise-free data. This comparison is called the signal to noise ratio, which, as its name suggests, is simply the ratio of the signal's amplitude (the maximum image value that could be observed) to the noise amplitude that we have measured. The ratio is usually quoted in decibels:

$$SNR = 20 \log_{10} \frac{signal}{noise} \qquad (2.4)$$

The signal to noise ratio also has consequences for the system's amplitude resolution that will be discussed below. The value used for *signal* is usually the maximum it can take: 255 in most instances.

2.5 Image resolution

When a vision system is being designed, the resolution of the images that are to be processed must be specified. This determines what objects can be seen in the data. Three resolutions must be defined: spatial (loosely the number of pixels), brightness (the number of shades of grey or colours in the image) and temporal (the number of frames captured or processed per second).

Whilst these resolutions are defined and discussed separately, they do have a mutual dependency which will also be discussed.

2.5.1 Spatial resolution

It is tempting to define spatial resolution as the number of pixels in an image. Thus an image with 600,000 pixels is said to have a higher resolution than one with only 300,000. However, this figure is misleading as it ignores factors such as the distance of the object from the camera and the field of view of the system. Rather, the definition of spatial resolution must consider the interaction between the optics of the camera and the detector.

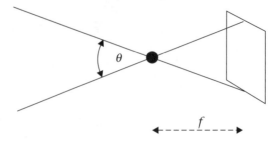

Figure 2.11   Relationship between field of view, θ, and camera's detector and focal length, f.

Figure 2.11 illustrates the interaction between a camera's field of view and the light-sensitive element that converts incoming photons into an electrical signal. The field of view is the angle subtended by rays of light that hit the detector at the extreme edges of the image. To fully define the optical system, we must define two fields of view, in the planes containing the detector's edges and parallel to the camera's optical axis. If these angles are divided by the number of light-sensitive elements across the detector in those directions (that is, the number of pixels in the digitised image in these directions) then we can compute the system's angular resolution. Although there are two angular resolutions, imaging systems are designed such that they are equal. An imaging system that has a horizontal field of view of 15° and 760 pixels across the image will have a horizontal angular resolution of just over one arc minute (1/60th of a degree).

The angular resolution can be used to specify how close an object must be for it to be resolved (seen), or what objects can be resolved at a certain range. Figure 2.11 illustrates this relationship. The angular resolution, θ, measured in radians, is equal to the ratio of the smallest resolvable object, r, to the range, Z:

$$\theta = \frac{r}{Z} \tag{2.5}$$

Therefore, to resolve an object 2 mm in diameter at a range of 1 m requires a system with an angular resolution of 0.002 radians (0.1°).

An alternative way of specifying the spatial resolution of a system bypasses all consideration of the optics and uses a variant of Nyquist's theorem. Nyquist was the first to formally set a limit on sampling rates for representing a digital signal. He observed that to represent a periodic signal unambiguously required at least two samples per period (see Figure 2.12). This observation can be translated into a requirement for a vision system: two pixels must span the smallest dimension of an object in order for it to be seen in the image.

If a signal is sampled at the Nyquist rate, little information is gained other than knowledge of the presence of the signal. Similarly, if an image is sampled at this rate, the presence of objects of this size is determined. To discover

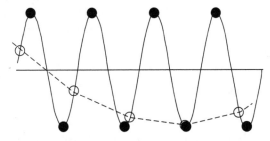

Figure 2.12 Sampling a continuous function at and below the Nyquist frequency.

Figure 2.13 Sampling an image with progressively more samples per unit length.

more about the objects requires higher sampling rates. Figure 2.13 illustrates the effect of progressively increasing the number of samples that span a simple image. Reading across the diagram, each image has four times the number of samples of the previous image, i.e. the number of samples in the images increases from $n \times m$ to $2n \times 2m$ from one image to the next. It is apparent that objects can be discerned in the earlier images but not recognised until the later ones.

2.5.2 Brightness and colour resolution

The brightness resolution of a system can be defined as the number of shades of grey that may be discerned in a monochrome image, or the number of distinct colours that may be observed in a colour image.

Given particular hardware, we may compute the brightness resolution of the system. Alternatively, we may investigate what a vision system is required to achieve and thus define the brightness resolution that will enable this task to be achieved.

Recall that the signal to noise ratio was defined using the ratio of the noise amplitude to the maximum amplitude in an image. The major contributor of noise in a digital system is the camera; the analogue to digital conversion adds very little noise. If we assume that the noise in a system is described by a normal (Gaussian) distribution, and the noise amplitude is measured as the standard deviation of this distribution, then our knowledge of statistics tells us that the probability of observing noise with amplitude more than three standard deviations from the mean is approximately 0.001, implying that there is a 1 in 1000 probability of observing a noise deviation with amplitude outside of this range: an unlikely occurrence. Therefore, if the total brightness scale is divided into bins of size six times the noise amplitude, then we can be sure that a sample that falls into the centre of one bin cannot be confused with a sample that falls into a neighbouring bin due to noise perturbing one value sufficiently for it to be confused with the other (Figure 2.14).

As an example, consider a black and white camera that has a signal to noise ratio of 55 dB. This equates to a ratio of signal to noise amplitudes of 562. If

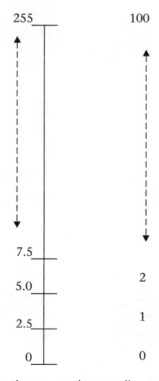

Figure 2.14 Dividing the grey scale according to the noise amplitude.

this magnitude is divided by six, we obtain the maximum number of grey values that this camera can give without confusion: 94.

Alternatively, by viewing typical images using varying numbers of shades of grey or colour we may also estimate the number of grey values required in an application. This is illustrated for a monochrome image in Figure 2.15; the first image has two shades, the second four shades, and the final one 256 shades. It is apparent that more detail becomes visible as the number of shades is increased. False contours are visible in areas of gradually changing brightness when there are insufficient shades of grey. The last few images do not show any apparent differences. Although there is a limited resolution in

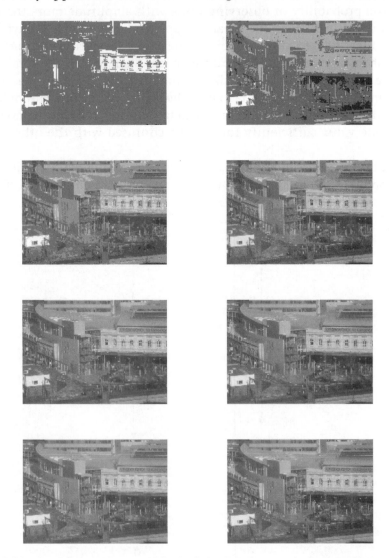

Figure 2.15 Sampling an image with pixels having progressively more grey values per sample.

the reproduction, this effect is due to the human visual system being unable to differentiate more than about 40 shades of grey. This is often given as justification for having this as a lower limit to the number of shades, but it ignores the requirement to allow for latitude in exposure.

It should be noted, finally, that image capture devices are limited in their capacities by what the manufacturers will provide. Most monochrome images are captured using eight bit values, and colour images are captured using three eight bit values.

2.5.3 Temporal resolution

Temporal resolution is defined either as the number of images that are captured and stored per second, or as the number of images that are captured and processed per second. When capturing analogue video, the national standards dictate that a maximum of 25 frames per second are available (or 30 in the USA). Digital video data may be captured at higher frame rates; the exact rate will depend on the rate that data may be transferred between the camera and the host computer and the size of the images that are captured.

When processing digital video, a lower limit on the rate at which results should be calculated can be set if we require the appearance of real-time processing. Psychological studies have suggested that this rate is in the region of twelve frames per second.

2.5.4 Interactions

It is helpful to consider spatial and brightness resolution separately to avoid confusing the effects of these causes. However, the two resolutions can interact in affecting the overall perception of an image: a poor spatial resolution can sometimes be compensated for by a good brightness resolution. In fact, for each brightness resolution it is usually possible to define a threshold spatial resolution above which the image appears of an acceptable quality and below which it does not. The combinations of resolutions will define a border between acceptable and unacceptable qualities. This border will be different for all types of images. As an example, consider the images of Figures 2.16 and 2.17. In each of these diagrams we have combinations of differing brightness and spatial resolutions that represent different points in the resolution space. It is apparent that somewhere along a diagonal of these diagrams lies the border between the acceptable and unacceptable images.

2.6 Connectivity and distance

In many cases when processing a digital image, one must decide whether one pixel is connected to another; that is, can one pixel be reached from another

Figure 2.16 An image presented with varying sample densities and grey values. Each row has half the number of grey values per pixel as the row above. The columns have 10%, 25% and 50% of the samples per unit length of the images in the rightmost column. (*Continued opposite*)

by tracing a path between connected pixels? The question can be reduced to 'How do we decide whether two adjacent pixels are connected or not?'.

Figure 2.18(a) illustrates the problem. Is the central pixel connected to the four nearest neighbours (north, south, east and west) or to all eight nearest neighbours? If four-connectivity is assumed, then the diagonal line of shaded pixels in Figure 2.18(b) is not connected, and the underlying line will

Figure 2.16 (*continued*)

not be detected. However, the two regions on either side of the diagonal line will not be connected, since no two of the closest neighbours are adjacent, which is intuitively the correct answer.

If eight-connectivity is assumed (that is, a pixel may be connected to the four nearest neighbours and the four next nearest) then the diagonally adjacent pixels of Figure 2.18(b) are connected. However, the two regions on either side of the line are also connected, since pixels in one region are diagonally adjacent to pixels in the region on the line's other side.

Figure 2.17 Another image presented with varying sample densities and grey values. See Figure 2.16 for details. (*Continued opposite*)

The solution to this contradiction is to be flexible in choosing a connectivity model. For some purposes four-connectivity is appropriate; for others eight-connectivity is a better approach.

Similarly, there are a multitude of methods of measuring distances in digital images. The Euclidean distance between a pair of pixels is measured by Pythagoras' theorem:

$$D(p_1, p_2) = \sqrt{(x_1 - x_2)^2 + (y_1 - y_2)^2} \tag{2.6}$$

Figure 2.17 (*continued*)

In some cases an approximation to this distance may be made – the so-called city-block distance:

$$D(p_1, p_2) = \mid x_1 - x_2 \mid + \mid y_1 - y_2 \mid \tag{2.7}$$

Which distance measure is used will be a compromise between speed of computation and accuracy.

Other measures of distance have been suggested, but are not widely used.

(a)

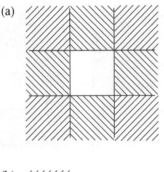

(b)

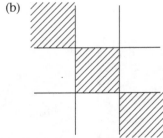

Figure 2.18 Pixel connectivity. (a) A 3 × 3 grid of pixels: is the central pixel connected to the four nearest neighbours, or the eight nearest neighbours? (b) A diagonal line of shaded pixels: are the pixels on the line and the two regions on either side of the line connected?

2.7 Colour representation models

Young's tristimulus theory was mentioned above. An important consequence of the theory is that it suggested that colours could be synthesised by suitable combinations of a red, a green and a blue primary colour. This was formalised by the CIE (Commission Internationale d'Eclairage), which in 1931 specified the spectral characteristics of the red (R), green (G) and blue (B) primary sources to be monochromatic light of wavelengths 700 nm, 546.1 nm and 435.8 nm respectively. These light sources could be combined linearly to match almost any colour, C:

$$C = rR + gG + bB \qquad (2.8)$$

The relative amounts of these primary sources required to match the range of visible colours were shown in Figure 2.2. Note that negative amounts of the red primary are required to match certain colours. To overcome this problem the CIE defined the curves shown in the graph sketched in Figure 2.19. These show the amounts of each idealised primary colour, X, Y and Z, that are required to match any arbitrary test colour. It is common for the amounts of X, Y and Z to be normalised and to present the two of them as the so-called

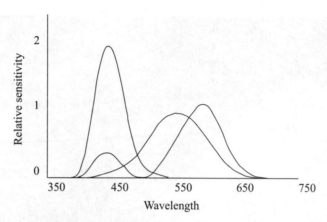

Figure 2.19 CIE colour matching functions for the standard colorimetric observer.

CIE chromaticity diagram. In this diagram, the values of x and y are presented according to the following formula:

$$x = \frac{X}{X + Y + Z} \quad \text{and} \quad y = \frac{Y}{X + Y + Z} \tag{2.9}$$

The diagram is shown in Figure 2.20. Around the outside of the horseshoe are shown the equivalent wavelengths of monochromatic light that are generated by these combinations of the CIE primaries. White lies at the coordinates (1/3, 1/3).

Although using the RGB colour space is convenient as colour images are captured in this format, it is not the only colour representation method, and is indeed probably not the best. A significant problem with the RGB colour space is that it is perceptually non-linear. This means that if we change a colour's RGB value by a fixed amount, the perceived effect it generates is dependent on the original RGB values. It is also difficult to predict the change that will occur to a colour by changing one of its components by a certain amount: what colour will result if we change the red component of the colour represented by the RGB triplet (0.57, 0.37, 0.06) by 0.30?

It was this type of consideration that led to the adoption of perceptual colour spaces. One of these, HSV, uses three components that represent:

- the intensity of the sample or its brightness (V)
- the underlying colour of the sample – the hue (H)
- the saturation or depth of the sample's colour (S)

Thus reddish colours will have similar hue values but will be differentiated according to their saturations. The HSV colour space is represented by the cone of colours in Figure 2.21.

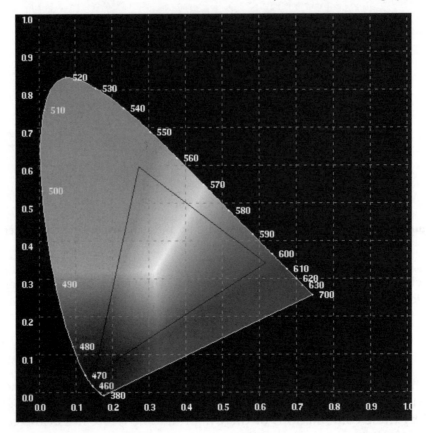

Figure 2.20   CIE chromaticity diagram. The range of colours realised by a typical monitor is indicated by the triangle. Numbers around the horseshoe indicate the wavelength of monochromatic light of the equivalent colour.

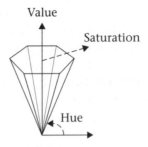

Figure 2.21   Definition of HSV colour space.

Finally, it should be noted that colour data is broadcast using colour difference values. These are again a triplet of values: one represents the brightness to be assigned a pixel, and the other two components represent colour difference values.

2.8 Camera calibration

In the final section of this chapter we examine the problem of camera calibration; that is, how can we relate the coordinates of pixels to coordinates in a frame of reference in the real world?

The calibration process divides into two stages: one that relates image coordinates to a coordinate frame aligned to the camera, and one that relates the camera coordinate frame to an arbitrary coordinate frame fixed to some point in the physical world. Related to these two transformations are two sets of parameters: extrinsic parameters relate to the camera to world coordinate transform and intrinsic parameters relate to the image to camera coordinate transform. Figure 2.22 summarises the process.

The extrinsic parameters simply define the translation and rotation of the camera coordinate frame such that it aligns with the world coordinate frame. In principle it is sufficient to determine the location of the camera's optical centre with respect to the origin of the world coordinates and the orientation of the camera's optical axis and image plane with respect to the world coordinate frame's axes (Figure 2.23). (The camera's optical centre is the point in the optical system through which all rays of light will pass undeviated. The optical axis is the line that is perpendicular to the image plane and passes through the optical centre.)

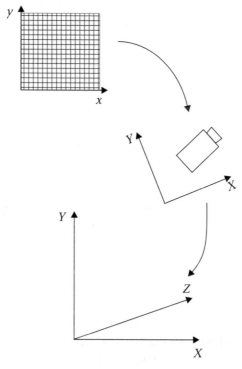

Figure 2.22 Coordinate frame transformations: image → camera and camera → world.

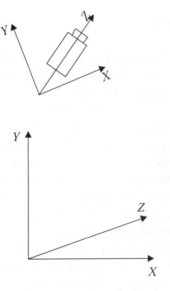

Figure 2.23   World to camera transformation parameters.

The intrinsic parameters of the camera are slightly more complex. We shall consider two cases: one in which there are no optical aberrations (i.e. the imaging process does not distort the image) and one in which distortions are introduced.

If the imaging process does not distort the image and the image is sampled uniformly in the x- and y-directions, then a linear relationship exists between the image and camera coordinates. We must offset the origin (since the camera coordinate system's origin coincides with the centre of the image) and scale the data:

$$x = -(x_{im} - o_x)s_x$$
$$y = -(y_{im} - o_y)s_y$$

(2.10)

If the imaging process does distort the data, it is usually sufficient to assume that a first-order spherical correction is sufficient:

$$x = (1 + k_x(x^2 + y^2))x_d$$
$$y = (1 + k_y(x^2 + y^2))y_d$$

(2.11)

This correction must be applied prior to the linear shifting and scaling. Its purpose is to remove the warping that is inevitable when an image is generated. Figure 2.24 illustrates its use: the original image plus the corrected one are shown. Dewarping is a topic that will be examined in greater detail in the following chapter.

(a)

(b)

Figure 2.24   (a) Unwarped and (b) warped images.

Examples of the use of camera calibration will be examined in future chapters.

2.9 Summary

In this chapter we have attempted to lay foundations for the rest of the text. We have introduced image processing by analogy with the human visual system. We have examined the general principles that must be considered when specifying what data is to be captured and how for a specific task. Generally, these requirements reduce to the angular resolution of the system, the number of pixels an image should contain and the number of discrete brightness or colour values. Camera calibration was also considered.

2.10 Bibliography

Newton (1931), Young (1807) and Helmholtz (1881) laid the foundations for colour perception. Gregory (1997) and Frisby (1979) present readable accounts of visual perception.

Hecht (1998) provides a modern introduction to optics and optical processes.

Stroud (1956) and others gave a justification for interpreting 'real time' from a human perspective. Haralick and Shapiro (1992) discuss most aspects of camera calibration.

2.11 Exercises

2.1   Take an image and experiment with the interrelationship between spatial resolution (number of pixels) and dynamic range (number of grey values). Is it possible to identify a dynamic range at each spatial resolution at which the image's subject matter becomes recognisable? Repeat the experiment with images of different subject matter (faces, outdoor scenes etc.).

2.2   An image of a fence is captured. The fence is made of panels 10 cm wide separated by a gap of 10 cm. A length of 20 m of fence appears in the image. To what minimum resolution should the image be captured in order to observe the fence without error? Describe the errors that will be introduced if the data is sampled to a lower resolution.

2.3   Take a noise-free image and add random noise of varying amplitudes that affects a varying number of pixels to create a sequence of images with varying signal to noise ratios. Score each of the images on a scale of one to five according to the image's perceived quality. What relationship can you discover between quality, signal to noise ratio and number of pixels affected?

3

Image transforms and feature extraction

The subject of image processing can be defined to include all operations that manipulate image data. These will range from simple operations that manipulate pixel values to more complex ones that transform an image from one representation into an alternative.

Many schemes have been proposed for classifying image transformation algorithms. Some authors organise them according to the area of the input image that is involved, whether it be individual pixels, small groups of pixels or the whole image. Others use the sequences of operations that commonly occur when images are processed: algorithms that correct the image for any defects introduced during capture are presented first, and so on. In this treatment we are taking the former option.

Feature extraction is defined as any operation that extracts information from an image. This information would normally then be used in further processing stages of a system to identify objects etc.

After studying this chapter you will be familiar with a range of commonly used methods for processing images and extracting information from them. Feature extraction is an important topic that will reappear in the following two chapters.

3.1 A classification of image transforms

An image processing operation is defined simply as an operation that somehow manipulates image data to generate another image. The size of the image will not be altered, but the size of each storage unit (pixel) might; see Figure 3.1. A large multitude of image transforms have been defined, and they can be highly confusing when presented to the novice all at once. All authors therefore attempt a systematic presentation. Some classify algorithms according to their task, thereby creating a recipe book of operations. This has its advantages in that if we are able to identify the task we are attempting to perform, then we can discover what algorithms might perform it. The approach does, however, assume some prior knowledge: the

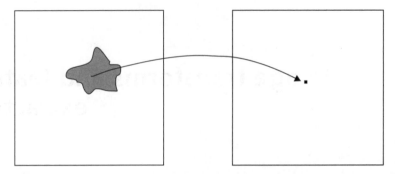

Figure 3.1   Image to image transformation, possible changes and invariants.

reader is expected to be able to determine what tasks are necessary when designing a system; this is probably beyond the ability of a novice approaching this subject for the first time. It is also possible to present algorithms according to their place in the processing hierarchy. Thus the description would follow the logical order of the algorithm's use. This is what we have used in the organisation of this text, where we have chapters devoted to image manipulation, feature extraction and feature recognition, but it is not necessarily appropriate when investigating image manipulation itself. Rather, in this chapter we have organised image processing functions according to the area of the input image that is involved. Thus we discuss point transforms that involve a single pixel; local transforms that involve a small region of pixels surrounding the one of interest; and global transforms that generally involve the entire image in computing the transformed value of a single pixel.

The aims of the image transformation being discussed are as follows:

- to remove or correct for degradations introduced by the image capture process
- to improve the appearance of the image for human perception or for further processing
- to identify and quantify structures in the image that may be indicative of the objects in the scene being viewed
- to transform the image into an alternative representation in which some operations may be performed more efficiently

After studying this chapter you should be able to design and implement systems that improve the appearance of images, either by removing exposure defects, or correcting for optical aberrations. You should also be able to implement simple enhancement systems that will form the basis of the further processing to be discussed in subsequent chapters.

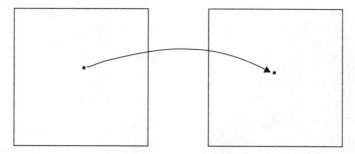

Figure 3.2 Point transform.

3.2 Point transforms

As discussed above, a point transform will manipulate the grey or colour value of an individual pixel without considering the neighbouring values (Figure 3.2). Since the only information that an individual pixel carries is its brightness or colour, and it is only this information that can be manipulated. This is achieved by a mapping between input and output grey values (Figure 3.3). The mapping must define an output value (along the *y*-axis) for each input value (along the *x*-axis). Every input value must have an associated output, but this need not be unique: more than one input might share the same output.

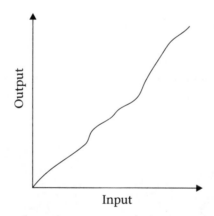

Figure 3.3 Mapping between input and output grey values.

The material of this section deals with how various mappings might be determined.

3.2.1 Grey scale manipulation

The grey values of an image may be manipulated in many ways to modify the image's appearance. The methods that are applied are generally interactive;

Figure 3.4 Adding a constant to each pixel of a grey image.

that is, the user of a vision system must decide how the modification is to be performed, rather than have the system determine the mapping automatically.

The two simplest methods of modifying the image are to add a constant and to scale the values by a constant multiplier (Figures 3.4 and 3.5). This might be necessary if, for example, the exposure of the image had been incorrect. It is important to emphasise that this will not alter the information content of the image, but it will make that information easier for a human observer to perceive.

These methods are quite arbitrary: how much should be added to the image or what scaling factor ought to be used are determined specifically for each image being processed according to the desired outcome. To reduce this arbitrariness, the images are often manipulated such that the mean grey level

Figure 3.5 Multiplying each pixel of a grey image by a constant.

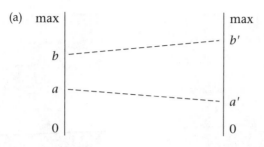

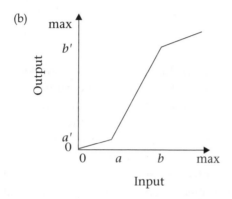

Figure 3.6 Interactive grey scale manipulation. (a) Mapping between input and output grey scales; (b) grey scale mapping.

is matched to a previously determined value. Thus we would add an amount equal to the difference between the target and actual grey values, or scale by a factor equal to the ratio of the target to actual values. Some applications also scale the image such that the variance of the data takes a standard value.

The grey scale of the image can also be manipulated interactively such that certain portions of it are expanded at the expense of others that are compressed. This must be done manually, as the ranges to be manipulated cannot be determined automatically. The mechanism of this process is illustrated in Figure 3.6(a). The left column indicates the input grey scale and the right column the output. Without any manipulation, the columns will match exactly: grey values on one column map to the same grey value on the other. The user may choose to connect values on the two columns to indicate that they should be mapped to each other: in this example value a has been connected to value a', indicating that the input grey value a is mapped onto the output grey value a'. The extreme values of the scale, normally 0 and 255, will always remain unchanged. Thus the input values between 0 and a will be mapped onto the output values between 0 and a'. Since, in this example, a' is less than a, this range of grey values has been compressed, which introduces the possibility that all or part of the range from a to 255 could be expanded. The user has also connected values b and b', which indicates that the values

Figure 3.7   Image manipulated with the transform of Figure 3.6.

in the range [*a*, *b*] will map to the values [*a'*, *b'*]. And since the range [*a'*, *b'*] contains more grey values than the input range, there is an expansion of the grey scale over this interval. Finally, the input range [*b*, 255] is mapped to the output range [*b'*, 255]. Figure 3.6(b) indicates the grey scale mapping that is generated, and Figure 3.7 shows an image manipulated with this transform.

The aim of manipulating the grey map in this way is to expand certain portions of its range and thus make the objects that have this range of brightnesses appear more clearly in the manipulated image. The problem with the techniques discussed is that they require an operator to recognise what range of brightness should be expanded. Two methods exist that achieve the same aim automatically.

False contouring applies a grey scale map of the type shown in Figure 3.8 to an image; the result is shown in Figure 3.9. The aim of this transformation is to enhance gradual changes in brightness by changing them into a

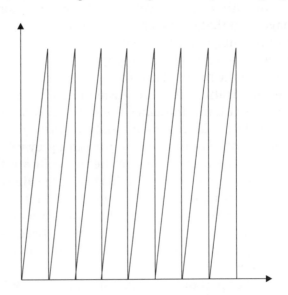

Figure 3.8   Grey scale map for false contouring.

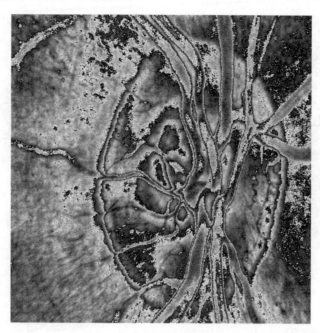

Figure 3.9 False contouring. An input image has had its pixels mapped according to the scale of Figure 3.8.

succession of rapid changes from dark values to bright values. An alternative is to map the input grey values into a set of colour values; rainbow sets of colours – gradations through shades of yellow or blue – have been used. Figure 3.10 presents an example using shades of red and orange.

3.2.2 Thresholding

From the discussion of the previous section, it should be apparent that many of the grey value manipulation algorithms are designed to improve the appearance of an image or to make certain structures more obvious. One family of techniques that do this is so important that it deserves a separate discussion: thresholding.

Thresholding is the operation that transforms an input image, be it a monochrome or colour one, into a binary image, that is an image whose pixels can take one of two values only. The following discussion is of monochrome data only, but the methods are readily adapted to colour data. In order to do this, a threshold value, θ, is defined. The thresholding operation is achieved by comparing each pixel value, $f(i, j)$, against the threshold and setting the output appropriately:

$$g(i,j) = \begin{cases} 0 & \text{if } f(i,j) \le \theta \\ 1 & \text{otherwise} \end{cases} \tag{3.1}$$

Figure 3.10   A false colour mapping.

Thresholding has a multitude of uses in image processing, mainly in making decisions regarding the identity of objects or pixels. Crucial to the operation is deciding a suitable value for θ. This will be discussed in later chapters.

3.2.3 Histogram manipulation

Transforming the grey scale of an image using the methods defined above is not necessarily an intuitive process. By manipulating the histogram we may achieve certain well-defined and well-founded results. Notable among these is histogram equalisation.

Histogram equalisation is based on the argument that the image's appearance will be improved if the distribution of pixels over the available grey levels is even. This transform would change the grey level histogram of Figure 3.11(a), which is shown with the image from which it was derived, into the histogram and image of Figure 3.11(b). Two things are apparent: one is that the histogram is not even; the second is that the image's appearance has been improved in some respects.

The transform is derived from the cumulative histogram, which is in turn derived from the image's grey level histogram. The grey level histogram records the frequency of occurrence of each grey value in the image. The

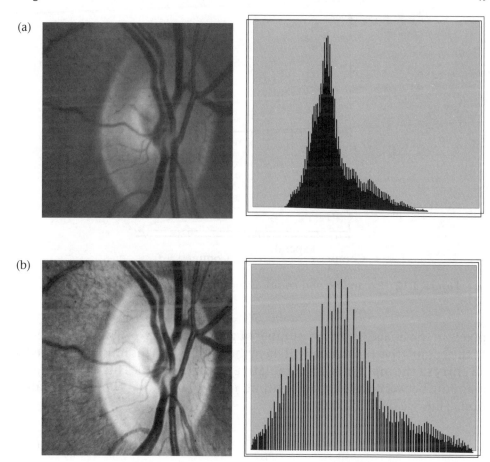

Figure 3.11 Histogram equalisation. (a) Image and histogram; (b) equalised image and histogram.

cumulative histogram records the number of pixels in the image with grey values less than or equal to each index. The cumulative histogram, $C(i)$, is derived from the grey level histogram, $g(i)$:

$$C(i) = \sum_{k=0}^{k=i} g(k) \qquad (3.2)$$

One interpretation of the equalisation transformation is that it warps the horizontal axis of the histogram, stretching it in some regions and compressing it in others, such that the frequencies become more uniform. The compressed regions correspond to those grey levels that are less occupied than they should be, as shown in Figure 3.12.

In the ideal case the equalised image will contain an equal number of pixels having each grey value. This number will be the ratio of the number of

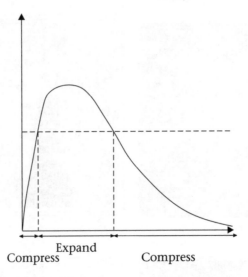

Expand
Compress   Compress

Figure 3.12 Expanding and compressing the histogram to make it uniform.

pixels in the image, N, to the number of grey values, l: N/l. Thus the jth entry of the cumulative histogram will have the value jN/l. This must be equated to an entry in the input image's cumulative histogram, $C(i)$. This will define the mapping between input, i, and output, j, grey values that achieves equalisation. Thus we may equate:

$$\frac{jN}{l} = C(i)$$ (3.3)

and rearrange:

$$j = \frac{l}{N} C(i)$$ (3.4)

One proviso must be observed: the range of grey values is 0 to $l - 1$, and the maximum value of j derived using this formula is l. It is therefore appropriate to subtract 1 from the result to obtain the correct maximum. The consequence of this, however, is that the minimum value of j could be -1 rather than zero. This is readily corrected. Thus the full expression for the transform is:

$$j = \max\left(0, \frac{l}{N} C(i) - 1\right)$$ (3.5)

It has also been suggested that equalising the histogram is not the best method of improving the image's appearance. Rather, the histogram should

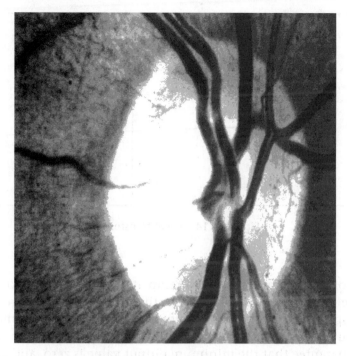

Figure 3.13 Example of the effect of histogram hyperbolisation.

be hyperbolised (Figure 3.13). Despite the apparent improvement in the data, this operation is rarely used.

3.3 Local transforms

Local transforms are those that are computed using a small region surrounding the pixel of interest (Figure 3.14). 'Small' is obviously a term that must be interpreted flexibly, as there could be some overlap between these and global transforms discussed below, but it can be assumed that the region involved in a local transform is much smaller than the image.

3.3.1 Convolution

This operation is fundamental to local transforms. Mathematically it is defined by Equation (3.6):

$$g(r,c) = \sum_{x=-\infty}^{\infty} \sum_{y=-\infty}^{\infty} f(r-x, c-y) t(x,y) \tag{3.6}$$

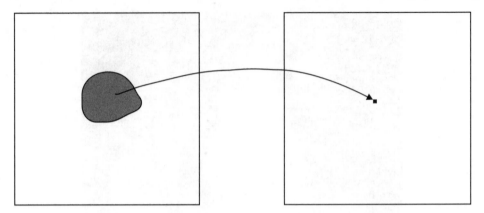

Figure 3.14   Local transforms.

The effect of this operation is that a template, $t(x, y)$, is placed over all possible image locations. At each location, the product of an image value and the overlapping template value is computed. The products are summed. This is the output value at that location. Optional further steps are to subtract an offset, to guarantee that the minimum output value is zero, and to scale the result such that the maximum value will lie within the range allocated to an image value. The offset to be subtracted would be the smallest result that could be computed. The multiplicative scaling factor could be the ratio of the maximum image value to the largest result that could be expected, or it could be the sum of the template values.

Whilst the limits of the expression extend to $\pm\infty$ in both the x- and y-directions, this does not pose a problem in practice. Firstly, the image values are undefined (zero) outside of the image region, and secondly, the same can be said of the template. Thus the dimensions of the template define the practical limits of the summation. As an example of convolution, the image of Figure 3.15 illustrates the result of convolving an image and a small template of nine elements.

As expressed in Equation (3.6), convolution requires n^2 multiplications and additions per pixel, where n is the size of the template. Obviously, as n increases, n^2 will rapidly become large, indicating that alternative methods of computation are desirable. Two methods are used. One of these makes use of the Fourier transform and will be described later in the chapter. The other method can be used if the template can be separated into two simpler, one-dimensional templates. Thus a convolution of the image with one $n \times n$ element template is reduced to convolution with a $1 \times n$ template and an $n \times 1$ element template. In this way, n^2 additions and multiplications are reduced to two $2n$ pairs of operations.

Separating the template may or may not be a simple operation. For example, Figure 3.16 shows the separation of two frequently used templates

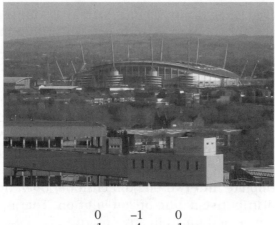

$$\begin{array}{ccc} 0 & -1 & 0 \\ -1 & 4 & -1 \\ 0 & -1 & 0 \end{array}$$

Figure 3.15 Simple example of convolution.

Figure 3.16 Separable templates. (a) Laplacian operator; (b) Laplacian of Gaussian.

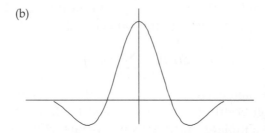

that can be derived analytically. Figure 3.16(a) is the separation of the Laplacian template; convolution of an image with this template is equivalent to double differentiation. The combination of the separated templates is intuitively equivalent to the original template, as will be discussed in the following paragraph. Figure 3.16(b) shows the separation of the Laplacian of Gaussian (LoG) template, which is used in edge enhancement and will also be described below. Since LoG templates can be large, it is desirable to find efficient ways of realising this convolution. The template is defined analytically, as is its separation: the diagram shows an oblique view of the two-dimensional template and profiles of the two one-dimensional templates.

Separating a template into two one-dimensional operations is only possible due to the distributive nature of convolution. That is, convolution of three templates can be performed in any order:

$$A \otimes (B \otimes C) \equiv (A \otimes B) \otimes C \tag{3.7}$$

Therefore, if B and C are the two separated templates, their convolution is equal to the combined template. The result obtained by convolving the image, A, with B (n multiplications and additions) and convolving the intermediate result with C (a further n multiplications and divisions) is identical to what is obtained by the original method.

The usefulness of the convolution operation lies in the results that it generates. Four applications will be covered: smoothing, sharpening (also known as edge detection), corner detection and template matching (in a later chapter).

3.3.2 Smoothing

The effect of smoothing on an image is to remove sharp, sudden changes in the brightness function. These might be caused by noise in the image capture device or small objects in the scene that might obscure the larger objects of the scene. The result of smoothing an image is thus another image with an improved signal to noise ratio, or an image in which the effect of distracting artefacts has been reduced.

The value of a smoothed pixel in an image is computed by combining a selection of the neighbouring pixels. The simplest method of achieving the combination is simply to average the values in the neighbourhood, N:

$$S(i,j) = \sum_{u,v \in N} P(u.v) \tag{3.8}$$

This can also be achieved by convolving the image with an appropriate template. The neighbourhood that is to be used defines the size and shape of the template. The template values are simply the reciprocal of the number of values included in the neighbourhood. Thus a neighbourhood of nine pixels would use template values of 1/9. By setting all template values to one and scaling the result of the convolution by 1/9, we achieve the same effect more efficiently.

In Figure 3.17, a 3 × 3 element template is used to smooth an image; before and after versions are shown to illustrate the effect of the process. It is

Figure 3.17   Smoothing an image using a 3 × 3 element template/kernel.

apparent that the smoothing has achieved the required effect, in that random noise fluctuations have been reduced. This is especially apparent in the smoother regions of the image. It is also apparent that some blurring of the image has taken place: sharp edges are no longer as sharp as they were. This is an undesirable side effect.

That this operation reduces the amount of noise in an image should not be a surprise. Earlier, some of the properties of image noise were defined. Among them was the property that the mean amplitude of the noise was zero. Therefore the sum of a set of noise values is likely to be closer to zero than the original values.

The deleterious blurring may be reduced by conditional smoothing. In this variant of the smoothing algorithm, the smoothed value, $S(i, j)$, is computed, but it will only replace the original, $P(i, j)$, if it differs by less than a preset value δ (Equation 3.9).

$$S(i,j) = \begin{cases} S(i,j) & \text{if } |S(i,j) - P(i,j)| < \delta \\ P(i,j) & \text{otherwise} \end{cases} \tag{3.9}$$

The reason for this may be understood by inspecting Figure 3.18, which shows a profile through an image feature. The brightness values are markedly

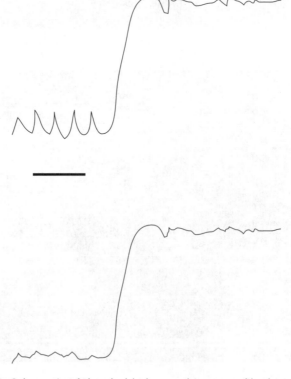

Figure 3.18 Schematic of thresholded smoothing – profile through an edge.

different on either side of the feature; they are uniform but are corrupted by noise. The horizontal bar beneath the profile indicates the size of the smoothing neighbourhood. When the neighbourhood lies entirely within either of the uniform regions, the smoothed value and the value that might be replaced are similar; they will differ by less than the threshold value that is selected. However, when the neighbourhood overlies the image feature, the smoothed and original values will be more different and smoothing will not occur. Thus, the original image features should be preserved, without smoothing, as shown in Figure 3.19. The minimum amplitude of the feature that is preserved is dependent on the threshold that is selected and the size of the neighbourhood.

These two operators are reasonably efficient, although they do not necessarily produce the best results. The so-called rank filters are often used in preference, as they yield a better result but at a higher computational cost.

A rank filter will select one value as the smoothed value from the set of pixels in a neighbourhood that have been ranked according to their magnitudes. For example, the median filter will select the value that is central in the ranked list or the average of the two central values. Figure 3.20 illustrates this filter used for smoothing, and Figure 3.21 demonstrates its use for removing small-scale objects from an image. In this case, the 'small' objects were blood vessels in an image of a retina; they were removed by using a neighbourhood of 15 × 15 pixels, significantly larger than the vessels' diameters.

The rank filters are computationally expensive, but rank filtering using a square neighbourhood may be approximated by repeated application of one-dimensional rank filters. Thus, a filter using an $n \times n$ neighbourhood may be approximated by using one with a $1 \times n$ neighbourhood followed by an $n \times 1$ neighbourhood. The number of pixels to be sorted to compute one filtered output is thereby reduced from n^2 to $2n$. The benefit that this gives far outweighs the fact that the result is not quite the same as that obtained by the two-dimensional filter.

Many smoothing filters introduce a ringing artefact that is especially visible in the neighbourhood of sharp boundaries: it is manifested as a sequence of echoes of the boundary. The cause of this artefact will be made clear in the discussion of the Fourier Transform below, but it is due to the shape of the template, which has a sharp spatial cutoff. If the template's values decayed smoothly to zero at its boundaries, then the echoing effect could be reduced – possibly even removed.

Such a template can be easily realised. A multitude of templates have been defined whose values are determined analytically. A common method is to use a Gaussian (normal) distribution to compute the template's elements:

$$T(r) = k \exp\left(-\frac{r^2}{2\sigma^2}\right) \qquad (3.10)$$

Figure 3.19 Example of thresholded smoothing. The lower image is a smoothed version of the upper one. smoothing has been performed only where the difference between the suggested smoothed value and the input value is below a threshold, in this case 5. Subtle differences are apparent in the vicinity of sharp discontinuities, e.g. window frames.

where r is the distance of the template element from the centre of the template, k is a normalising constant and σ defines the width and size of the template. An example of the use of this filter is shown in Figure 3.22.

Figure 3.20   An image smoothed by median filtering.

3.3.3 Sharpening and edge enhancement

Sharpening is often presented as the converse of smoothing: smoothing is intended to reduce the effect of significant local variations in the image data, whilst sharpening will exaggerate them. Thus sharpening is often referred to as edge enhancement.

Edges are extremely important structures in images and in image processing for two reasons. Firstly, it has been shown that the human visual system contains very specific edge-detecting subsystems. It has been shown that the retina performs a very low level edge-detecting operation, but there are higher level visual processes that combine this information in many ways to detect different types of edge structure: primarily differences in

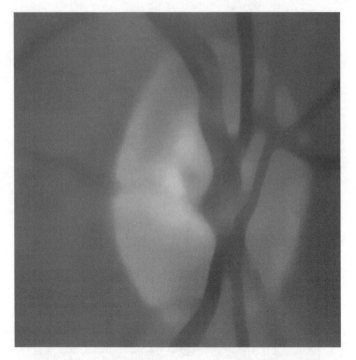

Figure 3.21 Median filter used to remove 'small' objects.

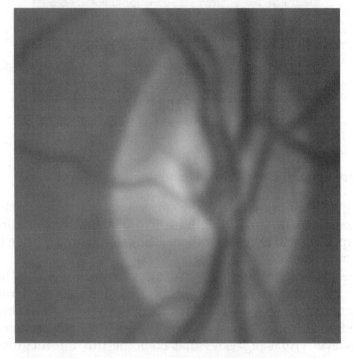

Figure 3.22 An image smoothed by Gaussian smoothing.

orientation and velocity in moving edges. So, if edge detection is such an important process for the human visual system, it ought to be important in computer vision systems.

Secondly, and consequent to the first reason, edges define the significant structures in a scene: the outlines of objects and parts of objects. An example of this is our ability to comprehend cartoons – a line drawing that includes only the significant structures of objects. This implies that scenes could be comprehended if only the edge information was present, which will allow us to process significantly less information than would otherwise be the case.

Many types of edge have been defined. An early catalogue defined three idealised types: step edges, line edges and roof edges (Figure 3.23). In practice, the step edge is the one most commonly encountered; however, the step is seldom as steep as the ideal case and the image values are not completely smooth on either side of the step. The grey level profile through a real edge is more likely to be similar to that shown in Figure 3.24.

For all practical purposes, we may define an edge thus:

An edge is a *significant, local* change in image intensity.

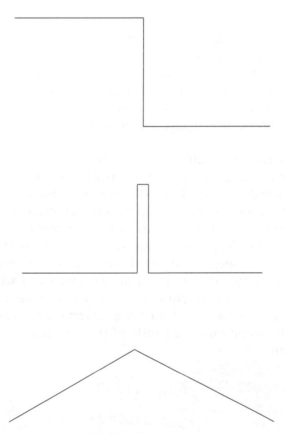

Figure 3.23   Schematic step, line and roof edges.

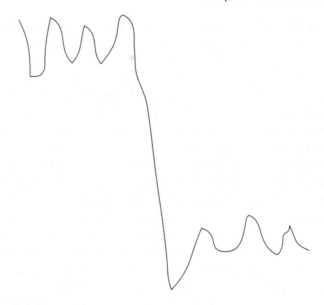

Figure 3.24 A schematic cross-section through a real step edge.

What is a significant difference? This question must be answered by investigating the difference between two pixels in relation to their brightness. Thus, if two monochrome pixels differ by 5 brightness values, this would be significant if their average value was 5, but probably not if their average value was 150. There will be a monotonic change from significant to insignificant as the proportional change in image intensity across the edge decreases.

What is a local change? A difference between two adjacent pixels will be of greater significance than the same difference between two pixels separated by the image's width. Again, there will be a monotonic increase in significance as the pixels being compared approach each other's locations.

Given this definition, it is not surprising that most edge enhancement operations involve differencing image values. The earliest was defined in 1965 by Roberts. This operator required the image to be convolved with two templates (Figure 3.25). This resulted in two images in which edges with orthogonal orientations were enhanced. These two images were then combined in two ways. The first combined edge magnitudes to estimate the edge strength, and the second used the ratio of the edge magnitudes to estimate edge orientation:

$$E_{mag} = \sqrt{E_1^2 + E_2^2}$$
$$E_{orient} = \tan^{-1} \frac{E_1}{E_2}$$

(3.11)

$$-1 \quad 0 \qquad\qquad 0 \quad -1$$

$$0 \quad +1 \qquad\qquad +1 \quad 0$$

Figure 3.25 Roberts edge enhancement templates.

The process is summarised in Figure 3.26.

The Roberts operator is possibly the simplest edge-enhancing operator that can be designed. It is, however, very susceptible to image noise. A simple analysis suggests that the same amount of noise present in a pixel value is also present in the estimate of edge magnitude.

To counter this problem, an element of smoothing can be introduced. We would therefore estimate the edge strength at a location using the difference between the averages of groups of pixels on either side of the edge. Two very simple operators have been defined: the Prewitt and Sobel. These differ only

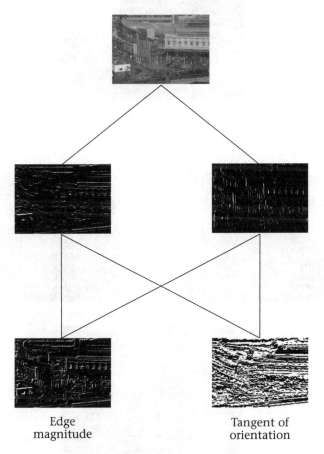

Edge
magnitude

Tangent of
orientation

Figure 3.26 Edge enhancement process. An image is convolved with two templates that enhance edges with orthogonal orientations. The enhanced images are combined to yield edge magnitude and edge orientation images.

in the weightings used in computing the averages. Figures 3.27 and 3.28 show the templates defined by these operators, the horizontal and vertical components of the edges they compute, and the combined edges.

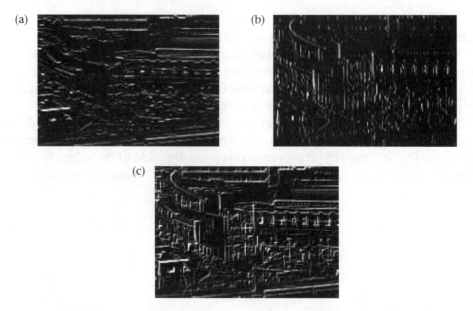

Figure 3.27 Prewitt edge enhancing template. (a) and (b) Responses of templates to an image; (c) combined response.

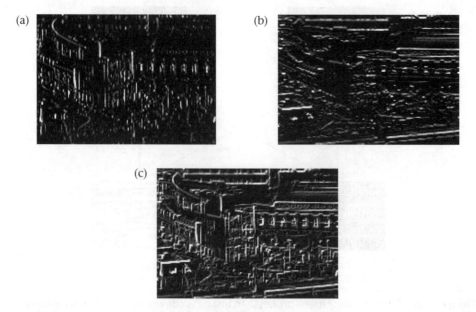

Figure 3.28 Sobel edge enhancing template. (a) and (b) Responses of templates to an image; (c) combined response.

The Prewitt and Sobel edge enhancement operators are slightly less sensitive to noise than the Roberts operator. The cost of this benefit is that these operators are slightly less sensitive to small (on the pixel scale) fluctuations in the data; this is not normally a problem.

Is it possible to select one of these operators as superior to the others? One study compared the operators according to their responses to the outline of a circular target and their performance when processing noisy images. Figure 3.29 was typical of the results that were obtained. The columns show the response of each operator when applied to an image containing a circular target on a contrasting background. Each row was derived from a source image with progressively more noise than the image used for the previous row. The interpretation of the result is that the Sobel operator has a superior

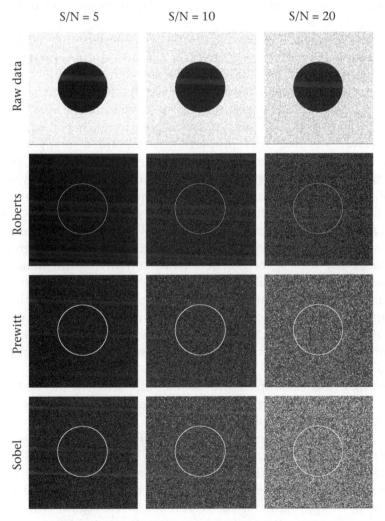

Figure 3.29 Response of Roberts, Prewitt and Sobel edge enhancement operators when detecting the outline of a circular target in the presence of noise at varying amplitudes.

edge detection performance to edges at all orientations, and a superior behaviour in the presence of noise.

The Sobel operator, whilst it partially addresses the problem of image noise, does not completely solve it. Neither does it address a further problem in image processing: scale.

When one of the simple 3 × 3 element templates is used to enhance edge features, they respond to features with a typical dimension of one pixel. However, when humans view a scene, they see objects at a range of scales: for example, a tree is composed of a trunk with branches, and the branches have smaller branches and ultimately twigs, all of which carry leaves. The tree can be observed at the leaf, twig, branch or whole tree scale. This is an alternative view of 'local'; previously, local was defined as a small pixel distance, but the present definition suggests that 'local' must be interpreted according to the object being viewed.

Edge enhancement operators have been suggested that address these issues. Computationally, they involve smoothing the image, using a Gaussian template which includes σ, the scale parameter, followed by differentiation or double differentiation. Canny suggested the former; Marr and Hildreth the latter. Interestingly, the scale behaviour of the operator was not the primary goal of these investigators. Canny was seeking an edge enhancement operator that had three properties: it responded to edges, it yielded accurate edge localisation and it gave a single response to each edge. Marr and Hildreth were investigating properties of the human visual system. Figures 3.30 and 3.31 illustrate the response of these two operators to an image using a range of scale parameters. One useful property is that the operators respond to objects of a different size as the scale parameter is varied. To illustrate this, Figure 3.32 shows a cross section through what is often termed a 'scale space'. The scale space is generated by convolving the image with the templates generated using all values of σ. Thus we generate a volume of data; two dimensions correspond to the image's dimensions and the third to the scale parameter. The cross-section illustrates how all objects are detected at small values of σ, but smaller ones are removed by the processing as σ increases. Ultimately, only the largest objects survive. The scale space will be revisited in a later chapter.

Processing in the scale space provides a more efficient method of implementing many image recognition and feature detection operations, as will be seen in subsequent chapters.

The Marr–Hildreth operator included a double differential operator. The operation of double differentiation can result in more accurate localisation of an edge pixel. Consider the profile across a real step edge (Figure 3.33(a)). If the profile is differentiated (Figure 3.33(b)), regions of constant grey value yield a zero, or approximately zero, response. The region where the grey value changes, which will correspond to the edge region – a region that will contain the point we wish to label as the edge – will yield a finite result.

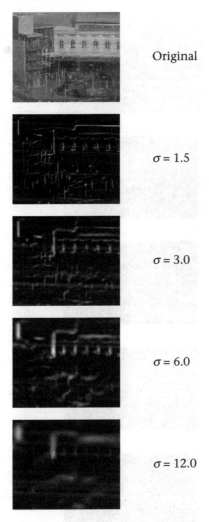

Original

$\sigma = 1.5$

$\sigma = 3.0$

$\sigma = 6.0$

$\sigma = 12.0$

Figure 3.30   Canny response to an image using $\sigma = 1.5$, 3, 6 and 12.

Often there will be a local maximum within this region, which defines the location of the edge. If there is no local maximum, the region of greatest magnitude is defined to contain the edge pixel, which will be determined subsequently by other methods. However, if the profile is double differentiated, we obtain the result of Figure 3.33(c). Again, uniform regions yield a zero result and the edge region a finite result. In this case, the result is positive where the profile's gradient is increasing and negative where it is decreasing; the position of maximum slope is located where the doubly differentiated profile crosses the zero. This position may or may not coincide with the centre of a pixel. In fact, we may use curve fitting techniques to locate the edge position to sub-pixel accuracy should this be desirable.

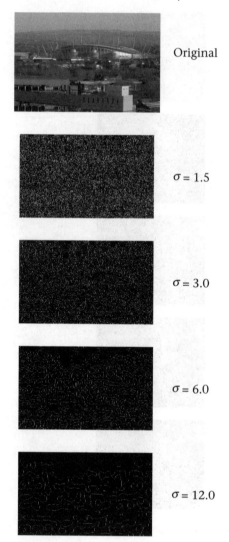

Original

$\sigma = 1.5$

$\sigma = 3.0$

$\sigma = 6.0$

$\sigma = 12.0$

Figure 3.31   Marr–Hildreth response to an image using $\sigma = 1.5$, 3, 6 and 12.

3.3.4 Corner detection

Edges are linear features that define the boundaries between objects and parts of objects. In many image matching applications a point location is required. Such a location can be matched with other similarly derived locations in other images. The correspondence between features' locations can inform us of the objects' motions or three-dimensional shape. Such applications will be considered in a later chapter, here we are concerned with methods of locating point features.

It has been suggested that regions that have a locally maximum variance will be good features. Finding these might be computationally expensive. It

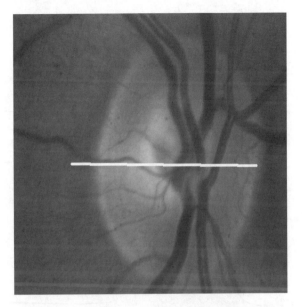

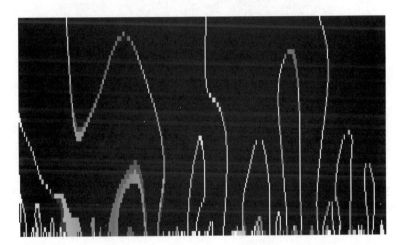

Figure 3.32 Cross-section through a scale space. The location of the cross-section is indicated. The scale space was computing by convolving the image with a Laplacian of Gaussian (Marr–Hildreth) template with increasing values of σ and detecting the zero crossings.

is therefore more efficient to use alternative features – corners have been suggested.

A corner feature is formed at the boundary between two image brightness regions where the boundary curvature is high. The following chapter will describe methods of locating a corner point by tracing these boundaries. It is also possible to locate potential corner features directly in the image.

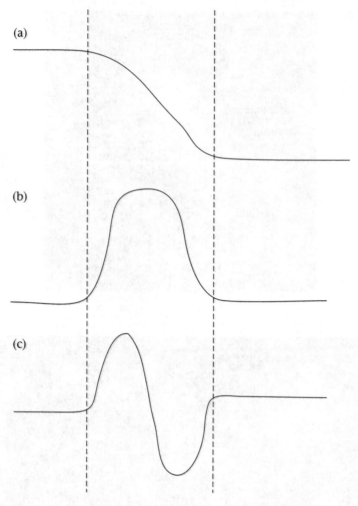

Figure 3.33 Edge detection by double differentiation. (a) Noise free, blurred step edge; (b) differentiation; (c) double differentiation.

One algorithm for achieving this goal is due to Moravec, and is summarised in Figure 3.34. This algorithm relies on the fact that at a corner, the image intensity will have large variations in more than one direction, unlike at an edge, where the image intensity has a large change in only one direction. The operator estimates the edge strength in four directions and takes the minimum as being a measure of interest. After thresholding the response and suppressing non-local maxima, a set of 'points of interest' remain, which may be useful for matching features. Modifications of this algorithm have been defined, principally using different numbers of edge operators or different methods of estimating the measure of interest. As stated previously, other corner detection methods rely on finding boundaries between edge segments and will be discussed in the next chapter.

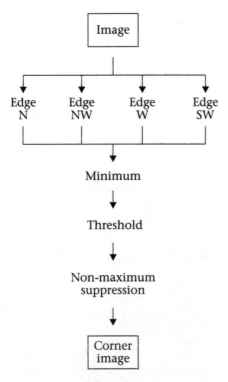

Figure 3.34 Moravec operator.

3.4 Global transforms

Global transforms are those in which the output value of a pixel is computed using all of the pixels in the input image. Differing effects are achieved by weighting the input values differently. These transforms can be used to modify the representation of the data to make it more suitable for certain types of processing. In this section, four commonly used transforms are described: the Fourier, wavelet, Hough and principal component transforms.

3.4.1 Fourier transform

The Fourier transform is a method of transforming an image into its frequency components. An image $f(k, l)$, is transformed to its Fourier representation, $F(u, v)$, and the Fourier representation is transformed back to the image by the pair of transforms:

$$F(u,v) = \frac{1}{N}\sum_{k=0}^{n-1}\sum_{l=0}^{m-1} f(k,l)\exp\left(\frac{-2\pi iku}{n}\right)\exp\left(\frac{-2\pi ilv}{m}\right) \qquad (3.12)$$

$$f(k,l) = \frac{1}{N} \sum_{k=}^{n-1} \sum_{l=0}^{m-1} F(u,v) \exp\left(\frac{2\pi iku}{n}\right) \exp\left(\frac{2\pi ilv}{m}\right) \qquad (3.13)$$

The N in the two equations requires some explanation. The Fourier transform is computed using an algorithm known as the fast Fourier Transform. This is an algorithm that computes the Fourier transform of an array of length 2^n. The two-dimensional transform requires that the image is square, that is, n and m are equal. In this case N is equal to this number, i.e. the width or height of the image. In some versions of this pair of equations, N is replaced by $\sqrt{N}$.

Figure 3.35 illustrates an image and its transform. The origin of the transform is at the centre. The u and v indices are values of spatial frequency and the elements of the transform, i.e. the $F(u, v)$, are termed the transform

Figure 3.35 An image and its Fourier transform. The origin of the transform is at the centre.

coefficients. Values near the origin, i.e. low u and v values, are low-frequency coefficients and contribute to the gross image features. Conversely, those coefficients that are more distant from the origin are termed the high-frequency components and make contributions to the small-scale image structure. Without the high-frequency coefficients, the image would appear blurred to a greater or lesser degree. Note that the transform is symmetrical, i.e. $F(u, v) = F(-u, -v)$. Applications of the Fourier transform in image processing will be discussed below.

The Fourier transform of an image is computed in two stages. As the definition of Equation (3.11) suggests, the inner sum may be computed first and independently of the outer sum. Therefore we transform an image by first transforming the rows (or columns). The columns (or rows) of the partial transform are then transformed to complete the operation.

It can be shown, by taking the Fourier transform of both sides of Equation (3.6), that convolving an image with some template is equivalent to multiplying the image's and template's Fourier transforms. Therefore we may convolve an image with a large template more efficiently in the frequency domain: it is more efficient to transform the image, multiply this by the template's transformation and reverse transform the result. By comparing the numbers of multiplications and additions required to do the convolution by both routes, it is possible to estimate a size of template above which the convolution is more efficient computed by the Fourier transform. This size is in the region of 15 elements on a side.

3.4.2 Wavelet transform

The Fourier transform provides a method of analysing an image's global properties. It determines how the image may be synthesised using a weighted sum of a set of basis functions, which in this case are sines and cosines of varying frequency. Equation (3.13) defines an alternative representation of a one-dimensional signal, the coefficients a_0, a_i and b_i are determined by the Fourier transform. The basis functions are not spatially localised; they are global and therefore exist everywhere. The basis functions are tightly localised in frequency; hence the property of the Fourier transform of determining an image's frequency make-up. This is a desirable property for frequency analysis, but not for many other signal and image processing operations in which localised basis functions are required.

$$f(x) = a_0 + \sum_{i=0}^{\infty} (a_i \cos kx + b_i \sin kx) \tag{3.14}$$

Wavelet analysis was proposed as an alternative method of representing a function (a signal or image) using frequency and spatially localised basis functions; that is, functions that are finite over a restricted range of frequencies and locations.

An infinite number of functions can be defined that have this property. It is not possible to determine in advance which might be useful. However, once a function has been identified, it is used to derive the set of basis functions by translating and dilating (Equation 3.15). The function Φ is usually called the mother wavelet.

$$\Phi_{sl}(x) = 2^{-s/2}\,\Phi(2^{-s}x - l) \tag{3.15}$$

The index l defines the wavelet's location and s its scale.

The data domain is spanned at varying resolutions by using the mother wavelet in a scaling equation:

$$W(x) = \sum_{k=-1}^{N-2} (-1)^k c_{k+1} \Phi(2x + k) \tag{3.16}$$

Four other conditions must be satisfied before the coefficients c_k can qualify as wavelet coefficients:

- Even numbered coefficients must sum to one.
- Odd numbered coefficients must sum to one.
- The sum of the products of adjacent odd or even coefficients must be zero.
- The sum of the products of a coefficient and its complex conjugate must be two.

Having created a wavelet system, it may be used to expand a function, $g(t)$, in terms of the basis functions of Equations (3.15) and (3.16); $g(t)$ might be a time-dependent signal or an image.

$$g(t) = \sum_{l \in Z} c(l)\phi_l(t) + \sum_{j=0}^{j-1} \sum_{k \in Z} d(j,k)W_{j,k}(t) \tag{3.17}$$

The $c(l)$ are known as the wavelet coefficients and represent the approximation of the original signal with a resolution of one point per $2j$ in the original. The expansion coefficients, $d(j, k)$, represent the detail of the original signal at different levels of resolution. The wavelet transform is therefore the process of determining the $c(l)$ and $d(j, k)$ for a given input signal and wavelet family. It is realised by the transforms of Equation (3.18).

$$\begin{aligned} c(l) &= \sum g(t)\phi_l \\ d(j,k) &= \sum g(t)w_{j,k} \end{aligned} \tag{3.18}$$

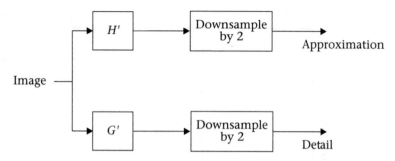

Figure 3.36 Computation of the 1D forward wavelet transform.

In practice, the transform of a one-dimensional signal is computed by convolution with a pair of appropriately designed low- and high-pass filters (H and G respectively), followed by a downsampling operation (Figure 3.36). The transformation of an image is achieved by separating the G and H and treating the horizontal and vertical directions independently (Figure 3.37). At each level of the transformation, there will be four combinations of low- and high-pass filtered data in the two orientations (Figure 3.38). At each level, the L_hL_v (low-pass horizontal, low-pass vertical) band can be further decomposed. The number of decompositions is dependent on the image being transformed and the size of the filters being used. Having completed the transform, an approximation signal and detail signals at a number of scales are returned.

A wavelet transform of an image is shown in Figure 3.39. The detail signals at the various scales of the transformed data are apparent, as is the sparseness of the transformed signal. It is these properties that make the wavelet transform suitable for use in certain feature extraction applications and image coding.

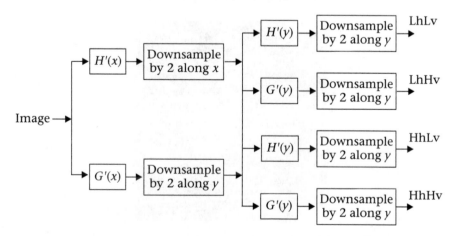

Figure 3.37 Computation of the 2D forward wavelet transform.

Horizontal coordinate

Vertical coordinate

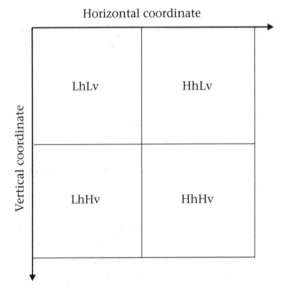

| LhLv | HhLv |
| LhHv | HhHv |

Figure 3.38   Wavelet quadrant diagram.

Figure 3.39   Source image and wavelet transform.

3.4.3 Hough transform

The Hough transform was first proposed as a means of detecting linear features in an image. It depends on being able to represent the object being sought in an analytical manner using a small number of parameters. Each point in the image that might contribute to the object is then transformed into the set of parameters corresponding to all of the objects it might contribute to. Having transformed all of the image points in this way, the sets of parameters are examined; those that have contributions from many points are assumed to be the parameters of objects that really are present in the image.

The transform is best explained with an example.

Consider a straight line. It may be represented by Equation (3.19). This has two parameters: m, the line's gradient, and c, the intercept (the point where the line and the vertical axis intersect).

$$y = mx + c \qquad (3.19)$$

We may rearrange this equation:

$$c = mx - y \qquad (3.20)$$

If we define a space using m and c as coordinates, instead of x and y, then this equation also represents a straight line, with gradient x and intercept $-y$. We can therefore make a transformation between the image space and the Hough accumulator: the image has coordinates x and y, the accumulator has m and c. A point in the image with a specific x, y combination will transform to a line in the accumulator, with that gradient (x) and intercept ($-y$) (Figure 3.40).

The accumulator is a simple array of counters used to record the number of contributions made to each parameter combination. When it is designed,

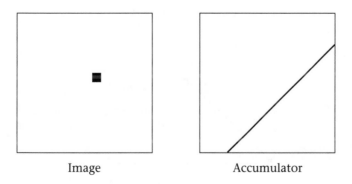

Image   Accumulator

Figure 3.40   Image and Hough accumulator correspondences.

the implementer must decide the appropriate range of parameter values and the resolution of values, i.e. the difference in value between adjacent cells.

The Hough transform is used to locate lines in an image by firstly enhancing the edges in the image and then thresholding them. We then have a set of points, some of which lie on the lines that exist in the image while others do not. Each point is considered in turn; the line it defines in the accumulator is computed and the values in the cells in the accumulator that it passes through are incremented. Having processed all points in this way, the accumulator is searched for local maxima. These define the parameters of lines in the image and the number of points that contributed to this line. No information is available that relates to the start and end points of the line. These must be determined from the original image data.

In practice, this form of the line's equation is not used as it does not represent vertical lines: these have infinite gradient and intercept, which clearly cannot be represented in the accumulator. Instead, the line representation of Figure 3.41 is used. In this, r is the perpendicular distance from the line to the origin and θ is the angle between the perpendicular and the x-axis:

$$r = x\cos\theta + y\sin\theta \qquad (3.21)$$

The Hough transform can be defined for all analytically defined shapes. For a circle, we would use the form:

$$r^2 = (x - x_0)^2 + (y - y_0)^2 \qquad (3.22)$$

where r, x_0 and y_0 represent the circle's radius and origin. The parameter space would be three-dimensional and points would transform into a conical surface.

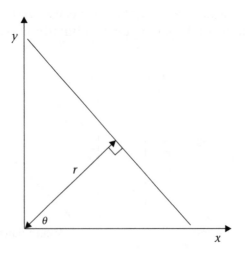

Figure 3.41   Line equation used for the Hough transform.

The transform has also been extended for arbitrarily shaped objects by defining a look-up table that dictates the cells to be incremented. This is not often used.

3.4.4 Principal component transform

The principal component (PC) transform (also known as the Karhunen–Loeve or Hotelling transform) was first suggested as a means of statistically identifying different species of irises. It is essentially a method of ranking the modes of variations in a data set from the most to the least significant. For example, if we measured the heights and weights of a group of people and plotted them on a scatter diagram, we might discover something like Figure 3.42. (The plot of a set of sample measurements in this manner is known as a scatter diagram.) The diagram clearly illustrates a relationship between a person's height and weight: taller people tend to weigh more. There is no significant inverse relationship: we do not often find tall lightweight people or very short heavy people.

The PC transform will identify an alternative representation of the data. This is achieved by firstly subtracting the average values from each point in the dataset, effectively moving the origin of the axes to the centre of the cloud of points. The transform then computes a rotation such that the first PC axis lies along the major axis of the data cloud. The other axis will be at right angles to this (Figure 3.43). The PC axes are given by the eigenvectors of the data's covariance matrix. The amount of the variation accounted for by each axis is given by the eigenvalues of this transform (see Appendix C).

The transform has identified the significant modes of variation of the data; that is, the way in which the most significant changes in the data occur. The values along these modes of variation can be used to recognise the original

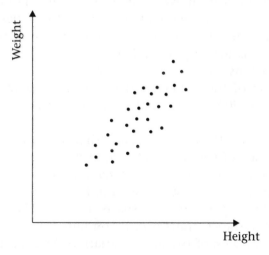

Figure 3.42 Scatter diagram of heights and weights for a sample population.

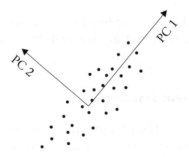

Figure 3.43   Principal component transformed axes.

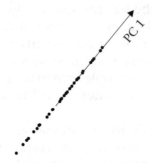

Figure 3.44   The effect of deleting the second component.

data. For example, if we deleted the second principal component of our height–weight data, in effect deleting the second component of Figure 3.43 and projecting all the data onto the axis of the first one (Figure 3.44), we would lose some information but would still be able to identify the tall and heavy individuals and the short and light ones.

In any practical application, we would be using much more than two variables. The PC transform can be used to represent the shapes of objects or the development of a time series of images. In either case we would have a few tens or a few thousands of points. The scatter diagram would have this number of dimensions. Whilst this is a large amount of data, much of it is redundant because of the correlations between the data points. It is not uncommon for over 90% of the total variation to be accounted for by five principal components.

Figure 3.45 illustrates the range of shapes that can be generated using samples along one mode of variation. The input data were 72 *x*- and *y*-coordinates from around the outline of a hand making a certain gesture. Therefore we have a 144-dimensional scatter diagram. Each sample of a hand making the gesture defines a point in this space. Having taken a representative number of samples, the PC transform is computed. In this case, 10 components accounted for 99% of the data's variation. The samples of the figure were derived by inserting appropriate values along one of these components

Figure 3.45 Samples of gestures derived from one significant mode of variation of a hand gesture dataset.

while keeping the others fixed. It is apparent that a significant amount of natural variation is represented by this change in a single value. This topic will be revisited in Chapter 7 when we investigate methods of recognising objects.

3.5 Processing in the frequency domain

3.5.1 Convolution theorem

An appreciation of the convolution theorem is central to an understanding of how the Fourier transform is used in image processing. The theorem states that the convolution of an image and a template will give the identical result to that obtained by multiplying their Fourier transforms. This is summarised

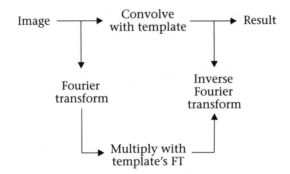

Figure 3.46   Convolution theorem.

in Figure 3.46, where the top row shows the direct computation of the convolution. The alternative path from source to result indicates the Fourier
transform of the image data, multiplication with the template's transform
(which is precomputed for efficiency reasons) and the reverse transform of
the result.

Therefore we may derive equivalent frequency domain operations simply
by deriving the Fourier transform of the template that was used in the spatial
domain. That is, to derive the smoothing operator we must compute the Fourier transform of the smoothing template.

3.5.2 Smoothing

Smoothing of an image was achieved by convolving the image with a uniform template (Figure 3.47(a)). The Fourier transform of this template is
shown in Figure 3.47(b). The desirable property of this function is its cutoff:
low-frequency components are retained to a greater or lesser degree, while
high-frequency components are attenuated or even removed. The less desirable property of the function is its leakage: there are rings surrounding the
central peak at which the transform has finite values: the ideal smoothing
filter would have zeros at all frequencies above the cutoff. The effect of this is
to introduce the ringing that was observed above.

A better smoothing filter may be obtained by using Gaussian smoothing.
The Gaussian template and its transform are shown in Figure 3.48. The transform pair are identical apart from their sizes. The Gaussian filter shows no
leakage and would therefore be expected not to exhibit the ringing effects of
the previous filter. This is indeed the case, as Figure 3.49 shows.

3.5.3 Sharpening

Sharpening is achieved by differentiating the image. The Fourier transform
of the differential operator is shown in Figure 3.50: it gives a uniformly

(a)

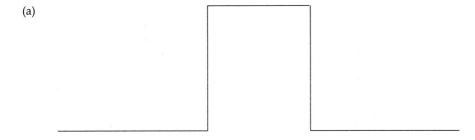

(b)

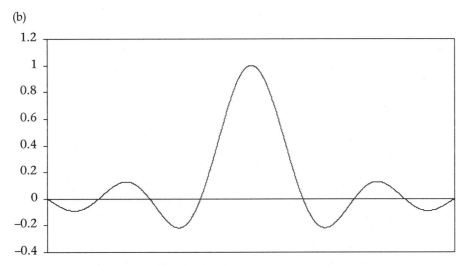

Figure 3.47 Smoothing with the Fourier transform. (a) Uniform template used to smooth an image by convolution; (b) Fourier transform of this template. Note that the template and its transform are circularly symmetrical; Cross-sections only are shown.

increasing amplification to all frequency components. Its effect is shown in Figure 3.51. Although the differential operator amplifies to a degree proportional to frequency, there is an upper limit to the frequency components present in the image; therefore, there are no very high-frequency components in the differentiated data. Likewise, the filter has suppressed low-frequency data. Double differentiation can be realised with a filter whose response increases as the square of frequency.

A frequency domain equivalent of the Marr–Hildreth or Canny operators can be created using the convolution theorem. Recall that these operators were defined as the convolution of a Gaussian function with a double or a single differential operator. Therefore the frequency domain equivalents can be defined by taking the products of the Fourier transforms of the components. In both cases, the operators are bandpass filters (Figure 3.52). The width of the band of frequencies that is passed and the frequency of the peak response are dependent on the operator's parameter, σ.

(a)   (b)

Figure 3.48   Gaussian template and its Fourier transform.

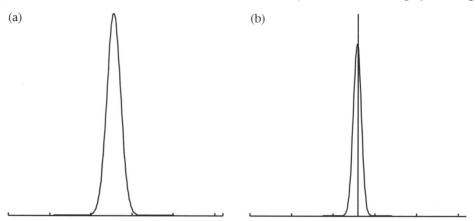

Figure 3.49   An image smoothed using a Gaussian template ($\sigma = 4$).

3.6 Geometrical transformations

Previous section of this chapter have examined methods that process the values of pixels *in situ*; that is, the location of the pixel is not affected. In this section we shall discuss two sets of transforms that change pixels' locations in a carefully defined manner: linear and non-linear transforms.

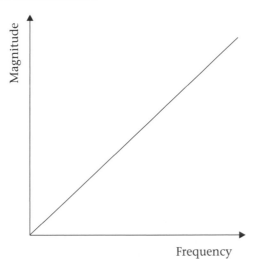

Figure 3.50 Fourier transform of the differential operator. Note that the template and its transform are circularly symmetrical; a cross-section only is shown.

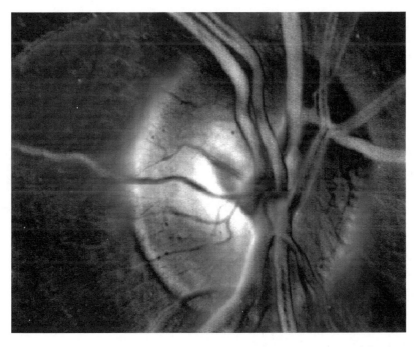

Figure 3.51 Effect of the transform of Figure 3.50 on an image, i.e. we take the product of the image's transform and the differential's transform and inverse transform the data.

Having moved a pixel, we often find that its new location does not correspond to one of the allowed locations: the new location is a non-integer coordinate. We must therefore examine methods of overcoming this problem.

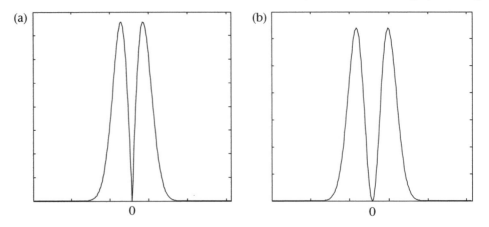

Figure 3.52 Cross-sections through frequency domain equivalent optimal edge detectors. (a) The Canny operator; (b) the Marr–Hildreth operator.

3.6.1 Linear transformations

An arbitrary geometrical transformation will move a pixel at coordinates (x, y) to coordinates (x', y'). The pairs of coordinates are related by the pair of transformation equations:

$$x' = T_x(x, y)$$
$$y' = T_y(x, y)$$

(3.23)

For all linear transformations, the two equations will be expanded to the linear polynomial:

$$x' = a_0 x + a_1 y + a_2$$
$$y' = b_0 x + b_1 y + b_2$$

(3.24)

These equations can in turn be expressed in matrix terms as:

$$\begin{bmatrix} x' \\ y' \\ 1 \end{bmatrix} = \begin{bmatrix} a_0 & a_1 & a_2 \\ b_0 & b_1 & b_2 \\ 0 & 0 & 1 \end{bmatrix} \begin{bmatrix} x \\ y \\ 1 \end{bmatrix}$$

(3.25)

The coordinates are represented using homogeneous coordinates. This is simply so that the whole transform can be represented using a single matrix product, rather than a matrix multiplication followed by a matrix addition.

By using the appropriate values for the six parameters, the various linear transformations of translation, rotation, scaling and shearing can be realised. The values are listed in Table 3.1.

Table 3.1 Transformation coefficient values for linear transformations.

Transformation	a_0	a_1	a_2	b_0	b_1	b_2
Translation by (x, y)	1	0	x	0	1	y
Rotation by θ	$\cos\theta$	$-\sin\theta$	0	$\sin\theta$	$\cos\theta$	0
Uniform scaling by a factor s	s	0	0	0	s	0
Vertical shear by a factor s	1	0	0	0	s	0

These transformations may be applied in sequence and the resulting transformation will also be a linear one. Thus we may translate the image, rotate it and translate it again. The net effect will be a rotation about a point other than the origin. Further, rather than apply each transformation to the image, we may compute a compound transformation matrix by multiplying the individual matrices, and simply transform the image using this single transformation.

One important effect of linear transformations is that straight lines remain straight lines and parallel lines remain parallel. The angle between a pair of intersecting lines might be changed, as might the area enclosed by a polygon.

3.6.2 Non-linear transformations

Non-linear transformations will involve higher order terms in the polynomial expansion of Equation (3.23). We might have a pair of second order transformation equations:

$$x' = a_0 x^2 + a_1 xy + a_2 y^2 + a_3 x + a_4 y + a_5$$
$$y' = b_0 x^2 + b_1 xy + b_2 y^2 + b_3 x + b_4 y + b_5$$

(3.26)

The effect of this type of transformation is to introduce a degree of warping to the data. Depending on the relative magnitudes of the first three coefficients (subscripts 0, 1 and 2) the image will be distorted according to Figure 3.53: pincushion (in which the sides of the image are distorted less than the corners) or barrel distorted. Not only does this transformation produce interesting graphic effects, it also models very accurately the types of distortion introduced by many camera lenses. For accurate measurement work, or for mosaicking a set of images, these distortions must be measured and removed: it is a non-linear transformation that achieves this correction. Figure 3.54 illustrates this process, showing a pair of images and their best overlap before and after correction.

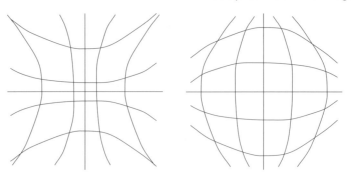

Figure 3.53   Pincushion and barrel distortion.

Figure 3.54   Distortion removed for mosaicking. (a) A pair of input images having a significant overlap. (b) The two images overlapped without any correction for distortion. The misalignment is most apparent in the profile of the mountain on the left hand side and the cloud immediately above it. (c) The same images with the distortions corrected. The misalignment is much less obvious.

3.6.3 Image resampling

Thus far, image transformations have been discussed that map an input image to an output image. Is this a sensible manner to implement the transformation?

Consider a rotation that involves multiplying each coordinate value with a sine or cosine. Only four angles have integer values of these functions: $0°$, $90°$, $180°$ and $270°$. All other angles have non-integer values. Therefore, unless a rotation through these specific angles is required, each input pixel might be transformed to a non-integer output pixel.

Several methods have been suggested for solving this problem: truncating or rounding the coordinate values, or sharing the pixel's value among the neighbouring destination locations. All of these methods suffer from the problem that many pixels in the output image will not be addressed by the transformation. Perhaps the most elegant solution is to apply the transformation in reverse. In this case, we would take an output location and use the reverse transformation to determine where it originated in the input image. This location might still be non-integral, but we are able to guarantee that all output pixels will be populated. Figure 3.55 illustrates the problem: the output pixels (x', y') are reverse mapped to the input pixels (x, y), which might be non-integral.

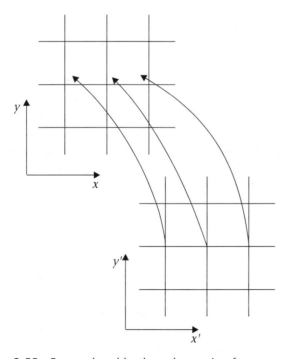

Figure 3.55 Forward and backward mapping for resampling.

How then should the output pixels' values be computed? Two solutions are widely used:

- Nearest neighbour interpolation simply rounds (x, y) to the nearest neighbour. Its value is given to the output (x', y').
- Bilinear interpolation takes a weighted sum of the four nearest neighbours to (x, y). The values of the four neighbours are weighted inversely by their distance from (x, y). Whilst this transformation requires more computations than simple nearest neighbour interpolation, it results in visually more pleasing output; specifically, the jagged effects generated by rotating straight edges are reduced.

3.7 Summary

This chapter has discussed the most significant image transformations. These are the basic building blocks of all image processing/computer vision systems. Their place in such systems will become more apparent as we negotiate the following chapters.

3.8 Bibliography

Myler and Weeks (1993) and Umbaugh (1998) provide useful accounts of low-level image processing. Marr and Hildreth (1980) and Canny (1986) were instrumental in originating what have become optimal edge detectors. Kittler *et al.* (1983) presented an early account of the analysis of the accuracy of simple edge detectors. The analysis has been repeated often since, looking at many different detectors. The corner detector is described in Moravec (1977). Other detectors have been defined, notably SUSAN (Smith, 1996). Hubel (1988) performed much early research into understanding the primate visual system, which had a strong influence on the design of edge detectors and indeed on computer vision systems.

3.9 Exercises

3.1 The perception of the grey values of an image may be improved by changing the grey scale from a linear one to a logarithmic scale, in which the output value is proportional to the logarithm of the input value. Suggest circumstances in which this mapping would be useful and compare the processing times required to perform the transform by (a) using the logarithm function and (b) using a look-up table.

3.2 Implement the histogram equalisation algorithm and verify that it improves the appearance of images under certain conditions.

3.3 Implement the thresholding algorithms and use them to segment a simple image. By how much do the results differ? Are these differences significant?

3.4 Implement software that convolves an image with a 3 × 3 element template. Explore the effects that can be achieved by using various values in the template.

3.5 If a 2D template can be separated into two 1D templates, estimate the numbers of operations that must be performed to convolve an $N \times N$ pixel image with the 2D template and with the two 1D templates.

3.6 The Laplacian of Gaussian (Marr–Hildreth) operator can be approximated by subtracting two Gaussians with different values of σ. For a given LoG, estimate the two values of σ that give the best match and the difference between the LoG and this approximation.

3.7 Estimate the number of operations required to compute the FFT of an image. Hence compare the number of operations required to convolve the image with a $k \times k$ element template with the number of operations required to transform the image, multiply the transform with the previously computed transform of the template and reverse transform the result. For what value of k does the Fourier method become more efficient?

4

Morphology

Morphology is defined as the 'study of the form of things'; that is, the structure of objects. Morphological transforms are those that are designed to elucidate this structure. Morphological techniques are also frequently used to improve the appearance of a thresholded image: we shall see that thresholding seldom, if ever, gives perfect results and will show how these operators may redeem the situation.

Whilst morphological algorithms are usually applied to binary (bilevel) images, they can be adapted to grey scale images. This chapter will describe thresholding, binary morphology and grey level morphology. It concludes with an examination of some specific transforms for extracting structural information from a region: the distance transform, skeletonisation and the convex hull.

4.1 Thresholding

4.1.1 Thresholding monochrome images

Thresholding is the process of reducing the grey scale of a monochrome image to two values. It is defined according to Equation (3.1), which is repeated here:

$$g(i,j) = \begin{cases} 0 & \text{if } f(i,j) \le \theta \\ 1 & \text{otherwise} \end{cases} \tag{4.1}$$

where $f(x, y)$ and $g(x, y)$ are the input and output images respectively and θ is a threshold value. The two output values need not be zero and one. Any two different values are sufficient: 0 and 255 are often used, as this maximises the contrast between the values.

Thresholding is an operation that can also be applied to colour images, which is discussed below.

The execution of the thresholding function is simple; the difficulty lies in selecting the correct value for the threshold. This is done by using the grey

(a)

(b)

Figure 4.1 Two contrasting objects. (a) Dark typed character on a bright background; (b) dark coloured toy on a light background.

level histogram, which records the frequency of occurrence of each grey value in the image. In the ideal case, the threshold would clearly distinguish between contrasting object (foreground) and background: for example, the typed dark letter on the white background, or the dark coloured toy on the light background in Figure 4.1. Figure 4.2 shows the histograms derived from these images. Clearly, we may select some value in the trough between the two peaks as our threshold. If we then applied Equation (4.1), we could distinguish between object and background (but would not be able to identify which was which).

Identifying the threshold in this way is an operation that may be performed manually, or it is a process that is easily automated. This method of determining the threshold is known as the modal method (even though this is a misuse of the term, since the mode is defined as the value that occurs most frequently).

But what would happen if there were no clear division between the foreground and background? Figure 4.3(a) shows an image of part of the retina called the optic nerve head, the region where blood vessels and nerve fibres pass into and out of the eye. It is possible to distinguish between the brighter nerve head region and the darker regions that are due to the retina. However, Figure 4.3(b), the histogram of this image, reveals no such clear division. The same effect is observed if the values of the foreground and background are very similar: imagine the peaks in Figure 4.2(b) sliding towards each other until they overlap. In these cases we cannot threshold at the mode; indeed, the modal threshold may not exist.

(a)

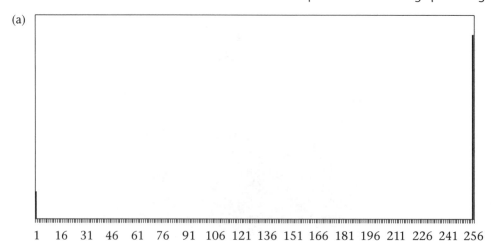

1   16   31   46   61   76   91 106 121 136 151 166 181 196 211 226 241 256

(b)

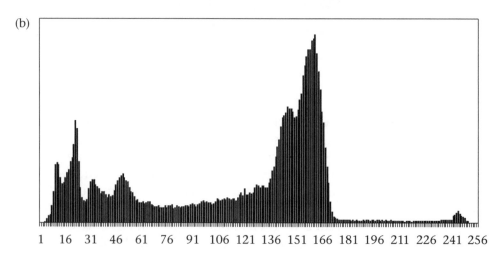

1   16   31   46   61   76   91 106 121 136 151 166 181 196 211 226 241 256

Figure 4.2   The histograms of the images of Figure 4.1.

A simple method of determining the threshold relies on knowing what proportion of the image is occupied by the foreground and whether the foreground is brighter or darker than the background. This method simply defines the threshold as that grey level which selects the correct proportion of the grey levels. If the foreground occupies p% of the image and is brighter than the background, then the threshold we require is the one shown in Figure 4.4. It divides the area under the histogram into one region containing $(100 - p)$% of the pixels, corresponding to the background, and a region containing p% of the pixels: the foreground. Naturally, this method is only effective if the size of the object is known in advance.

In other cases, two iterative methods have been suggested; both are equally effective and differ only in detail.

(a)

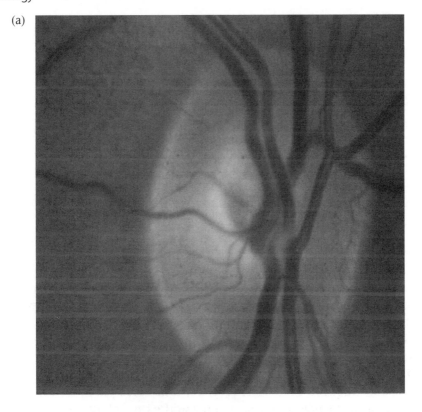

(b)

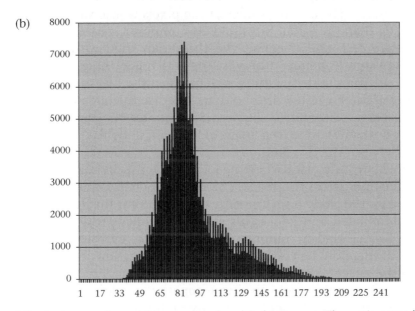

Figure 4.3 An image of an optic nerve head and its histogram. The optic nerve head is the region on the retina where blood vessels and nerve fibres pass through the eyeball.

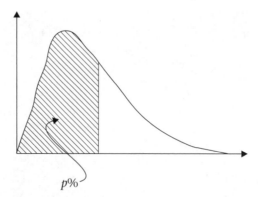

$p\%$

Figure 4.4   Histogram and P-tile threshold.

The first method searches incrementally through the histogram for a threshold. Starting at the lower end of the histogram, we compute the average of the pixels with grey values less than the suggested threshold, L, and the average of the pixels with grey values greater than the suggested threshold, G. We then compute the average of L and G. This value will be the threshold if it is equal to the suggested threshold, otherwise we increment the suggested threshold and repeat the process.

The second method searches the histogram more purposefully. An initial threshold value is suggested: the average of the image's four corner pixels is a suitable choice. The average values of the pixels whose values are less than and greater than the initial threshold are computed, L and G respectively. If the average of L and G equals the threshold, then we have found the threshold value, as before; otherwise the search continues with an updated value of the threshold. The difference between the two methods lies in the updating of the suggested threshold: in this case the updated value is equal to the average of L and G. Figure 4.5 illustrates the results obtained by applying both methods to the image of Figure 4.3; there is no significant difference between the two methods.

A problem will also arise when the local average in an image varies in a systematic manner across the image. This can happen if, for example, the scene is illuminated strongly from one side: the side nearer the light source will be better illuminated and hence this side of the image will be brighter. Any threshold value that is computed using statistics derived from the whole image will therefore be correct in a few image locations but incorrect over most of the image.

The solution to this problem is to estimate the value of the threshold at each pixel. This is usually achieved by inspecting the pixels in the region surrounding the pixel and computing a threshold using one of the methods discussed. The size of the region to be inspected should be decided by experimentation. It should also be realised that inspecting all of the image's

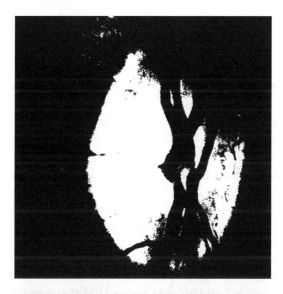

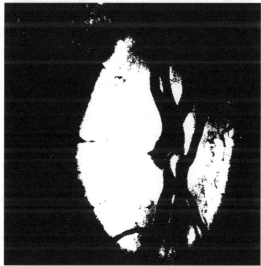

Figure 4.5 Thresholded images derived from Figure 4.3 using two iterative threshold finding methods. No significant differences are apparent.

pixels is an expensive operation; instead, a subset could be chosen and the intervening thresholds could be interpolated. Again, the number of thresholds to be computed should be determined by experimentation.

There are occasions when the foreground occupies a range of grey values that is between two ranges of background. That is, there are background pixels that are darker and brighter than the foreground. The solution to this difficulty is to define two threshold values, θ_1 and θ_2. The thresholding rule of Equation (4.1) now becomes:

$$g(x,y) = \begin{cases} 1 & \text{if } \theta_1 \leq f(x,y) \leq \theta_2 \\ 0 & \text{otherwise} \end{cases} \qquad (4.2)$$

The output values have been exchanged to ensure that the foreground has a greater value in the output image. The process is known as band thresholding, the two thresholds can be supplied manually or using an adaptation of the mode method. The two iterative methods are inappropriate.

4.1.2 Thresholding colour images

As we know, a colour image is represented using three colour channels. This suggests a simple method of thresholding the data: supply a threshold for each colour channel independently of the others and combine the results by conjunction: the effect of this is to partition the RGB colour cube into octants; the thresholded region will be the cuboid furthest from the origin: Figure 4.6. The drawback of this method is that it is not particularly flexible as the required object will not often lie in an octant of the colour cube. It is of course possible to band threshold colour images, in which case six thresholds would be defined and the colour space would be partitioned into 27 regions.

Of more practical use is a method that thresholds the colour space according to each colour's distance from a user-specified one; that is, the user specifies a reference colour (R_0, G_0, B_0) and the thresholding operation selects those pixels having similar colours:

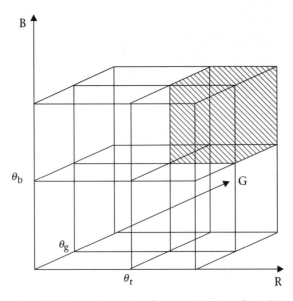

Figure 4.6 Thresholding colour data by partitioning the RGB colour cube.

$$g(x,y) = \begin{cases} 1 & \text{if } d(x,y) \le d_{\max} \\ 0 & \text{otherwise} \end{cases} \qquad (4.3)$$

where $d(x, y)$ is a distance function defined in the colour space:

$$d(x,y) = \sqrt{(f_R(x,y) - R_0)^2 + (f_G(x,y) - G_0)^2 + (f_B(x,y) - B_0)^2} \qquad (4.4)$$

Although performing this thresholding operation using RGB data will generally give satisfactory results, it may be more appropriate to use the perceptual colour space defined by the hue, saturation and value (HSV) components. Since HSV defines a perceptually uniform colour space, the value of $d_{\max}$ will give the same perceptual effect, irrespective of the location of the colour in the colour space. This is not the case with the RGB colour space: the same value of $d_{\max}$ may be perceived differently according to location within the colour space.

4.1.3 Outcome of thresholding operations

In the earlier example of a thresholded image (Figures 4.1 and 4.2), there was a clear distinction between foreground and background, and therefore there was no confusion between these regions in the thresholded images. In practice, such a state is rare. It is much more common to encounter the situation exemplified by Figure 4.3, in which the grey scale ranges occupied by foreground and background overlap and there are misclassified pixels in the output: some foreground pixels have been classified as background and vice versa. The number of erroneously classified pixels may be estimated by inspecting the histogram. Two Gaussian distributions are fitted to the curve, representing the distributions of foreground and background pixels. The threshold value can be defined at the lowest value of the histogram between the two peaks, as shown in Figure 4.7. Then the two shaded areas represent the proportion of misclassified pixels: the number of foreground pixels classified as background and vice versa. These pixels are revealed in the image as inconsistencies in the boundary between foreground and background, and isolated pixels of one class lying within the bulk of the other (isolated white or black pixels).

4.2 Processing binary images

Binary morphology relies on three key concepts:

- a structuring element
- fitting
- hitting

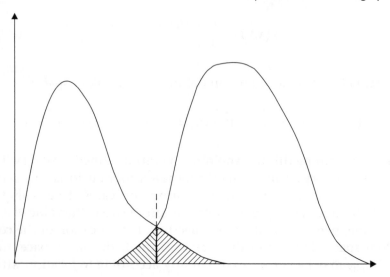

Figure 4.7 The histogram of an image containing two objects having different but over-lapping grey level distributions. The shaded regions indicate the proportions of misclassified pixels, either object 1 pixels classed as object 2, or vice versa.

The structuring element is a small template that is used to investigate the image. The structuring element's values, like the image it investigates, will be binary. Combinations of values making circular, square or cross-shaped templates are usually employed. The template will have an origin: it is this location that specifies the template's location in the image and therefore the position where the operation's result will be written. It is usual for the structuring element to have odd dimensions and for the origin to be at the centre.

A structuring element is said to fit at an image location if *all* the image pixels that overlap the structuring element pixels of value 1 are also 1. The image values are irrelevant if the structuring element value is 0. Therefore, in Figure 4.8 the structuring element fits at location A but not at location B.

$$
\begin{array}{ccc}
1 & 1 & 1 \\
1 & 1 & 1 \\
1 & 1 & 1
\end{array}
$$

Structuring element

```
0  0  0  0  0  0  0  0
0  0  1  1  0  0  0  0
0  1  1  1  0  0  0  0
0  1  1  1  1  1  1  0
0  0  0  1  1  1  0  0
0  0  0  1  1  1  0  0
0  0  0  0  0  0  0  0
```
B   A

Image

Figure 4.8 Structuring element fitting and not fitting a binary image.

Structuring element

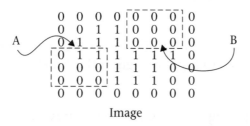

Image

Figure 4.9 Structuring element hitting and not hitting a binary image.

The structuring element is said to hit at an image location if *any* of the image pixels that overlap the 1 values in the structuring element are 1. In Figure 4.9, the structuring element hits at location A but not at location B.

Given these definitions, the two major morphological operations and their two combinations can be defined.

4.2.1 Erosion

Three definitions of erosion will be presented: using the fitting operation, a set theoretic definition and a very informal one.

Erosion of an image $f(x, y)$ by a structuring element $s(x, y)$, is denoted by $f \ominus s$ and is defined as:

$$f \ominus s = \begin{cases} 1 & \text{if } s \text{ fits } f \\ 0 & \text{otherwise} \end{cases} \tag{4.5}$$

The origin of s is placed in all possible locations in the image in this computation. Just as occurred with convolutions, there will be locations where the structuring element overlaps the image boundary. In such cases we proceed as we did with convolution previously: either we process just those pixels that lie within the image, ignoring the portions of the structuring element that are outside of the image, or we disregard these portions of the image entirely.

Secondly, the operation of erosion is defined formally using the set theoretic notation of Equation (4.7), which uses the operation defined in Equation (4.6).

$$A_x = \{c : c = a + x, \forall a \in A\} \tag{4.6}$$

$$A \ominus B = \{x : B_x \subseteq A\} \tag{4.7}$$

The first of these equations defines a displacement of the set of pixels A by an amount x (x will define a distance and direction). The second equation defines the erosion of A using the structuring element B.

Finally, we may also describe this operation informally as the following two steps:

- at each possible placement of the structuring element in the image
- remove the pixel overlying the origin if the structuring element overlies a non-object pixel

The effect of applying this operator to a binary image is shown in Figure 4.10. An image of an optic nerve head has been thresholded to give an initial binary image. The result of four iterations of erosion is shown. It is apparent that isolated object pixels are soon removed and the object itself shrinks at each iteration by an amount approximately equal to the size of the structuring element. The shrinkage is not only from the outside of the object; holes within the object are enlarged.

There are two obvious applications of erosion. The first is the removal of unwanted small-scale structures in an image. However, if we use erosion for this purpose, objects in the image that should be retained are also adversely affected. So, although erosion could be used for this purpose, in practice other operators are used. Secondly, erosion may be used to identify the boundaries of objects. By subtracting a suitably eroded version of the image from the original, we identify those pixels that were removed by the erosion: isolated noise pixels plus object boundaries (Figure 4.11).

Figure 4.10 Erosion of a binary image using a square structuring element.

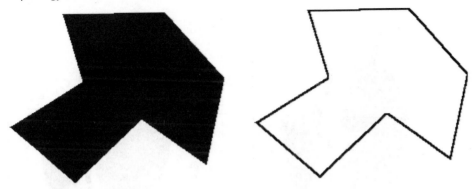

Figure 4.11 Boundary detection using erosion.

4.2.2 Dilation

The converse to erosion is dilation. Whereas erosion removes pixels from objects in an image, dilation adds pixels to the objects. Following the previous description, three definitions of dilation will be presented.

The dilation of an image, $f(x, y)$, by a structuring element $s(x, y)$, is denoted by $f \oplus s$. It is defined as:

$$f \oplus s = \begin{cases} 1 & \text{if } s \text{ hits } f \\ 0 & \text{otherwise} \end{cases} \tag{4.8}$$

Again, this is realised by placing the structuring element's origin at all locations in the image and performing this test. Overlaps of s with the image boundary are dealt with in the same manner.

The formal set theoretic definition of dilation requires the translation of Equation (4.6) and a reflection operator as defined in Equation (4.9). Using these, dilation is defined in Equation (4.10).

$$\hat{B} = \{x : x = -b, \forall b \in B\} \tag{4.9}$$

$$A \oplus B = \{x : \hat{B}_x \cap A \neq \varnothing\} \tag{4.10}$$

And finally, we have an informal definition of dilation:

- at each possible placement of the structuring element in the image
- add the pixel overlying the origin if the structuring element overlies an object pixel

What effect does this operator have on an image? Figure 4.12 shows the same source image as was used in Figure 4.10, but it is now dilated four times

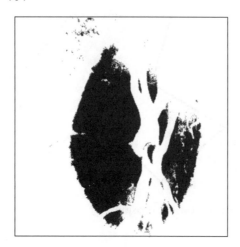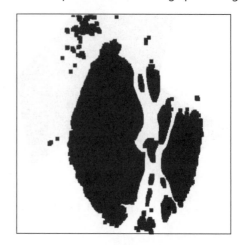

Figure 4.12   Dilation of a binary image using a square structuring element.

with the same structuring element. As might be expected, at each iteration the object expands: a layer of pixels whose thickness is approximately the size of the structuring element has been added to the boundaries of the objects. Isolated noise pixels have also been expanded. Small structures on the objects are more pronounced and small holes in the object boundary have been filled in.

4.2.3 Opening

Erosion and dilation both have positive effects: one removes isolated and small structures, the other fills in gaps. They also have a negative effect: the sizes of all objects are changed. Erosion and dilation operators may be combined to enhance the positive effects and suppress the negative. Opening of an image is defined as erosion followed by dilation using the same structuring element.

The erosion operator will remove noise pixels, be they isolated ones or spurs connected to an object. It will also shrink the object by removing some layers of boundary pixels and also expand any holes in the boundary, which could also be due to noise. The dilation operator will replace the boundary pixels and, to a certain extent, fill in the boundary holes. Figure 4.13 illustrates the effect of the operation, showing the original image, the intermediate result of erosion and the final result. It is apparent that a much smoother version of the object has been generated: isolated pixels have been removed and the object boundary is significantly straighter than it was originally.

Whereas further applications of erosion or dilation operators changed the image, further opening of the image with the same structuring element will produce no more changes.

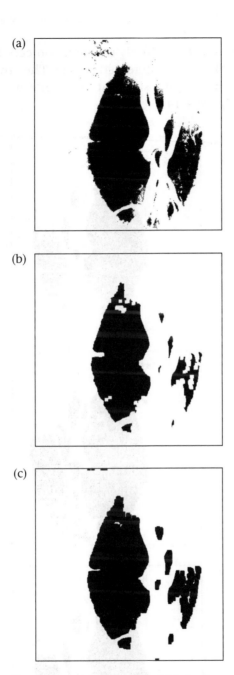

Figure 4.13 Opening of an image. (a) The original binary image; (b) the intermediate eroded version; (c) the final dilated version.

4.2.4 Closing

Closing uses the other combination of the two basic operators: it is defined as dilation followed by erosion. The dilation operator will fill holes in the object and possibly result in closely adjacent objects being merged. The objects themselves will also be increased in size. The erosion operation will restore the object to its original size, but holes that were filled will remain filled, as shown in Figure 4.14.

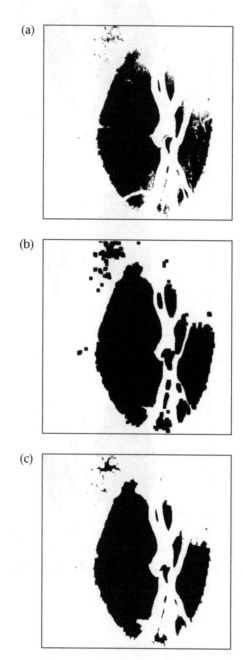

Figure 4.14 Closing of an image. (a) Original binary image; (b) intermediate dilated image; (c) final eroded image.

Like opening, repeated application of the closing operator, using the same structuring element, will have no further effect on the image.

4.3 Processing grey scale images

Although morphological operators have so far been applied exclusively to bilevel images, they may be modified for application to grey scale images.

In grey scale morphology, the structuring element will no longer be bilevel; it may take integer values, including zero and negative values. The formulation of the erosion and dilation operators must therefore be modified, and they must be understood in slightly different ways. The effects of eroding or dilating a grey scale image will be dramatically different to the equivalent binary operators.

4.3.1 Erosion and dilation

Formally, the grey scale erosion of an image, $f(x, y)$, with a structuring element, $s(x, y)$, at location m, n, is defined as:

$$f \ominus s(m,n) = \min_{j,k \in S}\{f(m-j,n-k) - s(j,k)\} \quad (4.11)$$

The output value is simply the minimum difference between the image and structuring element.

Informally, this operation may be understood by imagining the image as a landscape, with the intensity equating to height. We place the structuring element beneath the landscape and raise it as far as possible without it piercing the surface. The distance that the element is raised is the required output. Note that this distance could be negative if any of the structuring element's values is greater than the corresponding image value. The value could also exceed the maximum range of image values if the structuring element had negative values. The output of the erosion must therefore either be truncated to the correct range, or rescaled once the global minimum and maximum have been determined.

Figure 4.15 illustrates the effect of using a uniform structuring element to erode a simple grey scale image.

Once again, we may formally define the dilation of an image, $f(x, y)$, with a structuring element, $s(x, y)$, at location m, n:

$$f \oplus (m,n) = \max_{j,k \in S}\{f(m-j,n-k) + s(j,k)\} \quad (4.12)$$

The informal explanation of this is that we invert the structuring operator and lower it from above the landscape until one element makes contact with the surface. The height of this element is the value to be output. The same

Figure 4.15   Grey scale erosion.

comments may be made regarding the range of the output values, and an example result is presented in Figure 4.16.

4.3.2 Opening and closing

Opening and closing of a grey scale image are defined in exactly the same ways as for a bilevel image, except, of course, that the erosion and dilation operators are now defined differently. The effect of the operators is also

Figure 4.16   Grey scale dilation.

different: rather than smoothing the outlines of objects, we are now smoothing the topography of the landscape that is represented by the image. Opening and closing can be viewed as smoothing the landscape from underneath and above respectively (Figures 4.17 and 4.18).

Consider the structuring element to be a sphere. Then the opening operator can be thought of as rolling the sphere over the underside of the

Figure 4.17   Grey scale opening.

Figure 4.18 Grey scale closing.

landscape. The output of the operation will be the highest points reached by any part of the sphere. Peaks narrower than the sphere will be too small for it to enter and will therefore be reduced in amplitude and sharpness. The initial erosion removed the small details (small with respect to the structuring element), but also darkened the image. The following dilation brightened the image but could not reintroduce the details removed by erosion.

Conversely, closing can be thought of as rolling the sphere over the top of the surface and recording the lowest heights it reaches. Thus the brightest points in the image remain, but darker, smaller peaks will be removed.

4.3.3 Applications

Three particularly useful combinations of grey scale morphological operators have been defined and are discussed in this section. The section concludes with a description of two applications of these operators.

4.3.3.1 Morphological smoothing

Recall that images were smoothed by convolution with the appropriate template. Morphological operators may also be used to smooth an image. As described above, opening an image tended to remove bright peaks in the data while closing the image removed dark troughs. If both operators are used then the extrema are removed, as shown in Figure 4.19.

Figure 4.19 Morphological smoothing.

4.3.3.2 Morphological gradient

The morphological gradient is computed as the difference between the opened and closed image. It has the advantage of being less sensitive to orientation than the edge enhancement operators discussed previously, which computed edge strength in the two directions parallel to the image sides. Figure 4.20 illustrates the results of computing the morphological gradient of an image.

Figure 4.20 Morphological gradient.

Figure 4.21   Top-hat transformed image.

4.3.3.3 Top-hat transformation

The top-hat transformation is defined by the difference between an image and its opened version. Its strength lies in its ability to enhance detail in an image that would otherwise be obscured by shading; see Figure 4.21. The dual of the top-hat transform is the difference between the closed image and the original image; this will enhance slightly different structures.

4.3.3.4 Textural segmentation

Some uniformly textured images may be rendered smooth by repeated closing with progressively larger structuring elements. Consider the textured image of Figure 4.22. Starting with a small structuring element, smaller than

Figure 4.22   Texture segmentation. Adjacent regions having different textures may be detected easily.

the blobs, we may iteratively close the image, at each iteration increasing the size of the structuring element. Whilst the element is smaller than the blobs, they will not be removed. Once the element's size equals the blob size, the blobs will be removed.

If the image contained regions of differently sized blobs, continuing the operation would eventually render the entire image a uniform shade by gradually removing each region's blobs. Maintaining a record of the image's grey scale characteristics (mean grey value would be sufficient) during the closing operations will reveal the characteristic sizes of the blobs in each textured region.

4.3.3.5 Granulometry

Granulometry is the study of determining the size distributions of objects, usually in images. In some images it is possible to isolate the particles being viewed and hence measure their dimensions. Such cases are rare. It is more common for particles to be adjacent or overlapping. Isolating individual particles is therefore impossible. Opening or closing the image (which operation is used will depend on whether the particles are brighter or darker than the background) will remove particles whose size matches the structuring element. Therefore the difference between the original and the processed images will reveal information about the number of particles of that size. The image may therefore be characterised by iteratively opening or closing with increasingly large structuring elements. At each iteration, the difference between the original and processed images is computed. Finally, the size distribution is obtained.

4.4 Structural features

Several types of feature may be derived from binary images that are characteristic of the objects contained in them. The skeleton is a minimal representation of an object's shape. It includes just those pixels that define the structure of the object, excluding any extra detail such as brightness, colour or thickness. It is often computed using the distance transform. Finally, the convex hull is a minimal representation of the area covered by an object.

4.4.1 Distance transform

The distance transform is used to estimate the minimum distance between each point in an object and the background. All versions of the distance transform will compute the city block distance between a point inside an object and the image's background.

One intensive method of computing the distance transform is to use a 3 × 3 pixel structuring element to repeatedly erode an object until it is completely

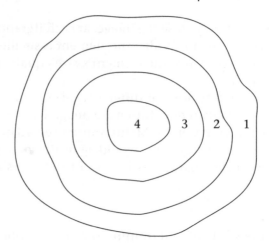

Figure 4.23 Distance transform using erosion.

removed. At each iteration a set of pixels will be removed from the object. The iteration number is the distance transform for these pixels; see Figure 4.23.

A slightly less intensive method uses the relationships of Equation (4.13):

$$f^0(x,y) = f(x,y)$$
$$f^m(x,y) = f^0(x,y) + \min(f^{m-1}(i,j)) \tag{4.14}$$

These simply state that the first iteration of the algorithm sets the pixels in the distance transform equal to the values of pixels in the original image (which will be zeros and ones).

At each successive iteration of the algorithm, m, the distance of a pixel, $f(x, y)$, is increased by the minimum distance of its four nearest neighbours. The increments to be used will depend on the distance measure employed. Figure 4.24 shows the increments to be used when Euclidean distances are used (Figure 4.24(a)) and the city block distances (Figure 4.24(b)).

The distance transform may be useful when computing the skeleton of an image, as discussed below. Figure 4.25 illustrates its use in detecting the centre of the palm of the hand in a gesture recognition system.

4.4.2 Skeleton

The skeleton of an object is a one pixel thick line that represents the object's shape. For example, in Figure 4.26 the lower half of each letter shows the skeleton of that part of the letter. It is apparent that the skeleton retains the characters' shapes and topological relationships, but has lost all information relating to their thicknesses.

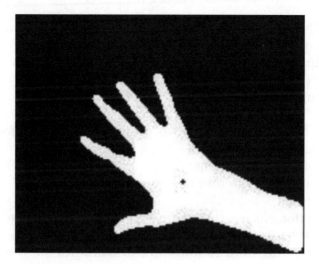

Figure 4.25 Distance transform applied to a hand image to detect the centre of the palm.

Figure 4.26 Skeletonisation. The image shows a set of characters whose bottom halves have been skeletonised.

The skeleton must retain the following properties:

- Connected image regions must thin to connected portions of the skeleton.
- The skeleton must be at least eight-connected.
- The locations of ends of lines must be maintained.
- The skeleton must approximate the medial line of the object.
- Extraneous spurs introduced by thinning must be minimised.

The medial line passes though the centre of the shape. This property is the most difficult to maintain due to the discrete nature of the data.

The skeleton is most often computed by repeated cycles of thinning operations. Each cycle consists of four applications of a thinning algorithm working from the top of the image to the bottom, the bottom to the top, left to right and right to left. These operations investigate a pixel and its eight neighbours. This ordering of the thinning is required to ensure that pixels are removed equally from all sides of the object.

During an application of the thinning algorithm all pixels are inspected in the context of their eight nearest neighbours. The pixel may be removed if all of the following conditions are met:

- its removal does not result in two portions of the skeleton becoming disconnected
- it is not the end point of a line
- it has at least one background neighbour

The first criterion ensures that connected regions of an image remain connected in the skeleton. The second ensures that the end points of objects are maintained. Thinning from all four directions ensures the symmetry of the operation and helps to ensure that the skeleton approximates the medial axis.

Whilst this is an effective method of skeletonising an image, it is not necessarily very efficient. Other methods have been defined that perform the task more quickly, which are cited in the bibliography. One method of interest uses the information derived from the distance transform: since the skeleton is defined by points that are furthest from the background, the value of the distance transform at these locations should be maximal in some sense: it will either be a local maximum or will lie on a ridge. The adjacent points on the ridge will be the adjacent points on the skeleton.

4.4.3 Convex hull

An object can be described as convex if a line connecting any two points in the object lies entirely within the object; see Figure 4.27. The convex hull of an arbitrary object is the smallest convex object that contains it; see Figure 4.28. The usefulness of the convex hull lies in its ability to define the area of the image that contains the object in question and to enable the discrepancies between it and the object to be identified. Both of these pieces of information are useful in the context of recognising the object.

One method of computing the convex hull relies on tracing the outline of the object. At each point on the outline, the angles defined by the tangent at this pixel and the vector between the current pixel and all other pixels on the boundary are computed; see Figure 4.29. The next point on the convex hull's outline will be the point for which this angle is minimised.

Other, set theoretic, methods of determining the convex hull have been defined. The interested reader is referred to the references cited in the bibliography.

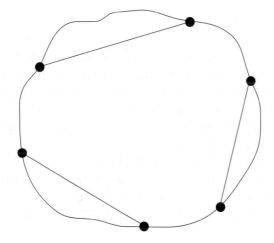

Figure 4.27 The definition of a convex object.

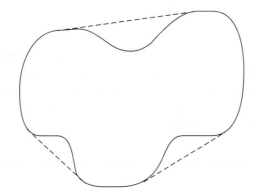

Figure 4.28 The convex hull of an arbitrary object.

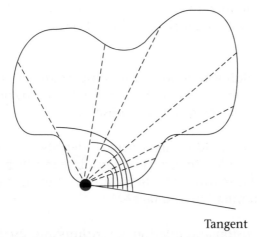

Tangent

Figure 4.29 Computing the convex hull.

4.5 Summary

This chapter has examined morphological image processing techniques. These are usually applied to binary images; therefore methods of reducing a grey scale image to a binary (bilevel) image were examined. The fundamental operations involved are erosion and dilation. These were defined and used to derive two further operations: opening and closing. Examples of the use of these operations have been given.

Morphological techniques are not exclusively applied to bilevel images. The modifications to the erosion and dilation operators to allow their application to grey scale images were therefore defined.

Finally, three methods of extracting structural information using morphological methods were discussed.

4.6 Bibliography

Serra (1982) was one of the originators of mathematical morphology applied to images. Dougherty (1992) also gives a useful summary. Parker (1997) discusses and evaluates various thresholding and other applications. Kalles and Morris (1993) presented a novel skeletonisation algorithm that was more efficient than any others at that time.

4.7 Exercises

4.1   Use one of the iterative methods to compute the optimum threshold value for separating an object from its background. Now repeat this exercise for another object. Are the thresholds the same? Can you explain why?

4.2   Use a thresholding function to investigate the effect of varying the threshold above and below the optimum defined by one of the iterative methods. Explain the results you observe.

4.3   Use a colour thresholding algorithm to identify skin-coloured pixels in a head and shoulders image. How can these results be used to identify the person's face? How will the skin colour value change as a consequence of illumination and race?

4.4   Implement erosion and dilation algorithms and use them to improve the quality of your thresholded images from earlier exercises.

4.5   Under what conditions could the medial axis transform be used to plan
the path of a mobile robot? (Think about the colour of the floor compared with the walls and other obstructions.)

5
Region detection

Region detection is the process of dividing an image into separate and non-overlapping regions. All of the pixels in an image must belong to some region or another.

A region can be specified by defining either the pixels that constitute it or the pixels that bound it. In this chapter we shall examine methods that have been designed to break an image into its constituent regions using these two definitions as starting points. We shall pay particular attention to those methods that are based entirely on the pixel data: that is, methods that do not attempt to identify any objects in the image. A later chapter will examine methods that segment an image by searching for particular structures within it.

Having separated an image into regions, the next step in processing the image will be to identify those regions and the relationships between them. This is the subject of the following chapter.

5.1 Introduction

Region detection, also known as image segmentation, is the process of dividing an image into a set of non-overlapping regions that completely cover the image. A region might be:

- an object
- part of an object
- the background

Figure 5.1 illustrates the type of results we could expect of a segmentation operator. Note that there are regions fitting into each of the three categories. This poses an interesting practical difficulty: how do we evaluate the success or failure of a segmentation function? An apocryphal story has it that a researcher was reporting the results of a simple experiment at a conference. He had sent a photograph of a simple object to a dozen of the world's leading computer vision laboratories, with the question: show the regions you would segment this image into. Not surprisingly, he received a dozen different

Figure 5.1 Illustrative segmentation results.

answers. Most revealing was the comment, 'I have drawn the regions you want, but they aren't the ones I see.' This suggests that we cannot evaluate these functions in isolation: we must include the context of the task we are performing. Therefore, if we are designing an optical character recognition system, does the segmentation algorithm separate characters from non-characters? If we are building a vision system for a mobile robot, does the segmentation algorithm separate the flat surfaces from the rest of the data? Can we recognise the characters from the regions we have identified, and can the robot safely move onto the flat surfaces it has found?

In general, we may state that having segmented an image, every pixel in the image will have been assigned to a region, so the union of all regions is the original image; each region will be homogeneous, or self-similar in some sense, and each region will be different from its neighbouring regions, or alternatively the union of two neighbouring regions is non-homogenous. These three criteria can be summed as:

$$\bigcup_{i=1}^{n} R_i = P$$
$$H(R_i) = True \qquad\qquad (5.1)$$
$$H(R_i \cup R_j) = False$$

where P defines a set of pixels that is being segmented (the image) and H some homogeneity predicate, which will return the value *True* for a region that is homogeneous.

A region is defined by the pixels that make it up. So we would say, 'this set of pixels represents an object' in some arbitrary image. The identity of the region is of no consequence at this moment; it is simply our concern to be able to identify areas of self-similar pixels. This suggests one method of segmenting the image: accumulate all the adjacent and self-similar pixels into the regions they represent.

Alternatively, a region may be defined by the pixels that form its border; that is, the outline of the region. It is a simple matter to convert from one representation to another. A region's boundary is readily derived from the pixels constituting the region: we could erode the image using a three by three structuring element and subtract this from the original region which would leave the pixels constituting the boundary. Alternative, the area surrounded by the boundary could be filled using some form of scanline algorithm, thus identifying the pixels making up the region (Figure 5.2).

Region detection algorithms are also sometimes classified according to how they isolate the regions. Point-based methods inspect individual pixels independently of their neighbours. If the pixel matches some global

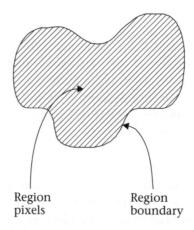

Region   Region
pixels   boundary

Figure 5.2 A region may be defined by its boundary or the pixels constituting it.

criterion, then it belongs to the region. Naturally, different criteria will be set for each region. After the initial labelling of the pixels, groups of contiguous pixels would be accumulated. Conversely, local methods will accumulate pixels into a region: starting from a single pixel we would inspect the neighbours, adding them to the region if they are similar.

In this chapter we shall discuss thresholding as an example of a point-based method, and region growing, the split and merge algorithm, and edge following as examples of local methods. Note that these methods divide the image into regions using only information available in the image; they are so called 'bottom-up' methods. Segmentation algorithms have also been defined that search for specific objects within an image; for example, a security application might segment an image into regions resembling people and other regions. Such algorithms will always include application-specific information: for example, information regarding the appearance of people in the type of image being captured. They will be closely coupled to the task they solve; they will perform this task well, but no other task.

Figure 5.1 also illustrates a further problem with segmentation algorithms. The tree has been separated into myriad small regions. When we view the image, we recognise that the object is a 'tree', irrespective of the further segmentation that could be performed to identify the trunk, branches, leaves and various shaded regions. But at a finer scale we could isolate large branches and the trunk, and at a finer scale still, perhaps we could identify leaves and shadows. The problem is: at what level should we segment the image? Is it appropriate to identify the leaves or the tree? This is a problem that is addressed by scale-based methods.

The final portion of this chapter will discuss methods of representing a segmented image.

5.2 Point based methods – thresholding

The methodology of thresholding was explained in the preceding chapter: what it achieves and how it is realised. In this section we shall examine how these methods are applied to practical situations in which we are attempting to separate an object, objects or parts of an object from each other and the background.

5.2.1 Global thresholds

We have seen how a single threshold that is to be applied to the image as a whole may be computed. We have also seen how variable illumination may cause this single threshold to give incorrect results. If it is possible, by illuminating the scene carefully and by judicious choice of the background, we can ensure that the object and background are contrasting shades or colours. We

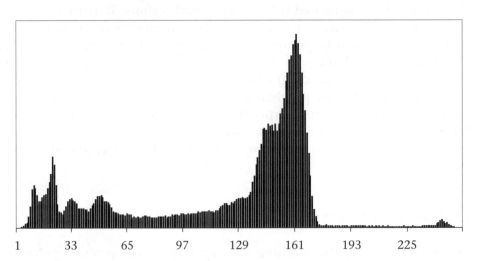

Figure 5.3 An image and its histogram. This illustrates that a unique threshold may not be suitable for separating the object from the background. Either some of the image will be classed as background, or, more likely in this case, some of the background will be classed as object.

may therefore guarantee that the image has a two-peaked (bimodal) histogram and a single threshold value will separate the object and background, as in Figure 5.3. Unfortunately, we do not always have control over the scene's properties, as Figure 5.4 illustrates. This is the image of Figure 4.3 with the threshold computed using one of the iterative methods. It is plain that the boundary is located correctly in some areas but not at most of them. Computing thresholds locally was suggested as the solution to this problem.

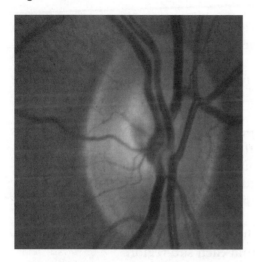

Figure 5.4 The image of Figure 4.3 and its thresholded version computed using a global threshold.

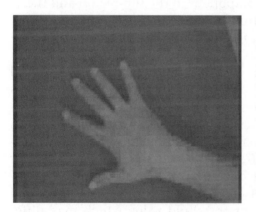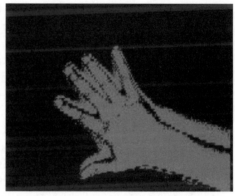

Figure 5.5 Skin thresholding. The skin-coloured pixels of the image have been selected using colour information.

Colour values can be used very effectively to isolate objects of known colour. Figure 5.5 shows how skin-coloured regions are selected; the image is one extracted from a gesture recognition system where finding the hands is the first stage in being able to recognise a set of gestures. The method works by defining the colour of the skin and isolating those pixels whose colour values are similar.

5.2.2 Local thresholds

Local thresholding methods are invoked in cases where the scene's illumination is spatially variant. They divide the image into sufficiently small regions that the illumination can be considered to be constant, and therefore each sub-region may be thresholded independently of its neighbours. Each sub-region will contain background, object or a mixture of the two. This leads to two difficulties that must be overcome in order for this approach to be effective:

- If the sub-region contains one component, we must determine which it is in order to set the threshold correctly.
- Adjacent sub-regions that both contain two components may have different thresholds. This will lead to discontinuities in the object boundary at the boundary between the two sub-regions.

Figure 5.6 shows the same source image divided into a number of sub-regions and the histograms derived from each sub-region.

If a sub-region contains one component, be it object or background, then its mean grey value will be significantly different from the image's mean. This will suggest the identity of the component in the sub-region and therefore allow us to infer the appropriate threshold. We should also take notice of the suggested identities of neighbouring single component sub-regions: they are likely to be the same.

Two neighbouring sub-regions that contain both object and background are shown enlarged in Figure 5.7(a). Figure 5.7(b) shows the histograms derived from the sub-regions; the threshold values are indicated on the histograms. Figure 5.7(c) shows the thresholded versions of the sub-regions. Since the sub-regions contained differing proportions of object and background, the two threshold values differed and consequently the boundary between object and background is discontinuous at the sub-regions. The discontinuity is due entirely to the discontinuous nature of the threshold values; each sub-region has a constant threshold value which may differ from its neighbour's. If the values merged smoothly across sub-region junctions then this problem would not occur.

5.3 Local methods – region growing

5.3.1 Region accumulation

Since all pixels belong to a region, we may select any pixel and it will be part of some region. Secondly, since a region is made up of adjacent pixels, this pixel's neighbours are possibly part of the same region. This is the essence of region growing algorithms.

The algorithm may be described in pseudocode as follows:

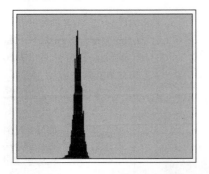
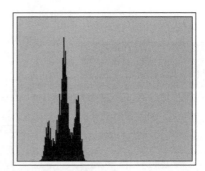
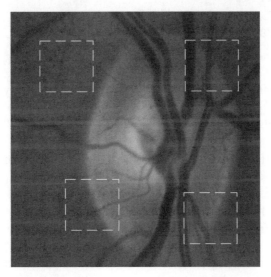
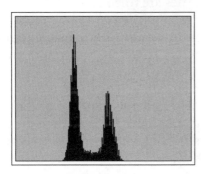
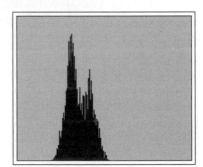

Figure 5.6 Local or adaptive thresholding. The image of Figure 4.3 divided into sub-regions and the histogram of each sub-region.

1   While there are pixels in the image that have not been assigned to a region.
2   Select an unassigned pixel and make it a new region. Initialise the region's properties.

(a)   (b)   (c)

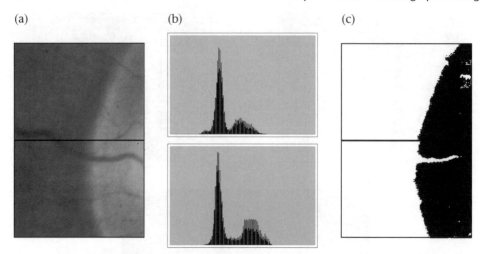

Figure 5.7 A problem of local thresholding. (a) Two neighbouring two-component sub-regions from Figure 5.6; (b) histograms of these sub-regions; (c) thresholded sub-regions. The boundaries on the thresholded subregions are not perfectly aligned.

3   If the properties of a neighbouring pixel are not inconsistent with the region:

     3.1   Add the pixel to the region.

     3.2   Update the region's properties.

     3.3   Repeat from step 3.0 using the newly added pixel.

This recursive algorithm provides a rapid means of growing regions. Two issues must be addressed: what region properties are to be used, and how do we decide that a pixel should be part of the region (the test in line 3.0)?

Since we are dealing with individual pixels, it would seem sensible to use grey or colour values as the region's property. Therefore we would grow regions of similar shade of grey or similar colour.

The properties of the region that we will maintain will be the average grey value (or averages of the three colour channels) plus the standard deviation of the grey value (or covariance of the colour channels). We may then decide statistically whether a region's neighbours belong to the region by computing the Z score of the grey or colour difference. If we assume that the region's values are normally distributed, then a Z score less than two would lead us to conclude that the neighbour is part of the region. The Z score is simply the difference between the region's and the neighbour's grey values normalised by the region's standard deviation.

If we decide that the pixel does belong to the region, then the region's properties will be updated by accumulating the values into the region's mean and standard deviation.

It should also be noted that other properties could be used as a homogeneity predicate. However, any other property will involve a number of pixels and the regions that will be derived will reflect this. Texture has been used for this purpose; texture measurement is discussed in the next chapter.

5.3.2 Split and merge

The region accumulation method will grow an arbitrarily shaped region with boundaries that are accurate to the pixel level. The disadvantage with the method is the time taken to execute it. Even if the recursive step (3.3) is removed it remains a time-consuming method of growing regions. The split and merge algorithm was suggested as an alternative: its execution is more rapid, but the outlines it generates are less accurate. In implementing a region identification algorithm, a compromise must be made between these two properties.

As its name suggests, the split and merge algorithm has two parts: a splitting phase that divides the image in a deterministic fashion according to the results of a homogeneity predicate, and a merging phase that combines adjacent regions that are similar.

The splitting stage will apply the homogeneity predicate to a region of the image; initially the whole image is used. If the region is non-homogeneous, then it is split into quadrants and each examined by the predicate in turn (Figure 5.8). The splitting will continue until either a region is homogeneous or it is too small for the homogeneity test to give sensible results.

The homogeneity predicates that will be used are texture measures that are applied to areas of the image larger than a single pixel. The implementer will be aware of the minimum region size that each measure will require in order to yield accurate results.

Given the sample image of Figure 5.9, the homogeneity predicate will determine that the whole image is non-uniform. The image is therefore split into quadrants. The predicate is applied to each quadrant in turn: some will be uniform and will not be further processed, and others will be non-uniform and will be divided into quadrants, which are in turn examined for homogeneity. The process terminates once all regions are uniform or too small to assess reliably.

At this stage, we can be sure that each region corresponds to a uniform area of the image. But uniform areas of the image may be represented by a number of adjacent regions, due to the deterministic nature of the splitting. The merging phase therefore inspects adjacent pairs of regions to correct this shortcoming. A pair of regions will be merged if:

- they are adjacent
- they have similar grey scale or colour properties
- the boundary between them is weak

A boundary is considered to be weak if it is of low contrast, i.e. the difference in brightness across the boundary is small in comparison with the

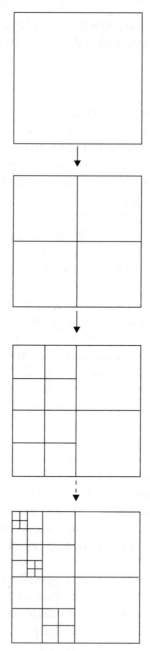

Figure 5.8 Split and merge.

average brightness, as shown in Figure 5.10. Most authors also take account of the length of the weak boundary compared with the total boundary length: if the ratio is small, then the regions should not be merged; see Figure 5.11.

Figure 5.9 Example of splitting.

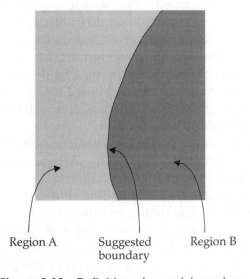

Region A   Suggested   Region B
                  boundary

Figure 5.10 Definition of a weak boundary.

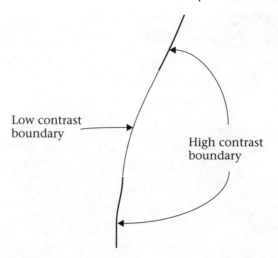

Low contrast boundary

High contrast boundary

Figure 5.11 Merging adjacent regions by strengthening weak boundaries.

5.4 Local methods – edge detection and following

5.4.1 Edge detection

Edge detection, as described in Chapter 3, was a process that enhanced the edge structures in an image. The operator that performed the enhancement could have been one of the simple 3 × 3 pixel templates or one of the optimal detectors: the Marr–Hildreth or Canny operators were described. The result of the process is an output image whose magnitudes are proportional to the like-lihood of the pixel actually being part of an edge in the image. Edge following is the process of tracking from one edge pixel to a neighbouring one and thus circumnavigating regions. In order to do this a binary image is required.

Figures 5.12(a–c) show respectively an image, its edge-enhanced version using the Sobel operator, and the histogram of the magnitude of the edge-enhanced image. Some threshold value must be determined for this histo-gram. One of the iterative techniques was used to define a threshold to gen-erate the binary image in Figure 5.12(d), which is suitable for identifying the boundaries in the image.

This is a case in which the pixels are eight-connected: each pixel may be connected to any of its eight neighbours. A boundary is determined by finding one pixel on it by scanning the image in a systematic fashion; nor-mally we would scan the image line by line starting at the top line. There-after, the boundary is tracked by passing from one pixel to one of its eight neighbours until a junction or an end point is found; see Figure 5.13. Tracking must then return to the start point and the boundary is tracked in the reverse direction, in this way we may gather the pixels that belong to boundary segments. The tracked pixels must be marked as tracked.

(a)

(b)

Figure 5.12 Identifying edge boundary candidates. (a) Input image; (b) edge enhanced version; (c) histogram of edge enhanced image; (d) thresholded edge enhanced image. (*Continued overleaf*)

Having completed a boundary segment, the next segment will be tracked. Its start point is usually found by continuing the systematic search of the image from the previous first start point. Ultimately, all of the unbroken segments in the image will be identified.

At this point the algorithm has defined a set of edge segments. Some of these might be so short that we may attribute them to noise in the image and delete them. The remainder must then be linked to define the outlines of regions. Two cases arise when considering how edge segments should be

(c)

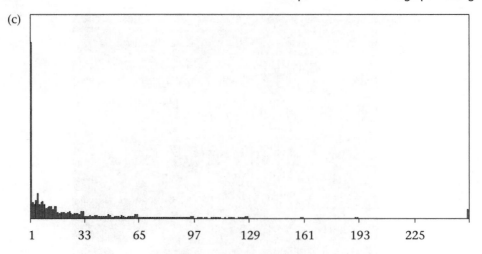

(d)

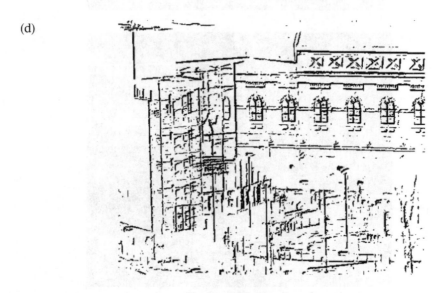

Figure 5.12 (*Continued*)

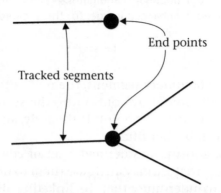

Figure 5.13   Boundary tracking.

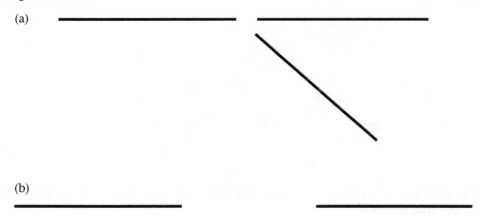

Figure 5.14 How should edge segments be joined? (a) At a bifurcation; (b) at a small gap.

linked. The first, shown in Figure 5.14(a), is a bifurcation: the end points of three edge segments are co-located. The second, in Figure 5.14(b), occurs when a finite distance separates two end points.

In the first case, as the diagram suggests, we would link the two segments that are most nearly collinear. In the second case, we would extend the two segments until they were linked. In this way we define a set of segments, many of which will form enclosed regions. Again, we may suggest that this process is simplified if we have any information regarding the shape and structure of the objects being sought.

The structure of the segments may be simplified by replacing sets of edge segments by more abstract structures. This is the topic of the following section.

5.4.2 Edge description

Edge segments have now been abstracted from the image. In many cases the object in the scene that produced the edge in the image has some regular structure: it may have a silhouette made of straight or regularly curved sections. A task that is sometimes performed is to replace a set of edge segments that approximate the real-world object with a linear or curved segment that approximates the image data but is believed to be a truer representation of the real-world structure. We shall discuss two methods of replacing a set of edge segments by a linear approximation. The techniques may be adapted to detect curved structures.

Edge segments may be accumulated into a linear approximation by aggregating segments and computing the best straight line that fits the data. This may be achieved using a least squares minimisation technique (Appendix C). This technique not only computes the best-fit line, but will also provide a measure of the error in the fit, i.e. the total distance between the data points

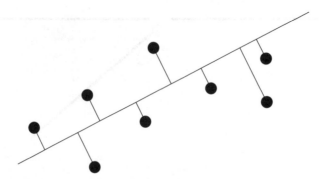

Figure 5.15 Accumulating edge segments into a linear approximation using least squares error minimisation.

and the line. Accumulation will continue while this total error is below some threshold. Once the total exceeds the threshold, the line is terminated and a new one initiated (Figure 5.15).

Segments may also be accumulated using the so-called hop-along algorithm. This algorithm will function as follows:

1   The next k edge segments are taken.
2   A straight line is fitted between the first and last points.
     2.1   The distance between the line and each point is computed. If the maximum distance is above a threshold, then the points up to the point of maximum distance become an approximated segment and the algorithm continues with the remaining points at Step 2.
     2.2   If the maximum error is blow the threshold, this approximation is compared with the previous one; if they are collinear, they are merged.
3   The next k edge segments are collected and the algorithm returns to Step 2.

The method is summarised in Figure 5.16.

5.5 Scale-based methods

5.5.1 Why scale?

Every object we observe has a characteristic scale or size: at either extreme of the scale range we have the universe and subatomic particles, while in between are objects of varying sizes. An image may contain objects exhibiting a fairly restricted range of scales. We have talked about the image of a tree: the whole tree is seen at a large scale, the trunk and branches at a smaller scale and leaves at an even smaller scale: Figure 5.17. Images of other objects will show similar ranges of scales.

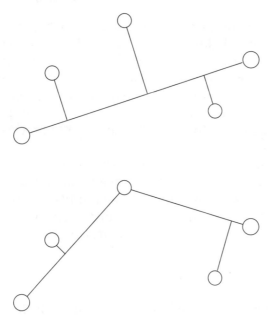

Figure 5.16   Hop-along algorithm.

Figure 5.17   The image of a tree, illustrating the structures that exist at various scales.

The image processing operations discussed in Chapter 3 will process an image at the scale of individual pixels, and, as discussed in Chapter 2, this is related to the size of the smallest object that is to be detected in the image. Therefore, most image processing will focus on the smallest scale objects that are present in our data. This may or may not be an appropriate scale for processing the image. It is therefore sensible either to resample the image at a range of scales and process some or all of them, or to process the image using scale-sensitive operators.

Images may be processed to create a pyramid representation of the original data. We may also generate a scale volume by applying a scale-dependent operator to the data: two axes of the volume would correspond to the image's dimensions and the third to the scale parameter. The wavelet transform may also be used to create a multiresolution representation.

5.5.2 Pyramids

As Figure 5.18 suggests, a pyramid representation of the image data will have at its base the original resolution data. Moving towards the apex of the pyramid, the resolution of the data will decrease, until, at the apex, we have the smallest resolution possible, which might be a single pixel or group of

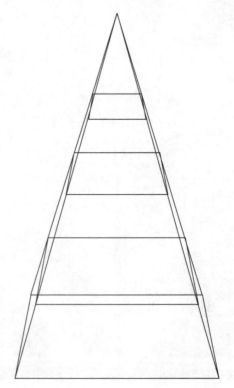

Figure 5.18 Pyramid representation of data.

features. As mentioned above, two methods of generating the pyramid are
available:

- image averaging
- feature extraction

5.5.2.1 Image averaging

When generating a pyramid by averaging, pixels in a layer above the base
layer are derived by averaging a set of pixels in the layer below. There will
always be a spatial relationship between a pixel and the set of pixels that
have contributed to it.

When designing a pyramid construction algorithm, three factors must be
considered (Figure 5.19):

- how the set of pixels is weighted when computing the average
- how the sets of pixels tile the image
- the size of the set of pixels

In the simplest case, we can compute a uniformly weighted average of a set
of four pixels and have no overlap between the sets. Then pixels in layer i of
the pyramid are derived from layer $i - 1$ according to:

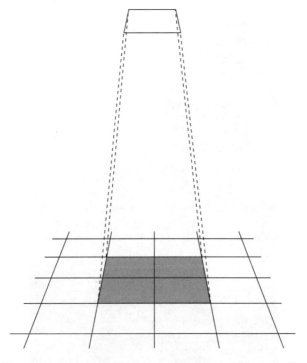

Figure 5.19 How sets of pixels are defined. How do the sets of pixels tile the image? How
are the members of the set weighted?

$$f^i(x,y) = \frac{1}{4}\sum_{u=2x-1}^{u=2x}\sum_{v=2y-1}^{v=2y} f^{i-1}(u,v) \tag{5.2}$$

A slightly more complex case takes a weighted average of 16 pixels with an overlap between tiles:

$$f^i(x,y) = \frac{1}{W}\sum_{u=2x-2}^{u=2x+1}\sum_{v=2y-2}^{v=2y+1} f^{i-1}(u,v)w(u,v) \tag{5.3}$$

where W represents the sum of the weighting factors $w(u, v)$. A smaller weighting would be given to the 12 boundary pixels than the central ones.

More complex tiling and weighting functions are possible, but few offer any great advantage.

Figure 5.20 shows the pyramid generated using the simplest scheme. Two properties of this method of representing the data are apparent:

Figure 5.20   Simple image pyramid.

- objects appear at a range of levels (scales) in the scheme
- each object has an appropriate level

Consequently, although it is possible to select a level in the pyramid at which to search for each size of object, we cannot isolate an object using size information alone: if we select a scale suitable for an object and investigate that level of the pyramid, we shall also find information relating to objects of similar scales.

Despite this apparent disadvantage, generating a pyramid does allow more rapid processing of the data. We may select a level of the pyramid at which to start processing and find the approximate locations of object boundaries. The approximate locations will be refined as we shift attention towards the base layer of the pyramid; however, as we move down the pyramid, information from the higher levels will direct the search. It is therefore unnecessary to process the entire image.

Finally, the image pyramid requires more storage than the original data: almost twice as much.

5.5.2.2 Image smoothing
Applying a set of smoothing operators to the data may also generate a multiresolution version of an image. Instead of a pyramid with less information at each level, this will generate a volume of data as we stack the smoothed versions of the image above each other (Figure 5.21).

Again it is not possible to associate a unique scale parameter to an object; each object will exist over a range of scales in the volume. This method of generating the multiresolution data offers little advantage: manipulating the information is simpler, but there is much redundant information to be stored.

5.5.3 Feature extraction

Creating the pyramid or scale-space representation is the first step in processing an image; subsequent processing stages would include processing the data to extract fundamental information, which will usually include some form of edge detection. Rather than create a multiresolution image pyramid and then perform feature extraction, it can be more efficient to perform multiresolution feature extraction using some form of edge detector that includes a scale-dependent parameter. The Marr–Hildreth and Canny operators include such a parameter in the form of the width of the smoothing function, σ.

By varying σ systematically, we may generate a scale volume that represents the features of the original data. As σ increases we locate progressively coarser features. This is as a consequence of smoothing the data with larger and larger smoothing kernels; see Figure 5.22. Whilst σ may be varied

Figure 5.21   Image scale space.

continuously, similar values will generate similar smoothed versions of the original data. It can be shown that the sequence of σ values that yields the best scale space (best in the sense that adjacent images are most dissimilar) is given by:

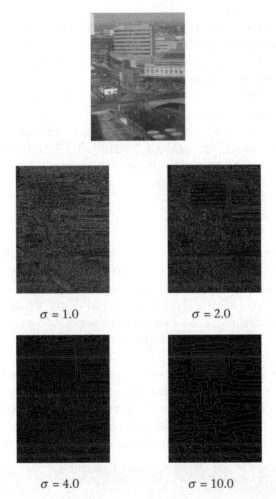

$\sigma = 1.0$ $\sigma = 2.0$

$\sigma = 4.0$ $\sigma = 10.0$

Figure 5.22   Feature scale space.

$$\sigma = e^{0.37n}$$
$$n = 0,1,2, \dots$$

(5.4)

It is also instructive to view a cross-section through a scale space generated in this manner, as shown in Figure 5.23. In this figure, the scale space has been generated using the Marr–Hildreth operator with uniformly increasing

Scale

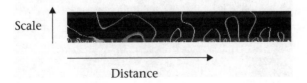

Distance

Figure 5.23   Cross-section through a feature scale space.

values of σ. The zero crossings of the data have been located and are plotted. The plot illustrates how the zero crossings occur in pairs: one for each side of an image feature. At a sufficiently high value of σ, the zero crossings due to a feature will disappear as that feature is effectively removed by smoothing. Finally, the lines due to the zero-crossings cannot cross each other.

A similar scale space can be obtained more efficiently by applying a simple edge-detecting operator to the image pyramid. The same comments will apply as were made at the end of Section 5.5.2.1: the feature pyramid requires almost twice as much storage of the raw data, but allows features in the original data to be localised more efficiently.

5.5.4 Wavelets

Wavelets have been described previously. We may use a wavelet transform to generate information from which we can derive a scale space. Referring to Figure 5.24, we can obtain a set of bandpass-filtered versions of an image by systematically setting all the data but one band to zero and computing the inverse transform. Similarly, we can obtain a set of low-pass filtered images at increasing cutoff frequency by setting more bands to zero and inverse transforming.

Using either method, the blurred images may be assembled into a scale space that may be inspected for features of interest (Figure 5.25).

Once again, a potential problem with this representation is the impossibility of identifying a unique scale that corresponds to an object, owing to the blurred nature of objects' boundaries in real images. It is therefore not

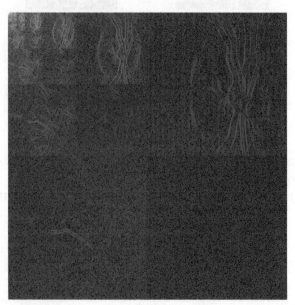

Figure 5.24 Wavelet transform of an image.

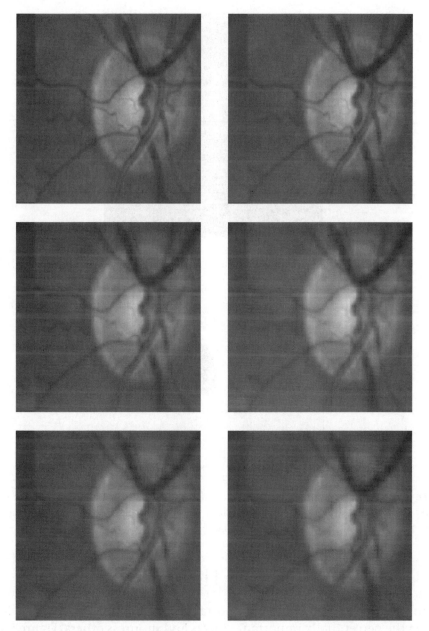

Figure 5.25 Scale space generated by a wavelet transform. Coefficients in the various iterations of the wavelet transform are set to zero and the data is reverse transformed.

possible to specify a scale for locating objects of a given size. It has been suggested, however, that objects that are perceptually important will be present in a large range of scales. One author has therefore suggested that an image of figures of importance, F, can be associated with each pixel by computing the product of all the scale coefficients, S, at this location:

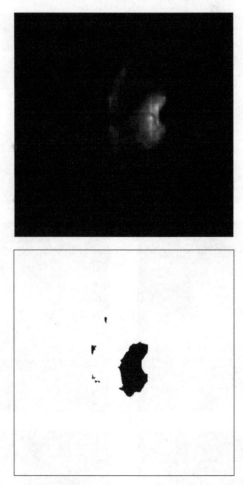

Figure 5.26   Image of figures of importance (the product of wavelet scale space coefficients) and the thresholded version. Locations that are highlighted in this image are sup-
posed to be of great perceptual importance.

$$F(i,j) = \prod_{\forall s} S(i,j,s) \qquad (5.5)$$

Having computing the figure of importance image, it may be thresholded to
extract the perceptually important objects and suppress others (Figure 5.26).

5.6 Watersheds

The methods of segmenting an image that have been discussed thus far
(thresholding, region growing and edge detection) have properties that make
them attractive in some circumstances and pose problems in others. The
watershed method of segmenting images combines many of the attributes of

the earlier techniques and is therefore potentially more stable than any of them. In particular, it is guaranteed to yield continuous region boundaries.

5.6.1 Definitions

A watershed in image processing applications is analogous to the geographical watershed. In a landform, a watershed is the line of separation between water flowing into different rivers or seas. The area enclosed by a watershed is known as a catchment basin. We may say with complete certainty that a drop of water falling to one side or the other of the watershed will eventually join one river or the other. We can say that a drop falling on the watershed is equally likely to flow into one river or the other.

By thinking of an image as a landform, similar definitions can be made, by identifying the geographical river or sea with a local minimum in the image. Simply, the algorithm locates local minima in the image and floods it from them. As adjacent floods meet, a barrier is made between them. Once the image is completely flooded, the network of barriers will constitute the watersheds. Figure 5.27 illustrates the process by viewing the cross-section through an image as the watersheds are built.

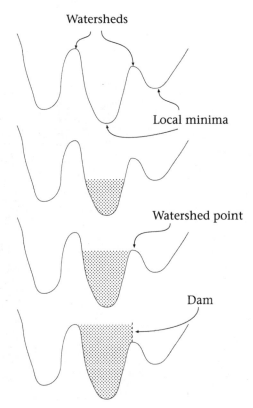

Figure 5.27 Watershed generation.

5.6.2 Practice

In practice the watershed algorithm is often the method of choice to detect uniformly shaded blob-like objects set against a uniform background. As we are searching for the boundary of objects, we would take the edge-enhanced image as input to the watershed algorithm, as this will result in the watersheds coinciding with the object boundaries.

The algorithm is then implemented as described in the previous section. The image is flooded, starting at local minima. The flooding is achieved by adding to the local minima all connected pixels that are below the flooding level. Morphological operations are used to build the barriers that prevent mixing of the floods.

The watershed algorithm is very sensitive to image noise: noise pixels will cause a plethora of erroneous regions to be detected. It is therefore necessary to smooth the image prior to edge enhancement and application of the watershed algorithm. It may also be appropriate to define other criteria that allow candidate local minima to be more accurately selected; these would be based on knowledge of the properties of the objects being sought and the characteristics of the image noise.

Finally, it should be noted that the watershed may select a region of the image surrounding the object, i.e. the object itself plus some background. In this case we would separately segment each watershed region using a simple thresholding operator. A sample result image is presented in Figure 5.28.

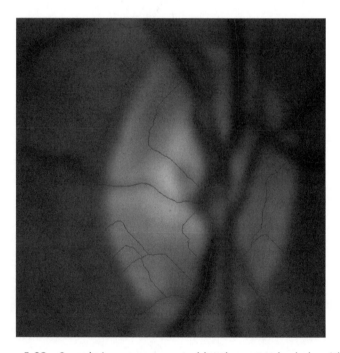

Figure 5.28 Sample image segmented by the watershed algorithm.

5.7 Representing regions

Region segmentation algorithms will identify regions of the image that correspond to different objects, parts of objects or the background. To be of any further use, these regions must be recorded: we must somehow be able to identify which pixels belong to which region. Three types of method have been suggested, two based directly on the image data and the third a hierarchical method.

5.7.1 Region map

The region map is considered to be the simplest but probably the most useful method of recording the regions that have been found in the image. It is simply an image of region identities. We define a numerical identity for each region which is placed in the equivalent pixel of the region map as that pixel is assigned to a region.

A variant on this scheme uses a separate image for each region that has been located. The image is a binary mask for that region: pixels with value 1 belong to the region, pixels with value 0 belong to other regions or the background.

5.7.2 Edge description

Since regions may also be defined by their outlines (boundaries), it is appropriate to use this information to delineate the regions of an image. Thus we could define the obverse to the region map: an image of the region boundaries.

Note that in many applications the exact boundary is not required; indeed, in many real-time applications, where speed is essential, the regions may be approximated by a bounding box: this is the smallest rectangle that is aligned with the image sides that completely encloses a region. Whilst the bounding boxes of adjacent regions often overlap to a considerable degree, the speed advantage that they confer more than compensates for any loss of precision.

5.7.3 Hierarchical representations

Hierarchical region representations are most frequently associated with hierarchical segmentation methods, notably split and merge. Quadtrees are the representation scheme most often used in this context.

A quadtree is a tree structure in which each node has zero or four child nodes, which are themselves quadtrees. The root node will correspond to the whole image and the leaf nodes to uniform rectangular regions. The linkage between regions (made in the merge phase of the algorithm) cannot be represented directly in this scheme; it must be a separate piece of information.

5.8 Summary

This chapter has been concerned with an examination of methods used to divide images into uniform and non-overlapping regions, which will correspond to some image structure. The next chapter will examine methods of extracting information from these regions that will be used in Chapter 7 to assign labels to the regions.

5.9 Bibliography

Threshold selection is a problem that is central to many autonomous systems and is therefore covered extensively, e.g. Shapiro and Stockman (2001) and Sonka *et al.* (1999). Scale spaces were first suggested by Lindberg (1994), who has since been active in this area. Edge following and edge segment linking are topics that are covered in most computer vision texts, e.g. Castleman (1996) and Haralick and Shapiro (1992). Image pyramids were first suggested as a means of compressing image data by Burt and Adelson (1983), but have since become more widely used for machine vision applications. Watersheds were presented in an early work by Serra (1988) and Beucher and Meyer (1992); after a period of lesser activity, they are now becoming a popular tool in the segmentation of suitable images.

5.10 Exercises

5.1   Think about the consequences of using grey level thresholding to separate objects with a view to counting and describing them and using an incorrect threshold.

5.2   If regions and boundaries are dual of each other, is one method more advantageous than the other? Why?

5.3   What will happen to the quadtree representation of an image if the image is scaled? Rotated? Translated?

5.4   Compute the number of pixels required to represent a simple image pyramid if the base is of size $n \times n$ pixels.

6
Region description

Region description is the generic term for all processes that extract descriptive information from a region. This information will subsequently be used to identify the region by comparison with the information derived previously from known regions. In this chapter we shall examine the various types of descriptive information that may be extracted from a region.

6.1 Introduction

Previous chapters have discussed methods of representing images, improving their appearance and of identifying uniform regions. In common image processing systems, the next stage of the processing scheme is to extract information from these regions. For this information to be useful, it must be characteristic of the region and therefore capable of being used to assign an identity to the region. Labelling (that is, actually identifying the region) will be the subject of the following chapter.

The method chosen to describe a region will be closely coupled to the problem being solved. When selecting a region description method it is therefore usual to work backwards by asking:

- What problem am I trying to solve?
- What information do I need to solve this problem?
- How do I find that information from the image?

For example, if we were asked to design a system to differentiate between potatoes and carrots, we might decide that the ratio of the maximum and minimum dimensions could be a reliable method of separating the vegetables because carrots are longer and thinner than potatoes, which are usually more compact. The designer must then solve the problem of how to measure these quantities and what operations must be performed in order to extract information from the image that will enable the measurement to be made.

In this chapter we shall examine some of the methods that have been suggested for achieving this task. We shall start by examining the features that can be derived from binary images, notably measurements of area and

151

perimeter shape. We shall discuss methods of representing the outline of an object and methods of quantifying the texture of a region. Finally in this chapter, we shall examine some of the methods that have been proposed for estimating the shape of an object using information derived from various sources: the shape from X problem, where X can be movement, stereo etc.

6.2 Features derived from binary images

Binary images provide a good starting point for deriving simple features that can be used to describe objects. The skeleton was presented in an earlier chapter as a means of giving a compact description of an object's shape. In this section we shall firstly examine how to group the pixels that belong to a single region and secondly discuss how the area and perimeter of the objects are computed. The following section will discuss methods of describing the shape of the object.

6.2.1 Connected component analysis

A contiguous set of pixels that share some property is known as a connected component. For example, the regions of a binary image are each connected components. The process of finding these components is known as connected component analysis. Several methods have been suggested for performing this task. One of the simplest is to use the dilation operator described in Chapter 4; this has the effect of adding a layer of pixels to a region at each iteration through the image; it is therefore an extremely slow method of identifying components. A recursive region growing can be used as defined in Section 5.3.1. This can grow regions very efficiently, especially if the tail recursion is removed.

An alternative method of identifying the pixels in a connected component uses a two-pass algorithm. In the first pass we are looking for pixels that could belong to a component. Each pixel is labelled with a numerical component label as it is found; the label it is given will be dependent on the labels of any previously labelled pixels (see Figure 6.1). As we are searching systematically through the image, only those pixels in the line above and to the left of the current pixel can have been labelled. Three possibilities can occur:

- None of the adjacent pixels (pixels A, B, C and D in the figure) has been labelled: the pixel is given the next free component label.
- One or more of the adjacent pixels have been labelled, but have the same label: then the pixel is given this label.
- Two or more adjacent pixels have been labelled with differing labels: the current pixel is given one of the labels and the equivalence between the newly connected regions' labels is recorded.

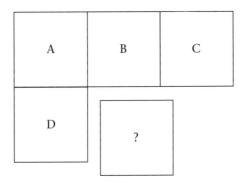

Figure 6.1 Connected component labelling. How the new pixels should be labelled depends on how the previously visited pixels (A to D) have been labelled.

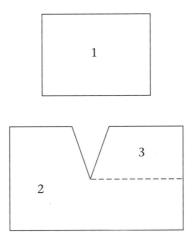

Figure 6.2 Situation after first pass of labelling. Some regions have a consistent label, others have multiple labels. The equivalence table will record the label to be recorded for inconsistent labels.

After the first pass, we will have a situation that resembles Figure 6.2: some regions will have a consistent label, i.e. all pixels in the region will have the same label. Other regions will have inconsistent labels: one region with portions having different labels. An equivalence table will record those labels that are parts of the inconsistently labelled regions and should therefore be seen as equivalent.

The second pass will simply relabel the inconsistent labels according to the equivalence table. A set of contiguous labels is not required, but can be achieved by examination of the equivalence table. The status of the labelling after the second pass is as shown in Figure 6.3.

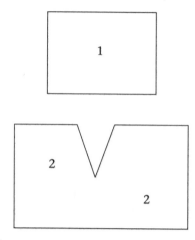

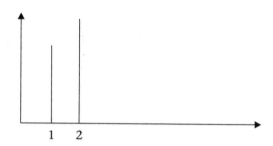

Figure 6.3 Situation after second pass. The inconsistently labelled regions have been relabelled consistently.

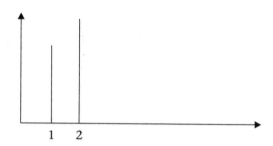

Figure 6.4 Histogram of the image labelled in Figure 6.3.

6.2.2 Area and perimeter

The area of a region is simply the number of pixels making up the region. Although this can be computed by counting the number of pixels as the region is grown, a simpler way is to compute the histogram of the labelled image, such as that of Figure 6.3. Figure 6.4 is the histogram of the labelled image of Figure 6.3. The histogram entries are zero apart from the entries that correspond to the labelled regions; these values are equal to the number of pixels in the region.

The perimeter of a region is the total length of its outline (Figure 6.5). A discussion of how to derive the perimeter will be postponed until we discuss chain codes below. At this point it is worth noting that a compactness measure, C, may be derived from the region's area, A, and perimeter length, p:

$$C = \frac{p^2}{A} \qquad (6.1)$$

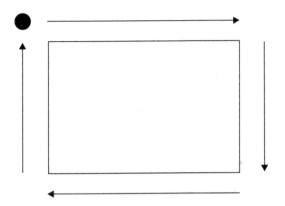

Figure 6.5   Definition of perimeter.

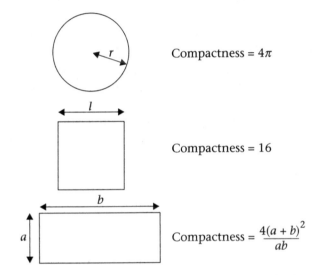

Figure 6.6   Compactness measure for three sample shapes.

This is a dimensionless quantity that is large for non-compact regions and small for compact ones. Figure 6.6 gives three examples.

6.3 Outline description

In the previous chapter we examined methods of tracing edges, in an attempt to locate the boundaries of regions. We also examined methods by which these boundaries might be simplified. In this section we shall examine methods of extracting and describing the boundaries of regions derived from binary images. These methods will range from ones that are very closely related to the image data to ones that are much more abstract. The abstract methods are, in effect, attempts to remove the effects of image capture from the data; image capture will always introduce degradations to the data, since it is an inherently noisy and approximating process. The abstract representations are an approximation to the data that we have captured, and we hope that this approximation is actually closer to the reality; this is justified since the noise is a random process and is equally likely to disturb pixels on either side of the boundary.

6.3.1 Chain codes

Chain codes were one of the earliest methods that were derived for describing the outline of a region. A chain code representation of a region will include the image coordinates of one point on the boundary of the region, plus a sequence of displacements that will take us from one pixel to the next connected one on the boundary and eventually return to the starting point; see Figure 6.7. The displacements are coded systematically, as in Figure 6.8, so a displacement towards the top of the image is always represented by a code '0', and so on. The direction in which the boundary is traversed is not important, provided the same direction is used consistently. Eight-connected chain codes are most frequently used, as they give a less jagged boundary.

The phrase 'on the boundary' must be clarified, as we may use one of two alternatives. The boundary pixels could be pixels inside the region that are adjacent to at least one background pixel (Figure 6.9(a)), or they could be pixels in the background that are adjacent to at least one region pixel (Figure 6.9(b)). Again, which alternative is chosen is not critical provided it is used consistently, as measurements derived from the chain code will differ according to which method is used.

Chain codes provide a position-independent means of representing the outline of an object. Wherever the object is located in the image, the chain codes defining its outline will be the same, but the coordinates locating the

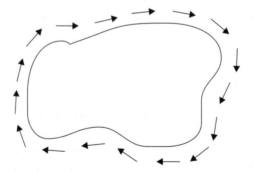

Figure 6.7   Chain code of an arbitrary region.

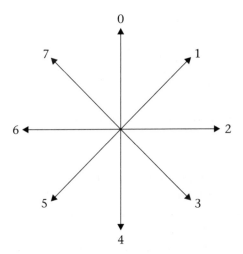

Figure 6.8 Chain codes using eight connectivity.

(a)

(b)

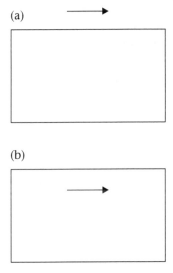

Figure 6.9 Explanation of 'on the boundary'. (a) Inside the region; (b) outside the region.

object will vary. It is also possible to modify the codes such that they become orientation-independent by making the chain codes' directions relative to the tangent of the boundary instead of fixed to the image's sides, as shown in Figure 6.10. This is occasionally used when this property is desirable; however, it does make deriving region properties a more involved process.

The perimeter and the area of a region are readily derived from the chain-coded boundary. Using eight-connected codes, even-numbered codes (0, 2, 4 and 6) represent a distance equal to the separation between pixels. Odd-numbered codes (1, 3, 5 and 7) represent a distance equal to $\sqrt{2}$ times the

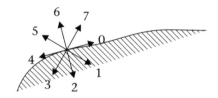

Figure 6.10 Direction-independent chain codes.

pixel separation. The total perimeter length is therefore the number of even-numbered codes plus $\sqrt{2}$ times the number of odd-numbered codes.

The area of a region is estimated by integrating the contributions due to each chain code. Figure 6.11 indicates how each code's contribution to the total area is computed. Starting from an arbitrary baseline, which could be the y-coordinate of the codes' starting points, and moving in a clockwise direction around the region, we have the following four cases:

- Codes with a start point above the baseline and moving clockwise will make a positive contribution to the area.
- Codes with a start point above the baseline and moving anticlockwise will make a negative contribution to the area.

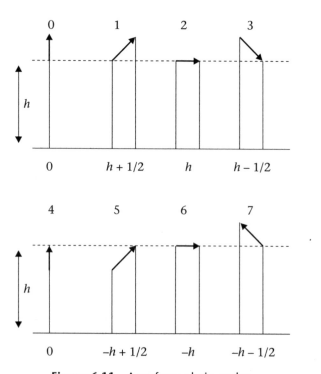

Figure 6.11 Area from chain codes.

- Codes with a start point below the baseline and moving clockwise will make a negative contribution to the area.
- Codes with a start point below the baseline and moving anticlockwise will make a positive contribution to the area.

The codes in Figure 6.11 all fall into the first two categories: codes 1, 2 and 3 into the first and codes 5, 6 and 7 into the second. The two codes that represent displacements parallel to the y-axis contribute nothing to the area.

If these codes had been below the baseline, their contributions to the area would change sign.

Finally, the magnitude of the area contributed by each codeword is the area of the quadrilateral bounded by the baseline, the displacement and the parallel lines joining the start and end points of the displacement to the baseline. The parallel lines will either be coincident (in the cases of codes 0 and 4), so these codewords will contribute nothing, or they will be separated by a distance of one pixel. Otherwise, the area is made up of the rectangle to the start of the displacement (codes 2 and 6), or this rectangle plus or minus the triangle defined by the displacement (codes 1, 3, 5 and 7).

Using these formalisms for perimeter length and area, these quantities can be derived as the region's boundary is being traced. This is obviously an efficient and rapid method of computation.

Finally, it was stated above that the region's boundary could be defined by the pixels immediately inside or outside the region. It is also possible to define the boundary by the cracks between the pixels that span the boundary, as in Figure 6.12. Although this gives a more accurate representation of the boundary, the additional expense incurred means that it is not often used.

Chain codes have been used as the basis of deriving higher level structures in the image. Particular groupings of codes may be recognised as more complex structures; for example, linear segments may replace a set of approximately linear chain codes, or a larger scale curve might replace a set of codes

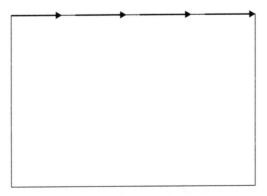

Figure 6.12   Crack-coded boundary.

that approximate the curve. Methods of realising and controlling this behaviour are the subject of Chapter 8.

6.3.2 Linear segments

The chain codes give a boundary representation that is accurate to the pixel level. The major disadvantage of this is that if the image is affected by noise, as it will be, then this will be at the pixel level and the chain codes will be directly affected, as shown in Figure 6.13.

This difficulty can be avoided if we replace approximately linear segments of the boundary by straight line segments. The boundary of an object is thereby reduced to a polygon.

This description is achieved in two stages, starting from a list of the pixels that constitute the boundary. In the first stage, sections of the boundary are divided into linear segments. In the second stage adjacent segments are merged, if necessary.

A section of boundary is represented in Figure 6.14. It has been selected by choosing an arbitrary set of connected pixels from the boundary list. This is reduced to a polyline, i.e. a set of linear segments, by firstly computing the distance from each point onto the line. The maximum distance is found; if it exceeds some threshold, then a vertex is inserted to bisect the original line. The process is then repeated for the newly formed segments. The threshold will, within limits, be a function of the line length; shorter lines will require a larger threshold.

The second stage of the process will investigate adjacent line segments that were split at the boundaries introduced in the first stage, i.e. the segments preceding and succeeding the segment of Figure 6.14. If these segments are collinear, then they should be merged.

The polyline representation is ideally suited to objects that have a boundary made up of linear segments. If any portion of the boundary is

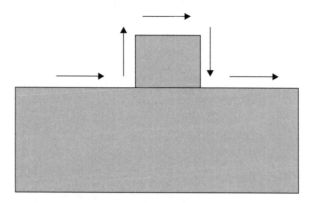

Figure 6.13 Chain codes affected by a single noise pixel. A noise contaminated image will cause erroneous additional codes to be introduced.

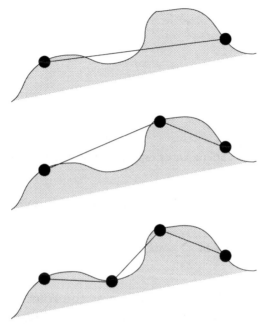

Figure 6.14 Polyline splitting.

curved, then this representation becomes inefficient, i.e. many small segments are generated. Inserting curved sections instead of linear ones may ameliorate this situation. Conic sections have been used, or the boundary may be approximated using a spline curve.

6.3.3 Spline curves

Splines were suggested as a method of approximating curves for computer-aided design systems using in the motor manufacturing industry. They provide a compact representation method in that two end points and two intermediate control points represent one curve section. Adjacent curve sections will share end points to ensure continuity: see Figure 6.15. Provided the control points can be identified reliably, this is an extremely compact method of representing curved sections.

6.3.4 Fourier descriptors

The boundary points, $s(k) = \{x(k), y(k)\}$, of a region may be represented as a set of complex numbers:

$$s(k) = x(k) + iy(k) \qquad 0 \le k < n \qquad (6.2)$$

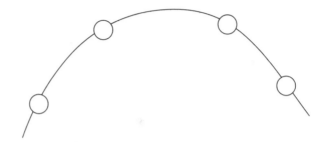

Figure 6.15   Spline curve representation of a curved section.

We may compute the discrete Fourier transform of $s(k)$ by:

$$a(u) = 1n \sum_{k=0}^{k=n-1} s(k)e^{-2\pi iku/n} \quad 0 \leq u < n \tag{6.3}$$

The complex coefficients $a(u)$ are known as the Fourier descriptors of the boundary. Naturally, the exact boundary may be regenerated using the inverse transforms:

$$s(k) = \sum_{u=0}^{u=n-1} a(u)e^{2\pi iku/n} \tag{6.4}$$

So far we have simply altered the way in which the points on a boundary are represented; they have not been manipulated in any way. The power of the Fourier representation is that it enables us to discard some information that may not contribute to the gross shape of the boundary. Suppose that the approximate $s(k)$ using fewer Fourier descriptors in the reconstruction is:

$$\hat{s}(k) = \sum_{u=0}^{u=P-1} a(u)e^{2\pi iku/n} \tag{6.5}$$

Although fewer descriptors are used in the reconstruction of each point, there will still be the same number of reconstructed points. The more descriptors that are used, i.e. the closer P is to n, the closer the reconstructed points are to the boundary. Recalling from the earlier discussion of the Fourier transform that high-frequency components account for fine detail, we may see that not including these descriptors will have the effect of removing fine detail from the reconstructed boundary, while retaining the overall shape. As Figure 6.16 shows, as more shape descriptors are removed, the less alike the original and reconstructed objects look.

Fourier descriptors have been used in shape recognition tasks; they are particularly suited to this, as, provided we can derive a suitable value for P, we

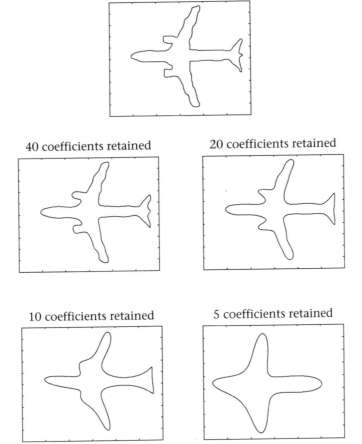

All coefficients retained

40 coefficients retained

20 coefficients retained

10 coefficients retained

5 coefficients retained

Figure 6.16 Fourier boundary descriptors. The plane's outline is represented by 1629 points. Removing coefficients in the transform results in an outline that resembles the original less accurately.

will have a set of descriptive coefficients that are insensitive to noise, object rotation and imaging artefacts.

6.3.5 Phi-s codes

The phi-s code is a representation of an object's border that creates a plot of distances from a point to the border as a radius is rotated about the point, shown in Figure 6.17. Although any point could be chosen as the centre of rotation, it is sensible to make a consistent choice, the region's centre of gravity is often used. Then simple shapes generate simple curves: simple geometric objects may be recognised easily from their phi-s curves by the number of maxima on it (Figure 6.18).

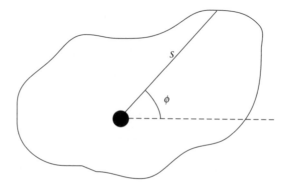

Figure 6.17   Phi-s curve. Definition of parameters.

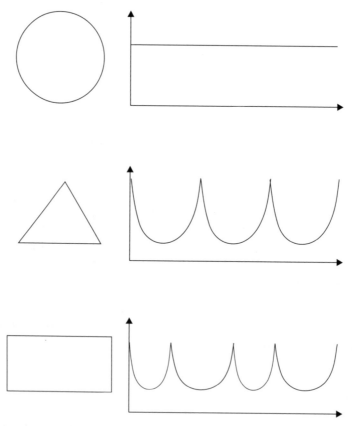

Figure 6.18   Phi-s curves of simple objects: circle, triangle, rectangle.

Real objects will generate more complex curves, but they may still be recognisable, as in Figure 6.19. Recognition will be achieved by comparison of the curve with curves derived from known objects.

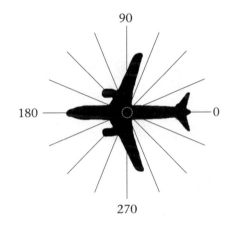

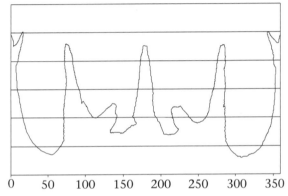

Figure 6.19 Phi-s curve of a real object.

6.3.6 Snakes or dynamic contours

Most boundary extraction and object recognition algorithms cannot process partially occluded objects; that is, partly hidden objects. Most methods will separate the object into its visible portions or combine the two objects: see Figure 6.20. Dynamic contours, also known as snakes after the story of two snakes eating each other's tails, were designed to solve the first problem: recombining the portions of the object.

We will require the boundary of an object to be continuous and smooth, i.e. to have no gaps and to change direction smoothly. The dynamic contour is therefore formulated to minimise the length and curvature of a line. But if a line's length is minimised, it will shrink to nothing (like the snakes eating each other). We must therefore introduce a force to oppose the shrinkage. This force will be derived from some image property: the gradient is usual. The following energy function is therefore evaluated along the length of the snake:

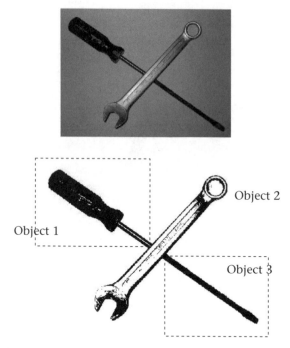

Figure 6.20 Occlusion. (a) Two objects illustrating occlusion; (b) occluded object segmented as two portions.

$$E_{total} = \alpha E_{length} + \beta E_{curvature} - \gamma E_{image} \tag{6.6}$$

E_{length} is simply the total length of the snake, $E_{curvature}$ is the total curvature measured along the snake and E_{image} is the opposing force. α, β and γ are constants used to control the relative importances of the energy terms.

Points on the snake are represented parametrically: $x = X(s)$ and $y = Y(s)$. E_{length} and $E_{curvature}$ are derived by summing each point's contribution according to:

$$E_{length} = \sum_i \left(\left(\frac{\partial x_i}{\partial s} \right)^2 + \left(\frac{\partial y_i}{\partial s} \right)^2 \right) \tag{6.7}$$

$$E_{curvature} = \sum_i \left(\left(\frac{\partial^2 x_i}{\partial s^2} \right)^2 + \left(\frac{\partial^2 y_i}{\partial s^2} \right)^2 \right) \tag{6.8}$$

and E_{image} is read from the edge-enhanced image.

A snake can be *open*, having different start and end points, or can be *closed*, having no start or end. When finding the outline of an object, the snake is initialised to a curve that is known to enclose the object. In many cases this

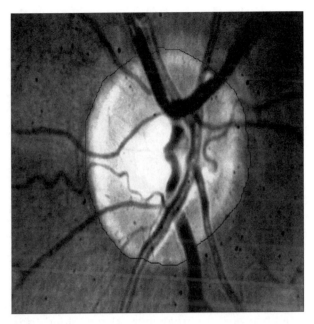

Figure 6.21 Snake surrounding an optic nerve head.

could be the image boundary. Shrinking the snake onto the object is an iterative minimisation process. E_{total} is evaluated along the snake and the snake is adjusted to a configuration that reduces its energy. Eventually the snake will settle at a minimum E_{total}; normally this will be a curve that fits tightly around the object and bridges gaps caused by occlusion. Figure 6.21 illustrates the final position of a snake shrunk onto an image of an optic nerve head. In this image, the nerve head region is discontinuous due to occlusion by blood vessels and poor thresholding.

The snake will have a variable length. It is therefore impractical to record all of the points on it; it would also be a computationally intensive process to evaluate the changes in snake energy during the minimisation steps. The snake is therefore usually represented by a spline curve: a set of control points is selected and the snake is interpolated through them. The number of control points will remain constant.

The values of α, β and γ must be determined by experimentation. They might be constant along the snake's length, or we might choose to vary them according to how tightly curved we wish the snake to be or the strength of the image feature in some region.

6.3.7 Boundary segments

Object boundaries can also be described as a sequence of structural building blocks that are extracted from the primitive boundary description elements.

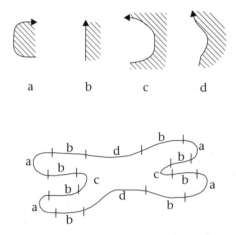

Figure 6.22 Shape primitives used to describe chromosome outline.

One of the first examples was used in a system for classifying chromosomes (Figure 6.22). The chromosome image was thresholded to isolate the chromosomes from the background. The outline of each chromosome was traced and the chain codes so derived translated into one of the building blocks shown.

The strength of this approach is its immunity to scale, rotation and translation: no transformation will have any effect on the description, beyond changing its start point. Further, comparatively simple rewrite rules may be used to recognise the chromosome, as will be described in the next chapter.

6.4 Texture

Texture is a visual or tactile property possessed by many surfaces, but there is no formal definition of texture that is widely accepted. Two definitions have been suggested that might enable us to formulate methods of quantifying texture and thereby quantifying an important region property. Texture measurements have been widely used in classifying aerial and medical imagery.

Texture could be defined as a pseudo-regular arrangement of a primitive element. This is a useful description for many artificial textured surfaces, such as a brick wall, in which the primitive element is a brick and which is actually arranged very regularly: see Figure 6.23. The definition can also be relaxed to include many natural textures in which the primitive element varies.

We may also define a textured region as having a unique distribution of brightness levels. Although this might seem to be a very weak definition, it does suggest that numerical measures of texture might be appropriate, and

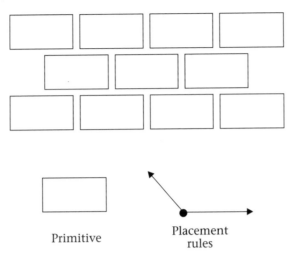

Primitive   Placement
                             rules

Figure 6.23 An example of how a synthetic texture is generated.

have been used in practice to discriminate textures that are visually subtly different.

In this section we shall examine some examples of statistical and structural approaches to quantifying texture. The aim is to derive a numerical description of the texture, which may later be used to give the textured region a label.

6.4.1 Statistical texture measurements

Statistical texture measurements invoke the second definition of texture. The underlying assumption is that the human visual system is able to discriminate between subtly different distributions of brightnesses in different regions and can therefore separate the regions. It has been found by experiment that statistics involving individual pixels (first-order statistics) and statistics derived from pairs of pixels (second-order statistics) are able to mimic human capabilities. Regions that differ in higher order statistics cannot be differentiated visually.

6.4.1.1 First-order statistics

First-order statistics are those that are derived from a single pixel, usually via the grey level histogram of the pixels in a region. The simplest of these are the mean and standard deviation of the distribution, as defined in Figure 6.24. Whilst the standard deviation of a distribution does give some descriptive information about the texture, it is too illumination-dependent to be of any practical use. We therefore divide it by the mean value of the

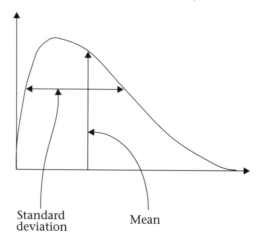

Figure 6.24 Definition of simple texture measures derived from grey level histogram.

distribution to remove this dependency: this quantity is known as the coefficient of variation and has been found to be of some use when describing texture.

Higher order measures (skew, kurtosis etc.) have also been infrequently used.

6.4.1.2 Second-order statistics

Second-order statistics are more robust against external influences that affect the texture, e.g. factors such as illumination. The co-occurrence matrix is the method that has received most attention.

The co-occurrence matrix records the number of times that we observe pairs of grey level values in a given relative displacement. To compute it, we must first specify what relative displacement we require: for example, three pixels to the right or two pixels to the right and one upwards. We then investigate the region, using the grey values of all pairs of pixels at this separation as matrix indices. The matrix element that each pair indicates will be incremented. When the process is completed, the matrix will record the number of times each pair of grey values occurred at that separation; see Figure 6.25.

Most monochrome images are captured with 256 grey levels. Since this creates a large and sparse matrix, the range of grey values is always reduced; 16 or 32 is a common range to use.

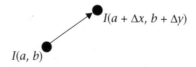

Figure 6.25 Definition of co-occurrence matrix displacement.

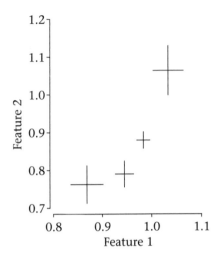

Figure 6.26 Differentiating samples of four differently textured regions by co-occurrence matrix analysis.

Having created the matrix, it is characterised by simple functions that are intended to measure the uniformity or otherwise of the textured region. Figure 6.26 illustrates some experimental results. Images were collected from samples of two populations and the textures characterised by two of the co-occurrence functions. The graph shows how the two functions manage to differentiate the two populations of textures.

6.4.2 Structural texture measurements

The first definition of a texture suggested a primitive element placed according to a set of simple placement rules. For example, the primitive element could be a rectangle and the placement rules could be 'to the right' and 'below'. Starting from a single rectangle, as shown in Figure 6.27, we may generate an array of rectangles and many other arrangements.

6.4.2.1 Fourier descriptors

Textures generated using placement rules will exhibit strong periodicity and might therefore be assessed using Fourier transformation techniques. For example, Figure 6.28 shows the Fourier transform of the textured image in Figure 6.27. The transform of this textured image shows peaks at regular intervals (the texture's periodicity) and also the texture's orientation. These may be characterised numerically by integrating the transform in sectors and annuli:

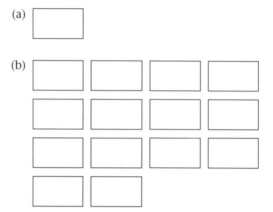

Figure 6.27   Generating a texture following simple rules. (a) Initial placing of the texture primitive; (b) a possible texture generated by repeated application of the placement rules 'place to the right' and 'place below'.

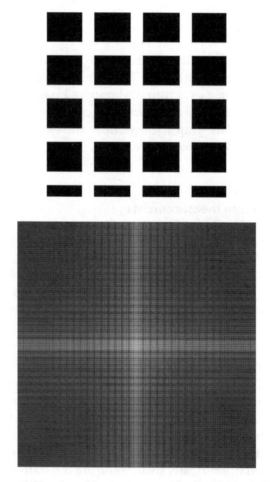

Figure 6.28   A regular texture and its Fourier transform.

$$S(r) = \frac{\sum_{\theta=0}^{2\pi} T(r,\theta)}{r}$$

(6.9)

$$S(\theta) = \sum_{r=0}^{R} T(r,\theta)$$

$S(r)$ is a one-dimensional function that will reveal the texture's periodicity. The normalisation factor of $1/r$ is included to reduce the contribution due to annuli of larger radius. $S(\theta)$ will also be a one-dimensional function, revealing the texture's directional properties.

6.4.2.2 Markov random fields

A Markov random field can be used to model a texture by making the value of each pixel a linear combination of its neighbours' values, plus additive noise:

$$f(i,j) = \sum_{k,l \in R} f(k,l) h(k,l) + n(i,j)$$

(6.10)

where R is the region containing the pixel's neighbours and $h(k, l)$ are the parameters of the Markov field. It is thought that each unique texture should have a unique set of parameters to characterise it. Therefore, if the parameters can be derived from a texture, using a least squares process, then we might be able to recognise the texture.

6.4.2.3 Fractal measures

If a texture exhibits self similarity at a range of scales, it is said to be a fractal texture. Formally, a texture is self-similar if it can be decomposed into the non-overlapping union of N copies of itself each scaled down in size by a factor r. Then the texture's fractal dimension, D, is given by:

$$D = \frac{\log N}{\log(1/r)}$$

(6.11)

Methods exist to compute the fractal dimension of regions of an image.

6.5 Shape from X

Humans are able to estimate the shape of an object using many clues, such as how the object moves, how it reflects light, its surface appearance and the slightly different views given by our two eyes. 'Shape from X' is the name given to the set of algorithms that implement these abilities. They all attempt to recover the shapes of objects in a scene by identifying the properties of surface patches on the objects. We shall examine five examples of shape from X algorithms

6.5.1 Motion

Relative motion between a rigid body and an observer can be decomposed into translation and rotation in the image plane (i.e. about the observer's optic axis). Therefore we may relate points on the object at time t to the same points on the object at $t-1$ using a rotation R and a translation T:

$$P_{i,t} = R_t P_{i,t-1} + T_t \qquad (6.12)$$

The two matrices will each have two terms. Given sufficient points on the object the equation may be solved for these terms and the relative locations of the points. We may therefore determine the shape of the object. It has been shown that four views of three non-collinear points are sufficient.

6.5.2 Stereo

Over a fairly short range of depths, humans are able to use the slight differences in the images of the world that are seen in the two eyes to estimate the distance to points on an object and thus the object's shape. The mechanism involves recognising the object in the two scenes and comparing the angles of vergence required to fuse the images. (The angle of vergence is the amount that an eye rotates about a vertical axis.) Humans do not measure distances, but this is possible for a computer vision system.

6.5.2.1 Depth from disparity

To implement a stereo vision system we will require two cameras. For simplicity, we shall assume that the cameras are optically identical (same sensor, same focal length) and are mounted such that their optical axes are parallel and the image planes are coplanar. We shall measure the separation between the two cameras, $2d$.

Figure 6.29 shows in plan view the situation when an object is seen in the two cameras' images. For simplicity, distances are measured from a point midway between the two optical centres. The images are coplanar and at a distance f from the origin and the object is at a range z at coordinates (x, y, z). The object is seen in camera 1 at coordinates $(x1, y1, f)$ and in camera 2 at $(x2, y2, f)$. We may identify two sets of similar triangles:

- The triangle formed by the object, the optical axis of camera 1 and the image in camera 1.
- The triangle formed by the object, the optical axis of camera 2 and the image in camera 2.

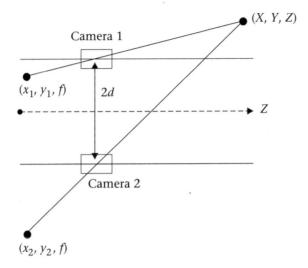

Figure 6.29   Stereo vision. Definition of parameters.

With reference to the measurements indicated in Figure 6.29:

$$\frac{x-d}{z} = \frac{x_1}{f}$$
$$\frac{x+d}{z} = \frac{x_2}{f}$$

(6.13)

Rearranging, we have:

$$x-d = \frac{zx_1}{f}$$
$$x+d = \frac{zx_2}{f}$$

(6.14)

Subtracting and rearranging, we obtain an expression that relates the object's range to the difference in the images' coordinates:

$$z = \frac{2df}{x_2 - x_1}$$

(6.15)

Similar methods may be used to derive expressions for the object's x- and y-coordinates.

The difference in the image coordinates is known as the disparity. It will be increased as the camera separation is increased, so increasing the camera separation will improve the accuracy of depth measurements. However, the separation cannot be increased without introducing further problems: as the separation is increased, fewer points will be common to both images as a consequence of the cameras' optic axes being parallel. Furthermore, the similarity of objects in the two images will be reduced, which will increase the difficulty of identifying the images of the object.

6.5.2.2 Correspondence

Implicit in the shape from shading technique is the ability to match the images of an object in the two cameras' images. This is known as the correspondence problem; the matching points are known as a conjugate pair. To solve the problem we must therefore take each point in one image and find its match in the second.

The brute force method of solving the correspondence problem is to identify a feature in one image and attempt to match it against all features in the other image. A simple calculation will reveal the impracticality of this: the number of matches to be assessed will be huge.

The number of potential matches can be reduced to a practical number by invoking the epipolar constraint. The epipolar plane is defined by the object point and the cameras' optical centres (Figure 6.30). The intersection of this plane and an image plane is an epipolar line. Given one point of a conjugate pair the other point will lie on the other image's epipolar line. This is true for all camera geometries, but is especially simple for the case of coplanar images: the epipolar lines will be the lines having the same y-coordinates. In practice the coordinates may not match exactly, given measurement and manufacturing errors. Therefore, if we have a feature in one image, we would ideally find its match by searching on the other image's epipolar line for

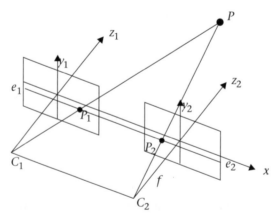

Figure 6.30 The geometry of stereo vision. A point P is projected to P_1 and P_2 in two coplanar images. The epipolar plane is defined by these three points. The epipolar lines (one in each image) are defined by the intersections of the image planes and the epipolar plane. In the case of coplanar images, the epipolar lines coincide.

matching features; in practice we would also search the lines adjacent to the epipolar line.

The question remains, what features should be used? There are two conflicting requirements. One is to have unique features that may be unambiguously matched, which will result in a small number of features. The other requirement is to have a large number of features to give a dense depth map, which suggests that simple features should be used. In practice, small regions having large variances are used and intervening depth values are interpolated.

6.5.3 Illumination

An object may be illuminated using a structured light source, such as a grid or an array of points. Knowing the relative locations and orientations of the light source and camera, the locations in space of the illuminated surfaces may be determined; see Figure 6.31. The separation between light source and camera is b; the other angles and distances are defined in the figure. We may relate object coordinates, (x, y, z), to image coordinates, (x', y', f), by:

$$(x,y,z) = \frac{b}{f \cot \beta - x'}(x',y',f) \qquad (6.16)$$

This method has been used to determine the shape a mouth makes when talking (information that is useful for speech therapists), and also by clothing manufacturers and retailers to tailor jeans to customers.

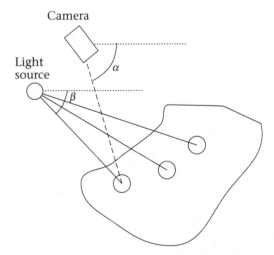

Figure 6.31 Shape from illumination. Knowing the relative locations of the camera and light source and the geometry of the structured light, the relative location of each spot may be determined from the image.

6.5.4 Shading

It can be shown that for matt surfaces, the proportion of light reflected to a detector is dependent on the surface reflectance and the orientation of the surface with respect to the light source:

$$\frac{I}{I_0} = k\cos\theta \qquad (6.17)$$

This expression gives an ambiguous estimate of surface orientation. If we invoke the additional constraint that the surface is smooth, then the problem may be solved using an iterative technique.

It should be noted that shape from shading techniques require that the reflectance of the object is constant. Any object with surface markings cannot be processed.

6.5.5 Texture

If we view a uniformly textured object from an oblique angle we notice two effects. The texture primitives are foreshortened and the texture exhibits a gradient (Figure 6.32). If we know the underlying texture primitive it is possible to estimate distances and orientations of the primitives relative to the observation point. It is not an accurate process and depends strongly on being able to identify the primitive and the texture being uniform. It is another method that has been proposed for a niche application.

Figure 6.32   Texture gradient.

6.6 Summary

This chapter has been concerned with the discussion of methods of describing regions; that is, regions' boundaries and the structure of regions. A description of a region is only of use for labelling the region, which is the subject of the following chapter.

When choosing a feature to be used for object description, four factors should be considered:

- The features should take significantly different values for objects belonging to different classes, e.g. maximum object length could separate carrots and potatoes.
- The features should take consistent values for objects of the same class, e.g. potatoes should have similar maximum lengths.
- The features derived should be uncorrelated, otherwise their discriminatory power is reduced.
- The smallest possible number of features should be used, consistent with producing correct results. A system's complexity increases dramatically as the number of features increases: the number of samples required to learn the characteristics of a problem increases exponentially, and the system's performance can even be degraded by adding more features.

6.7 Bibliography

Chain codes were first investigated by Freeman (1961, 1974), but continue to receive attention. The representation of outlines using polygonal segments has been investigated by, for example, Voss and Suesse (1997), Rosin (1997) and many others. The chromosome analysis is due to Ledley (1964) and is a very early example of computerised pattern recognition.

Fourier descriptors have often been used to recognise objects from silhouettes, e.g. Zahn and Roskies (1972). The phi-s curve is described by Ballard and Brown (1982). Although dynamic contours had been derived earlier, Kass *et al.*'s paper (1987) generated a flurry of interest. Finally, texture analysis was reviewed in an early paper by Haralick *et al.* (1973) and latterly by Haralick and Shapiro (1992).

Shape from X methods continue to receive much attention, but the foundations are summarised in many texts, e.g. Shapiro and Stockman (2001) and Haralick and Shapiro (1992).

6.8 Exercises

6.1   Implement the connected component labelling algorithms and compare the times taken to label an image using the two methods.

6.2   Compute the chain code of the shape in Figure 6.33. Suggest a method by which the description could be made to be independent of the shape's size.

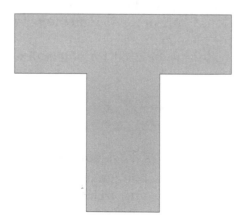

Figure 6.33   Shape for Exercise 6.2.

6.3   Explain why the snake algorithm is able to outline shapes such as the optic nerve head boundary of Figure 6.21. What are the consequences of changing the values of the parameters α, β and γ?

6.4   Describe how second-order texture measurements could be used to segment an image into self-similar regions that differ from their neighbours.

6.5   Outline the requirements of a system that will determine the shape of a simple object using the shape from stereo techniques described in this chapter.

7
Region labelling

Region labelling is the process of associating a label with a region of the image. Formally we may state the problem as: given an image containing one or more objects of interest and a set of labels corresponding to a set of models known to our system, how do we assign the correct labels to regions?

7.1 Introduction

The previous chapters have discussed methods of identifying regions and extracting information that was in some sense descriptive of them, whether that was the boundary of the region or statistics derived from the region itself. The present chapter deals with methods of recognising the regions, i.e. associating a label with the region by comparing the description of the region with the description derived from known samples; that is, comparing the processed data with a model. Humans perform this task effortlessly, rapidly and usually correctly. However, describing how we perform this task has been surprisingly difficult, and even now we do not have a complete description. Consequently, a wide variety of approaches to solving the problem have been suggested, all of which perform well in certain circumstances.

Four major factors make region labelling a difficult problem.

- The natural variability of the scene will cause an equal variability in the captured images. The characteristics of an object's image will depend strongly on the camera being used to capture data, the scene's illumination and other objects in the scene, as well as some other less important factors. This variability must either be captured in the descriptive model or removed somehow before the image is described.
- An image is a two-dimensional projection of a three-dimensional object. Any model must capture the object's 3D properties and allow a match with a 2D image. For example: as a car turns a corner it presents different aspects to the camera. The images are all valid examples of a car, but how do we represent these as a single model?
- Systems are often designed to recognise one object and make measurements of it. Sometimes we wish to recognise a small number of objects: car,

lorry, van, bicycle or pedestrian. This can be achieved using a brute force approach. But what if the object database is too large to make this feasible? Then different matching strategies are needed. For example, for Kanji (Chinese) character recognition, the dictionary includes several tens of thousands of characters.

• Occlusion – as the number of objects in the scene increases, so does the probability of one of them partially obscuring another. The object model ought to be robust against this problem and allow an object to be recognised given an image of part of it.

Figure 7.1 illustrates the significant stages of a region labelling system. The image is processed by the feature detector subsystem (described in Chapter 6). The other components of the system are:

• a database
• a hypothesis generator
• a hypothesis verifier

The database records the descriptions of the objects that the system can recognise. This represents the world as far as each recognition system is concerned: the world contains only those objects known to the system. The database can contain any number of models; it is common to have systems in which one object is represented, a small number of models or many models. The strategy used to recognise these models depends on the number of models.

Depending on the size of the database, a hypothesis generator might be required. For example, if we were recognising Kanji characters, the database might contain up to 44,000 entries. Clearly it is impractical to compare a candidate against each character in turn. One solution is to abstract from the database a set of possible matches using some simple technique, and compare the candidate against each one in turn. This strategy yields acceptable

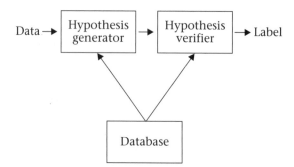

Figure 7.1 Components of an object labelling system. Depending on the complexity of the problem, some of these stages might be omitted.

results provided the number of candidate matches is small. Conversely, if the database contained one model, a brute force approach would be suitable.

The hypothesis verifier will deliver the system's final answer: either the object's identity or a negative result: the object is not.... The verifier must compare the descriptions in the database (if they are few) or the descriptions suggested by the hypothesis generator against the object's description. The object will either match a model or not.

We shall examine a number of approaches to solving the recognition task. We shall start by investigating familiar template-matching techniques, and look at their modification: flexible templates. We shall then examine statistical methods of pattern recognition and active shape models. Finally we shall examine syntactic methods of recognising patterns.

7.2 Object labelling

The simplest method of labelling an object is to compare it against a previously identified sample. If the object and sample resemble each other, then we have recognised it. This method is only appropriate when the object can appear in a small number of different views, for reasons that will become obvious. To overcome this difficulty, flexible templates have been defined.

7.2.1 Template matching

Template matching is the process of comparing regions of an image and a template. A measure of the similarity or dissimilarity between object and template is computed; we can therefore find the locations where the template matches a region of the image. Figure 7.2 is typical of the type of results that are obtained; it shows a scanned page of text, and the template is one character abstracted from the text. The third image shows the similarity measure, and part (d) is the profile of a cross-section through that image. It is large where the template matches a region of the image; the magnitude of the result is proportional to the degree of similarity.

Rather than measure similarity between region and template, it is simpler to first attempt to measure dissimilarity, D. How could a measure of dissimilarity be computed? We need a function that increases as the image and template become more dissimilar and is zero when they are the same. Three alternatives have been proposed:

- Compute the maximum absolute difference between the template and the region of the image it overlies:

$$D(u,v) = \max_{(i,j)\in R} | f(u+i,v+j) - t(i,j) | \qquad (7.1)$$

(c)

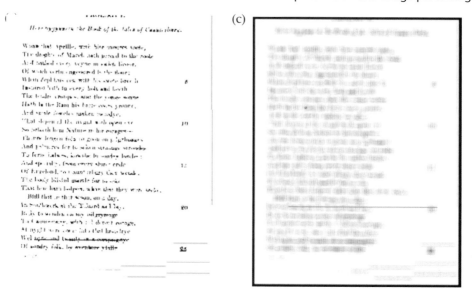

(b) (d)

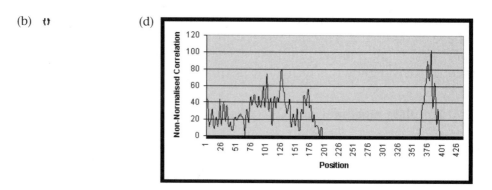

Figure 7.2   Template matching.

- Compute the sum of absolute differences:

$$D(u,v) = \sum_{(i,j) \in R} | f(u+i, v+j) - t(i,j) | \qquad (7.2)$$

- Compute the sum of squared differences:

$$D(u,v) = \sum_{(i,j) \in R} (f(u+i, v+j) - t(i,j))^2 \qquad (7.3)$$

Although all options fulfil our requirements, the third is preferable as it is easiest to compute.

If we expand the right-hand side of Equation (7.3), omitting the indices for brevity, we obtain:

$$D(u,v) = \sum_{(i,j)\in R}(f-t)^2$$

$$= \sum_{(i,j)\in R}f^2 + \sum_{(i,j)\in R}t^2 - 2\sum_{(i,j)\in R}ft \qquad (7.4)$$

Now the sum of the template elements is constant and can therefore be safely ignored. The sum of image values in nearby regions will be similar and can also be ignored, at least for a first attempt at deriving a dissimilarity measurement. Therefore if we ignore the first two terms of the expression and change the sign of the third term, we have a simple measure of similarity between a template and a region. It is the sum of the products of overlapping image and template values, which, for a symmetrical template, is the same as the convolution expression discussed in Chapter 3. We can therefore say that a reasonable measure of the similarity, S, between an image and a template is derived by computing the convolution (or cross-correlation, if the template is symmetrical) between them:

$$S(u,v) = \sum_{i=-k}^{k}\sum_{j=-l}^{l}f(u+i,v+j)t(i,j) \qquad (7.5)$$

This result is large in regions where the image and template are similar or the image values are high, and small in most other regions. It was the expression used to derive the result image of Figure 7.2. It is apparent that there are also high values in the output image that cannot be attributed to this reason but are caused simply because the image values are large in that region. Normalising S using the sum of image values in the region can suppress these false positives. The expression that results is the cross-correlation coefficient, C:

$$C(u,v) = \frac{\sum_{i=-k}^{k}\sum_{j=-l}^{l}f(u+i,v+j)t(i,j)}{\sqrt{\sum_{i=-k}^{k}\sum_{j=-l}^{l}f^2(u+i,v+j)}} \qquad (7.6)$$

Some authors also normalise using the sum of the template values, but since this factor is constant, we have omitted it. C will be large where the template and image are similar. Therefore we can locate and recognise an object in the image by setting up the appropriate template (Figure 7.3) and computing the normalised cross-correlation. The local maxima in this image will define regions of similarity. The implementer must decide a threshold value to differentiate true- from false-positives.

Although cross-correlation, or template matching, is extremely effective when used correctly, we must be aware of its severe limitations.

A specific template is required for each object to be recognised. To recognise printed text using this method we would require 26 templates for lower-

Figure 7.3 An example of normalised cross-correlation. The lower image is an enlargement of the region indicated in the upper image.

case characters, another 26 for upper-case, 10 for numerals and a small number for punctuation marks. If we change the font size, all the templates must be changed. If we rotate the text, another set of templates is required. The problem is exacerbated in real-world images, since there is infinite variability in the views of objects that we observe.

The matching fails catastrophically if the objects are partially occluded.

For these reasons, modifications to template matching algorithms are required, if they are to be deployed efficiently.

7.2.2 Flexible templates

We have seen how a rigid template is unable to tolerate deviations of the image data from the template: the template will fail to recognise such deviations. Consider also the problem of using a template to match natural shapes: the inherent variability will defeat any rigid template-matching scheme. Flexible templates have been suggested as a method of overcoming these problems. The idea of a flexible template is that it should in some way adapt itself to the image data, the amount of adaptation required to force the template to match the data is a measure of how closely the template and image resemble each other. The flexible template can also match related image features: the template might specify a spatial relationship between two substructures. The substructures might also be flexible templates.

In one of the earliest implementations of this strategy it was suggested that related image features could be built into a single template. The features would be represented by simple templates that would be connected by virtual springs. Stretching the springs to match the templates' locations against the image features and then distorting the templates to match the features exactly would achieve matching. Thus the closeness of the match could be evaluated by computing a weighted sum of the energies required to match the features and the energies required to displace the features:

$$E_{\text{total}} = W_{\text{internal}} E_{\text{internal}} + W_{\text{external}} E_{\text{external}} \tag{7.7}$$

The external energies are due to the distortion that must be applied to the templates to match the image features, and the internal energies to the displacements. The weight terms determine the relative importances attached to these quantities.

For example, the technique can be applied to the problem of identifying faces in images. The face template could be as represented in Figure 7.4. The facial features (mouth, nose, eyes, ears and hair) would be represented by simple templates, and their relative locations would be specified by the features' locations in the face template and by the relative lengths of the springs. The stiffnesses of the springs define the flexibility in the features' positions.

The simple template could also be defined by geometrical terms. For example, the eyes could be represented as a circle and a pair of parabolae, as in Figure 7.5. An eye would be located in an image by firstly searching for circles and parabolae and secondly finding the combinations of these primitives that fit the parameters of the eye template. The best match between the template and the image is the one that requires the least distortion of the template to match the image.

7.3 Active shape models

The principal component method was introduced in Chapter 3 and Appendix C. It is used here as an attempt to capture and represent the

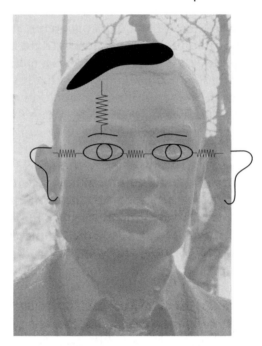

Figure 7.4 Flexible template representing a face.

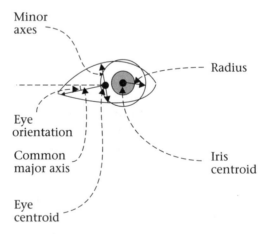

Figure 7.5 Flexible template representation of an eye as a pair of concentric circles and two parabolic sections.

significant intrinsic variation of a body of data and thereby provide a compact representation of this data. Having discovered this means of representing our information, the principal components will give a simple means of recognising future examples of this data. Two examples of applications of this technique will be given: principal component shapes and principal component images.

7.3.1 Principal component shapes

The shape of an object may be represented using a principal component model. To do this we will require a number of representative samples of the shape to be modelled (how many samples are required is an open question – sufficient are required to capture all the natural variation of the data, but more may not be advantageous). The images are normalised for the size and orientation of the object; these are variations in the data that do not contain useful information and should be excluded from the model.

We must then identify the outline of the object and locate a set of points on the boundary. These points must be located consistently in each sample. Again, any inconsistency at this stage would generate variability in the model that does not contribute useful information. The coordinates of these points provide the samples that are input to the principal component transform.

The transform will determine how many of the components contribute significantly to the model. The remaining components may be deleted. Systematically varying any of the remaining components through the range of values it can take will generate a representative set of samples of the shape, as Figures 3.45 and 7.6 show. Collectively, the components will define a hypervolume in the component space; the objects belonging to this set of samples will be represented by points inside the hypervolume. Other objects will lie outside the volume.

Recognising an object is achieved by preprocessing the data as before: the image must be normalised for size and orientation and the object's outline found. Points at the same locations must be determined. These points are then used as coordinates to plot a point in the principal component space (Appendix C); if the point lies within the hypervolume, then the object is recognised. Otherwise, one of the alternative models must be used to try to recognise the object.

7.3.2 Principal component images

Principal component images may also be computed. A similar process is followed. To create the model a representative selection of images must be gathered and normalised for brightness, orientation and size. The images are then vectorised and transformed. (An image is vectorised by stacking its columns to form a single column vector.) The principal component transformation will be computationally intensive as it involves diagonalising a square matrix whose dimension is equal to the number of pixels in the image. Although techniques exist for achieving this, even for large images, in practice the image is restricted to modest sizes for speed of processing. An image of several thousand pixels may often be reduced to the average image plus maybe a dozen component images. Figure 7.7 illustrates the average image

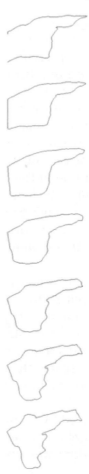

Figure 7.6 Another example of hand gestures generated by a principal component model.

and component images of the transform of a set of face images. Transform data such as this will allow these individuals to be recognised automatically using suitable source images.

7.4 Statistical recognition

Many of the techniques discussed in Chapter 6 generated numerical descriptions of a region. Statistical pattern recognition methods are appropriate for recognising these patterns. The data derived by these techniques are compared against the models using well-defined and mathematically rigorous statistical techniques that will yield probability values, the probability of the pattern being an instance of each of the models in the database.

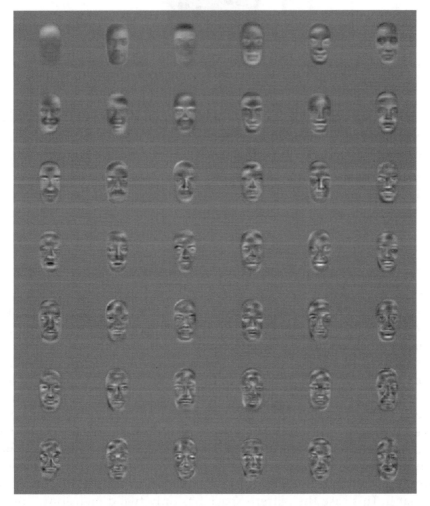

Figure 7.7 Principal component transform of face image set: the average face and 42 principal component basis functions.

The input to the recogniser will be a pattern vector (Equation (7.8), where the superscript T indicates matrix transposition). This is simply a vector formed of the measurements derived from the region. The vector's elements must therefore be numerical values. This might be thought to be a limitation of the technique, but it is usually possible to create a numerical coding of non-numerical values.

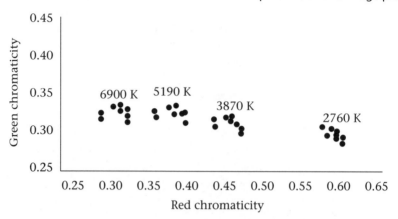

Figure 7.8 Sample pattern space. These are average normalised skin colours for a set of people of differing ethnicities. The images were captured under different lighting conditions.

$$\mathbf{x} = \begin{bmatrix} x_1 \\ x_2 \\ \vdots \\ x_n \end{bmatrix}$$
(7.8)

$$\mathbf{x} = [x_2 \quad x_2 \quad \cdots \quad x_n]^{\mathrm{T}}$$

The vector specifies a point in pattern space. Pattern space is the volume defined by the features: it has as many dimensions as there are features and is limited by the total range of the features' values.

Provided the features have been chosen using the guidelines stated at the end of Chapter 6, the features derived from instances of the same class of pattern will form a tight cluster in the pattern space and each class's cluster will be clearly separated from all others. Figure 7.8 illustrates this point. It was derived during a study into the effects of illumination on apparent skin colour. Each cluster represents the skin colours derived from a sample population under different illumination conditions. Note how the clusters are clearly separated, but there is also a finite variation within the cluster. Note also that in this case the pattern space has only two dimensions; normally many more features would be used to describe a region and the pattern space would therefore have many more dimensions.

The pattern recognition problem may be stated as the assignment of an unknown pattern x to one of a known set of W classes: ω_i.

7.4.1 Discriminant analysis

A discriminant function assesses the degree of membership of a sample to a class – how strongly does a sample belong to a class? In the case where we have W classes, we must define W discriminant functions, $d_1(x)$, $d_2(x)$, ..., $d_W(x)$. The sample, x, will be assigned to the class having the largest value of its discriminant function:

$$d_i(x) > d_j(x) \quad j = 1,2, ...,W; \quad j \neq i \tag{7.9}$$

A decision boundary that separates class ω_i from ω_j may be defined by the values of x for which the two discriminant functions are equal:

$$d_i(x) - d_j(x) = 0 \tag{7.10}$$

A decision function may therefore be defined that enables binary decisions to be made: does a sample belong to class i or class j?

$$d_{ij}(x) = d_i(x) - d_j(x) \tag{7.11}$$

In this formalism, a pattern may be assigned to a class depending on the value of d_{ij}; see Figure 7.9.

$$\text{if } \begin{cases} d_{ij}(x) < 0 & x \in \omega_j \\ d_{ij}(x) = 0 & x \text{ is unclassified} \\ d_{ij}(x) > 0 & x \in \omega_i \end{cases} \tag{7.12}$$

This approach can be extended to multiple classes using a voting approach, as shown in Figure 7.10. For each pair of classes we define a decision function. In the case of W classes, there will be $W(W - 1)/2$ decision functions, which must be evaluated for an unlabelled sample. $W - 1$ of the decisions will compare the correct classification of this sample against the other classes; the correct class will therefore receive $W - 1$ votes. The other decision functions will involve two incorrect classifications and will therefore be distributed

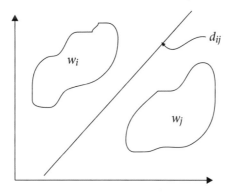

Figure 7.9 Linear discriminant analysis, binary case.

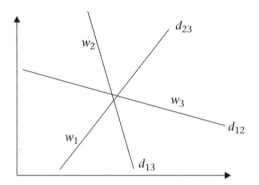

Figure 7.10 Linear discriminant analysis, general case. w_i represent regions of the pattern space occupied by measurements derived from different classes. d_{ij} represent the decision boundaries separating classes i and j.

randomly. It can be shown that the incorrect classes will each receive $W/2 - 1$ votes if the distribution is completely random.

How is the discriminant function defined? One simple possibility is to use the distance from the unknown sample to the centroid of the class (even though this gives a decision rule in which a sample is assigned to the class having the *smallest* discriminant function):

$$d_i(\mathbf{x}) = |\,\mathbf{x} - \mathbf{m}_i\,|$$

where   (7.13)

$$\mathbf{m}_i = \frac{1}{N_i} \sum_{x \backslash n \backslash arpi_i} \mathbf{x}_i$$

The decision function between two classes is then the perpendicular bisector of the line joining the centroids of the two classes.

7.4.2 Bayesian classification

Linear discriminant classification has a fundamental problem in that it takes no account of the distribution of values within a class. Consider the distributions of Figure 7.11. The two classes represented in the diagram have unequal distributions. The minimum distance classifier takes no account of this; in fact, the decision boundary that bisects the line joining the classes' centroids lies partly within one of the classes. Therefore a minimum distance classifier would have a significant misclassification rate.

An improvement on the minimum distance classifier would be to take account of the spread of values of the distribution and compute some form of Z score (the distance normalised by the variance). The discriminant function would then be:

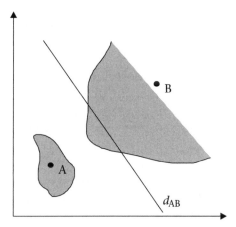

Figure 7.11 Two unequally distributed classes. An example where minimum distance classification can fail, as there are portions of distribution of class B within the area of pattern space assigned to class A.

$$d_i(x) = (x - m_i)^{\mathrm{T}} \sum_i^{-1} (x - m_i) \tag{7.14}$$

The Σ represents the covariance of the sample's distribution. If the pattern space were one-dimensional, this expression would reduce to the ratio of the square of the difference between the measurement and the mean to the variance of the sample.

Provided the variance matrix, Σ, can be measured, this is a satisfactory discriminant function. If this quantity cannot be measured, then a Bayesian approach may be taken, which assumes nothing about the distributions of pattern values.

Generally, the spread of the values of one component of a pattern vector sampled from two classes might be as shown in Figure 7.12, which shows a

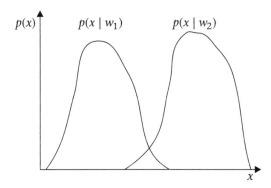

Figure 7.12 Probability distribution function of one feature value, x, derived from two sample populations.

significant overlap between the values derived from the two classes. Bayes' rule gives a rigorous method of assigning a sample to one class or the other with minimum error.

We define the probability of observing a member of class j as $P(\omega_j)$. Knowing nothing else about either the distributions of classes or the values of any measurements derived from a sample, we could minimise the classification error by assigning the sample to the class having the largest $P(\omega_j)$. This is not entirely satisfactory.

Suppose that we have previously measured the probabilities of observing pattern values for each class, as shown in Figure 7.12. These conditional probabilities are denoted by $p(\mathbf{x} \mid \omega_j)$. This distribution enables us to read off the probability of a sample belonging to a class if the observed feature value is x. Bayes' rule provides a means of combining both pieces of information: the conditional probability density, $p(\mathbf{x} \mid \omega_j)$, and the *a priori* probability $P(\omega_j)$ to give what is called the *a posteriori* probability:

$$p(\varpi_j \mid x) = \frac{p(x \mid \varpi_j) P(\varpi_j)}{p(x)} \tag{7.15}$$

where

$$p(x) = \sum_{j=1}^{W} p(x \mid \varpi_j) P(\varpi_j) \tag{7.16}$$

In the two-class case of Figure 7.12, the *a posteriori* probability density functions are as shown in Figure 7.13.

The sample should be assigned to the class having the largest *a posteriori* probability. It should also be noted that $p(x)$ is common to all *a posteriori*

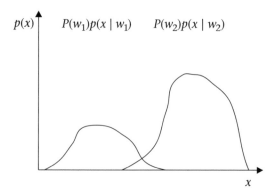

Figure 7.13   *A posteriori* probability distribution function of the distributions shown in Figure 7.12

measurement and could therefore be ignored. The discriminant function is therefore:

$$d_i(x) = p(x \mid \varpi_i) P(\varpi_i) \qquad (7.17)$$

So far, nothing has been said about the form of the conditional probability density, or how we might estimate the *a priori* probabilities that are required in order to use Bayes' rule. Determining the *a priori* probability is not difficult; it will often be dictated by the problem we are attempting to solve (for a system designed to identify items on a conveyor belt, the numbers of each type of item will be known in advance; therefore we know the *a priori* probabilities).

Determining the form of conditional probability densities is not a simple matter: they will generally be multiple-dimensioned and need not be smooth functions; only a few samples from each class may be available to build the distributions. Therefore it is usual to assume an analytical form for this distribution; the Gaussian, or normal, distribution is most often used. Since this may not be the correct distribution, the performance of the classifier will be degraded.

7.5 Syntactic recognition

Many object outlines are described structurally. The example of a chromosome was given in which the outline was represented by a sequence of elemental shapes. In a similar fashion, the outlines of characters have been represented using the appropriate shapes. Syntactic techniques are used to recognise such sequences of primitives.

A syntactic pattern recogniser requires three components:

- a set of pattern primitives: the elemental shapes used to describe the outline
- a set of rules, a grammar, that define how the primitives are combined
- a recogniser that processes the rules and generates a classification

The primitive elements may be considered to be words in the language generated by the grammar. The grammar, G, will be capable to generating every sentence in the language, $L(G)$; that is, every example of a valid outline in these examples.

For recognition to occur, the rules of the grammar are applied in reverse to a sentence. If it can be shown that the sentence is consistent with the grammar, then the pattern has been recognised. If more than one class of outline is to be recognised, then multiple grammars must be specified.

The grammar is composed of a 4-tuple:

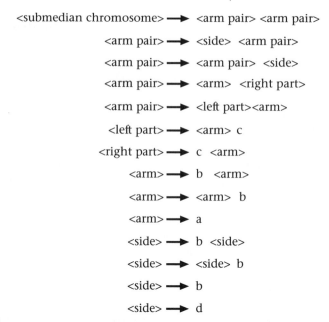

<submedian chromosome> ⟶ <arm pair> <arm pair>

<arm pair> ⟶ <side> <arm pair>

<arm pair> ⟶ <arm pair> <side>

<arm pair> ⟶ <arm> <right part>

<arm pair> ⟶ <left part><arm>

<left part> ⟶ <arm> c

<right part> ⟶ c <arm>

<arm> ⟶ b <arm>

<arm> ⟶ <arm> b

<arm> ⟶ a

<side> ⟶ b <side>

<side> ⟶ <side> b

<side> ⟶ b

<side> ⟶ d

Figure 7.14 Chromosome generation and recognition grammar.

$$G = (N, \Sigma, P, S) \tag{7.18}$$

where

N is a set of non-terminal symbols used as variables during recognition.
Σ is a set of terminal symbols corresponding to the pattern primitives to be extracted from the image.
P is the set of rules defining the grammar, called productions.
S is a start symbol, which is effectively a class label.

Consider the grammar derived to generate and recognise chromosomes (Figure 7.14) and the chromosome of Figure 7.15, which is represented by the string of symbols indicated. Then by applying the rule of this grammar to replace the terminal symbols and non-terminals, we eventually apply one rule that replaces some non-terminals with the start symbol. The chromosome has thus been recognised.

Different types of chromosome could be recognised by including rules with other start symbols.

7.6 Evaluation

Having designed and tested a classifier, it must be evaluated. Two quantities must be specified:

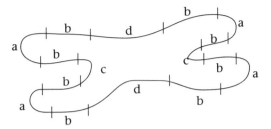

d b a b c b a b d b a b c b a b

→   <side> b <arm> c <arm> <side> b <arm> c <arm>

→   <side> <arm> c <arm> <side> <arm> c <arm>

→   <side> <arm> <right part> <side> <arm> <right part>

→   <side> <arm pair> <side> <arm pair>

→   <arm pair> <arm pair>

→   <submedian chromosome>

Figure 7.15 Chromosome classification.

- How accurately are the various classes recognised?
- Is there any pattern to the misclassification of samples?

The first of these quantities is evaluated using the classification rate: how frequently does the classifier correctly recognise a pattern. The second quantity is often described using the confusion matrix.

7.6.1 Classification rate

The classification rate, sometimes called the success rate, is simply the proportion of the patterns that are assigned to their correct classes. In the ideal case all patterns would be correctly classified. In practice, because of the variability of the data and errors in the measurements we are likely to observe, as indicated in the previous section, there are overlaps in the distribution functions of any two classes in the pattern space. This is particularly true when trying to classify natural objects.

A classifier's success rate is estimated using test data whose identities are known. Many strategies have been proposed to estimate the success rate, a large proportion of them for cases where there is little test data. Two of the simplest techniques are probably the most obvious ones.

The simplest method of assessing a classifier is to divide our data into two sets. The first, the learning data, is used to train the classifier; that is, to build the models in the database and evaluate the properties of the different classes. The second data set, the test data, is used for testing: the classifier will classify each pattern in this set and we will record the number of correct classifications. The classification or success rate is then simply the ratio of the number of correct classifications to the total number of patterns classified.

Two difficulties can arise when using this method. How can we be sure that the learning and test data are representative of the data as a whole? If there is a small amount of data, then the estimate of the success rate can be very uncertain: if we have ten patterns in the test set, then changing the classification of one could change the success rate by a significant amount.

These problems can be alleviated using the *leave one out* strategy. The classifier is trained using all the data but one sample, which is then classified. The outcome, success or failure, is recorded. This is repeated for all of the samples and the total success rate is obtained.

Both methods can only estimate the success rate. The true success rate can only be found by classifying all of the patterns, which is clearly impractical. Instead we must be aware that we have an estimate of the classification rate that is subject to some uncertainty. The question must then be asked: how big is the uncertainty in our estimate of the classification rate?

Suppose we wish to establish the proportion, p, of left-handed students in a class. Suppose we interview a random sample of N students and n claim to be left-handed. We may estimate p to be:

$$\hat{p} = \frac{n}{N} \tag{7.19}$$

The true proportion can only be found if our sample is the whole class. The larger N is, the more accurate the estimated proportion will be. If we interviewed different selections of students, then the estimated proportion might differ in each case. In fact, the estimates will be samples from a binomial distribution. For large values of N, more than about 25, the distribution is approximately Gaussian (normal) and has a mean and standard deviation of:

$$\mu = p$$
$$\sigma = \sqrt{\frac{p(1-p)}{N}} \tag{7.20}$$

We must use our estimate of p in these expressions, as we do not actually know it.

Given that approximately 95% of the Gaussian distribution lies within two standard deviations of the mean, we can be reasonably certain that the true value of p is within two standard deviations of our estimate.

This analysis is only appropriate if the outcome of our classifier is accurate – presumably the students know whether they are left-handed or not. In practice, the classifier will be subject to some error. In this case, the standard deviation remains the same, but the mean of the distribution is now:

$$\mu = p(1 - \varepsilon_1) + (1 - p)\varepsilon_2 \qquad (7.21)$$

where ε_1 and ε_2 are the two classifier error rates: the errors caused when a left-handed person claims to be right-handed and vice versa.

7.6.2 Confusion matrix

The confusion matrix is the appropriate method of reporting the results of a multiclass classifier. It is simply an array reporting the classifications of patterns. Thus the matrix element C_{ij} reports the number of patterns of class i that were assigned to class j. The matrix is sometimes presented as numbers of classifications and sometimes as classification probabilities.

7.7 Summary

In this chapter we have examined various methods of pattern recognition. We have taken the output of various region description algorithms from the previous chapter. These could have been numerical descriptions, symbolic descriptions coded numerically or symbolic descriptions. The numerical descriptions form a pattern vector. We hope that, given a good choice of region description, the pattern vectors associated with a class of regions will be similar; that is, they will be clustered in the same region of the pattern space. We also hope that different classes will occupy different regions of the pattern space, with no overlap. In practice, these properties are not often observed. We therefore need to be aware that when a pattern is classified there will be some uncertainty in the classification. This uncertainty can be measured and ought to be specified as part of the classification result.

7.8 Bibliography

Introductory pattern recognition material is expanded in many texts, for example, Duda *et al.* (2001) and Duda and Hatt (1973). Flexible templates were originated by Fishler and Elschlager (1973) and extended by Yuille *et al.* (1986). Active shape models have received considerable attention recently as they capture real objects' intrinsic variability, even though there are significant difficulties in building accurate models. Hotelling (1933) originated the principal component transform and Cootes *et al.* (1992, 1995) originated the active shape models as described here. Statistical pattern recognition techniques are described by Duda *et al.* (2001) and by Fukunaga (1972). Syntactic, or structural, pattern recognition is described in Ledley (1964) and Gonzalez and Thomason (1978). Evaluation of classifiers is also analysed extensively; see for example Haralick and Shapiro (1992).

7.9 Exercises

7.1   The *New Chinese Dictionary* has over 43,500 entries. Each entry is a symbol representing a word or part of a word. Outline a recognition strategy that is able to recognise a character from the strokes used for drawing the characters.

7.2   Although the discussion of template matching indicated that most image data had so much variability that this technique could not work, it has been used as a means of recognising cars in collision avoidance systems. From your knowledge of cars, design a template that could be used to recognise the widest possible range of cars.

7.3   Describe the tasks that must be performed in creating a statistical pattern recognition system that is to identify different organs in an ultrasound image. The organs differ in the textural pattern they reveal.

7.4   Written characters can be recognised by the strokes that they are drawn with, or by the corners that are discovered when tracing the characters' outlines. Suggest a set of shape primitives and rules that could be used for recognising upper-case Latin characters.

8
System architecture

In the preceding chapters we have presented techniques for achieving specific goals. The implication of this presentation is that a vision system is a linear sequence of operations: we capture an image, process it to remove degradations, extract some features, build these into more complex structures, and describe regions and label them. Given a simple problem to solve, this approach might be satisfactory. In most real-world applications it is too simple to be effective. Other strategies for controlling the execution of a vision system are the subject of this chapter.

8.1 Introduction

Early computer vision systems were designed by assembling a sequence of operations that gradually built an abstract description of an image from the pixel data. This was formalised by Marr (1982), who suggested that computer vision system design should be broadly similar to the human visual system (Figure 8.1).

At the bottom level of the hierarchy is a set of operators that extract simple pieces of information from the image. In Marr's original work, these were blob-like objects and edge segments. The next transform combined these simple tokens into more complex structures: edges and surfaces. Further transforms eventually generated what was termed the 2½-dimensional sketch. This contained more information than a map of surfaces' locations: some three-dimensional structure had been inferred, but it is impossible to recover all of an object's structure from a single image; parts of the object will be self occluded. Nevertheless, Marr's work laid a sound theoretical foundation for computer vision systems.

Several problems were not apparent at the time of Marr's work or were not addressed. One was the problem of knowledge representation: how should information regarding a particular problem be represented in a system? The other was how to actually control the system: was a bottom-up strategy such as Marr suggested appropriate for computer vision applications?

In this chapter we shall examine knowledge representation and system control.

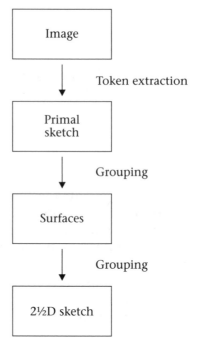

Figure 8.1   Marr's hierarchy of representations.

8.2 Knowledge representation

When the study of artificial intelligence was in its infancy it was thought that any problem could be solved given sufficiently powerful problem solving strategies. To prove the theory, software was implemented that was able to solve a relatively simple problem using a range of powerful strategies. Unfortunately, it was found that this system was not able to solve a wide range of problems. The conclusion was drawn that problems would be solved using relatively simple strategies but supplying information about the problem.

Six commonly used knowledge representation schemes will be described. When designing a system, the most appropriate scheme should be chosen. Account should be taken of the complexity of the problem being solved, as it would be inappropriate to use an overly complicated scheme for a simple problem.

Each knowledge representation scheme must include:

- *strategic* knowledge about the problem being investigated and potential solutions
- *algorithmic* knowledge about how potential solutions translate into computer vision algorithms and how the algorithms interact

- *data* knowledge about information derived from the image and how this can contribute to the solution

8.2.1 Implied

Any piece of software designed to solve some problem will implicitly represent knowledge without necessarily using an obvious knowledge representation scheme. So any image processing software written to solve a specific problem will implicitly encode strategic, algorithmic and data knowledge.

The system will usually be inflexible in that it will have been designed to solve a specific problem, possibly under specific conditions of scene illumination etc. If these conditions are changed, then it is highly likely that the system will fail to function correctly. The system will also be inflexible as regards reuse; since it will have been designed for a specific purpose, the system will not be suited to any other application.

Despite these disadvantages, this method of implementing vision systems remains more popular than any other, mainly because of the short development time and hence low development cost, and partly because of the high performance that can be achieved, since the system will usually be highly optimised for the task.

8.2.2 Feature vectors

Feature vectors have been encountered as a means of representing numerical data for input to statistical pattern recognisers. The feature vector is an ordered set of data: each element will record a specific property of the information extracted from the image. Thus, in Figure 8.2 we have a partial representation of a feature vector used for character recognition. The first element records the number of strokes used when writing the character, the second the number of loops in the character and the third the ratio of the character's width to height. Other elements of the vector will record other properties.

Non-numerical properties can also be coded numerically, for example colours and other abstract descriptions.

Data knowledge is represented explicitly in this scheme: it is present in the feature vector. All other knowledge types are implicitly represented in the

A   **N**

Strokes	3		Strokes	3
Loops	1		Loops	0
w–h ratio	1		w–h ratio	1

Figure 8.2 Feature vector knowledge representation.

software written to process the data and extract the information to fill the vector's elements. Whilst this makes the scheme inflexible, it is able to utilise commonly available pattern recognition software, as the feature vector may be exported to this software.

8.2.3 Relational structures

A relational structure will encode the relationships between objects or parts of objects in an image. Figure 8.3 shows an arch structure built of building blocks and the relational graph designed to represent it. The graph is reasonably complex, even for this simple image; it will be unwieldy for images of more complex objects.

The nodes of the graph represent objects, parts of objects and relationships. The arcs simply link the nodes and facilitate the recording of relationships. Thus we may have a relationship called 'above' which is linked by two directed arcs to nodes representing structures; the interpretation is that one of the structures is above the other.

It is possible to bind image processing functions into the graph. These would be invoked to establish the participants in relationships. Thus the 'above' relationship would have associated software for establishing the two regions involved and verifying which was above the other.

The graph may be used in one of two ways. Firstly, it may be used as a description of an object of recognition purposes. A graph-based description of objects found in the image would be prepared. Graphs that are isomorphically

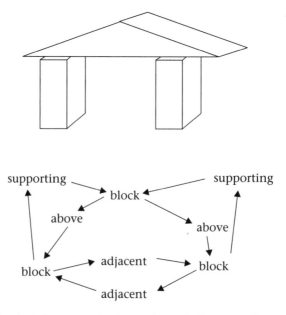

Figure 8.3 Arch image and relational graph that partially describes it.

identical must represent the same object. Secondly, we may use the graph to guide our interpretation of a scene: as the graph is traversed, the relationships are identified and so the scene is understood. This use of the graph is not as widespread, as the graph is too specific for most applications, although the hierarchical description that follows is closely related.

All types of knowledge are present in the graph.

8.2.4 Hierarchical structures

Hierarchical knowledge structures follow the hierarchical decomposition of structures in an image. Figure 8.4 illustrates how this could appear in practice: the tree's root node corresponds to the whole image. Nodes below this level will correspond to progressively finer levels of meaning and image detail. Figure 8.5 illustrates a practical application. The graph in this case is prepared in advance; it contains the strategic knowledge needed to solve the problem in that it defines the expected structure of the image. Functions required to identify the image regions corresponding to the node data are linked to each node: the implementation and algorithmic knowledge. At the lowest level, the leaf nodes will have links to operations that will locate simple structures in the image. Once these structures have been located, they will be linked into the structure.

Scene

↓

Objects

↓

Parts of objects

Figure 8.4   Conceptual hierarchical knowledge structure.

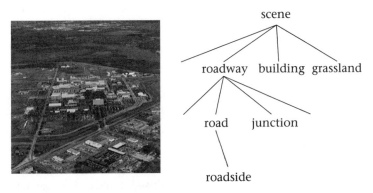

Figure 8.5   Hierarchical knowledge structure partially depicting an aerial photograph.

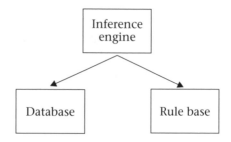

Figure 8.6   Architecture of a rule-based system.

8.2.5 Rules

A rule-based system has three major components, shown in Figure 8.6: a rule base, a database and an inference engine. The database contains all the information that is generated as the image is processed, starting with the image itself, i.e. the data knowledge. The rule base will contain all other types of knowledge required by the system. Rules encode quanta of knowledge in the form of left- and right-hand sides:

$$\langle \text{antecedent} \rangle \rightarrow \langle \text{consequent} \rangle \tag{8.1}$$

The interpretation of the rule depends on the inference engine.

$$\langle \text{two antiparallel lines} \rangle \rightarrow \langle \text{road} \rangle \tag{8.2}$$

The inference engine may function in one of two ways: forwards chaining, in which it infers conclusions from given facts, and backwards chaining in which it makes hypotheses and attempts to verify them given the available facts. For example, given the rule of Equation (8.2), the forwards chaining inference engine would observe two antiparallel lines and conclude that they formed a road. The backwards chaining engine would use the rule to guide its search for a road by focussing attention on finding pairs of antiparallel lines.

8.2.5.1 Forwards chaining
In the forwards chaining mode, the left-hand side of the rule will specify a pattern. This would normally involve some variables that could match elements from the database. The right-hand side of the rule might specify some action, which could be to modify an existing fact or to assert a new one.

In this mode, the inference engine will follow a cycle of matching, resolving and acting. In the matching phase, it will attempt to match the left-hand side of the rules against the facts in the database. A rule plus the matching facts is known as an instantiation. The set of instantiations is called the conflict set. One of the set's members must be chosen for firing, which is the term used for executing a rule's action. Each rule could match a different set of facts and might therefore appear multiple times in the conflict set.

Several mechanisms have been suggested for conflict resolution.

- Select the instantiation whose rule has the most complex pattern. This is likely to have been designed to handle an exceptional case and should therefore be fired in preference to other rules.
- Select the instantiation whose rule was most recently used. It is then likely that the system will remain focused on one task until it is completed.
- Select the instantiation whose data was most recently used so as to complete the processing of one portion of the data before processing any others.
- If all other mechanisms fail, an instantiation could be chosen randomly.

Having selected an instantiation, the action part of the rule is fired. This will modify the database by establishing new facts or modifying existing ones. Eventually, the data will be processed and conclusions will be reached.

Forwards chaining is a method of processing data that is suited to low-level processing, e.g. the lowest levels in Marr's hierarchy, as it concentrates on the data rather than any achieving any goal in a focused manner.

A major problem of rule-based systems is the number of comparisons that must be performed when identifying the conflict set. Even a modest rule-based system might contain 50 to 100 rules; the number of facts depends on the problem being solved and the state of processing, but is likely to be several hundred. Therefore, several tens of thousands of comparisons must be made during each cycle of processing. Naturally, this will have a serious effect on the system's performance, so much so that rule-based systems have fallen out of use. One technique that was intended to alleviate the problem was to divide the rule base into a multiple of smaller ones, only one of which would be active at any instant. Since the individual databases would be much smaller, creating the conflict set in each iteration could be achieved in a much shorter time.

8.2.5.2 Backwards chaining

Backwards chaining is usually presented as the antithesis of forwards chaining. Systems will postulate a hypothesis and attempt to prove it from the available data. For example, the following set of rules is abstracted from a system designed to label subtraction coronary angiograms of the type shown in Figure 8.7 (the figure shows a head X-ray, which is actually more complex than the neck). The strategy that is followed when labelling the vessels in the

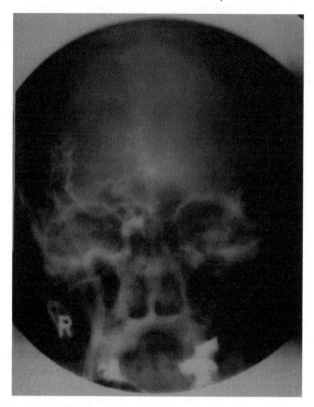

Figure 8.7 An angiogram. The X-ray shows bone structures and the blood vessels car-rying a contrast medium. Another X-ray image taken without contrast medium could be subtracted from this one to reveal only the blood vessels (plus imperfections in the sub-traction process).

angiogram is firstly to identify the bifurcation (that is the point at which a vessel divides into two smaller vessels) involving the common carotid artery (CCA). The CCA will be the widest vessel in the lower portion of the image. The other vessels involved in the bifurcation are the two carotid arteries. One of these has further vessels branching off it; the other does not. This fact enables these two vessels to be labelled, and the distances of the branching arteries from the bifurcation enable them to be labelled.

The interpretation of each rule is that in order to achieve the single goal on the right-hand side (the consequent), all of the goals on the left-hand side (the antecedents) must be achieved. The antecedents will themselves be achieved either by being the consequents of other rules or by evaluating some function applied to the image. There must be a single rule whose conse-quent does not appear as any other rule's antecedent: this goal is interpreted as the system goal – the goal that the system is designed to achieve. *Under-stand angiogram* was the system goal of the rule base from which the rules of Equation (8.3) were extracted.

$$\left.\begin{matrix} \text{find vessel sections AND} \\ \text{group and label vessel sections} \end{matrix}\right\} \rightarrow \langle\text{understand angiogram}\rangle$$

$$\left.\begin{matrix} \text{find carotid bifurcation AND} \\ \text{label main carotid arteries AND} \\ \text{label branch carotid arteries} \end{matrix}\right\} \qquad (8.3)$$

$$\rightarrow \langle\text{group and label vessel sections}\rangle$$

$$\left.\begin{matrix} \text{threshold the image AND} \\ \text{trace centre lines AND} \\ \text{identify vessel segments} \end{matrix}\right\} \rightarrow \langle\text{find vessel sections}\rangle$$

When the system is initialised, it will search for the system goal by identifying the consequents of all rules and then finding which one is not also an antecedent of another rule. Thereafter, the system can maintain a list of goals it needs to achieve: initially this will be just the system goal; then the antecedents of the rule defining how the system goal is achieved will be added; then the antecedents of the antecedents will be added; and so on. Eventually, goals must be achieved by performing some action that evaluates a result, in our example by performing an image processing task.

Since backwards chaining systems focus on how particular tasks will be achieved, they are also described as being goal-driven. They are suitable for high-level image processing or computer vision tasks where we have a significant amount of strategic knowledge.

8.2.6 Frames

A frame has been defined as a 'data structure for representing a stereotyped situation'. It was first suggested as a model of the organisation of human memories: related facts seem to be strongly associated and we seem to have a mental model for familiar objects, thus given a partial view of an object we are not surprised by the appearance of the remainder of the object, provided we are familiar with its prototype: we can see a car and not be surprised that it has a body, wheels, seats, doors, windows and a roof.

As Figure 8.8 illustrates, a frame is composed of an unordered sequence of slots and fillers. We could create a frame for any object that was to be described; it would contain the slots defined by the prototype, which would be filled as the object was described. The fillers could be a value derived from the image, a reference to a region of the image or even a link to another frame.

When processing an image, a frame would be instantiated for the object being sought. Practically, as with other knowledge representations, we must provide sufficient strategic knowledge for the system to suggest a frame that is likely to be correct, otherwise we would have to try to fit so many frames to

Slots (attributes)	Fillers value, atomic, link, ...

Figure 8.8 Frame data structure.

the data that the analysis would become totally impractical. Having suggested a likely frame, the analysis would proceed with the system attempting
to populate the frame. Each slot's filler would be populated according to the
filler's type. The analysis would be completed once the fillers were populated. Figure 8.9(b) suggests the frame structure that could represent the
image of Figure 8.9(a).

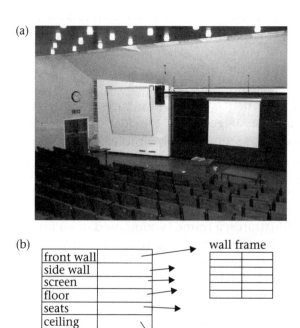

Figure 8.9 Populated frame example. (a) Sample image; (b) possible frame structure.

8.3 Hierarchical control

In discussing rule-based systems we alluded to two directions in which data might be processed when we discussed forwards and backwards chaining, or data-driven or goal-driven analysis. In this and the following section we shall discuss explicitly the methods used to control how an image is analysed.

Two alternative strategies have been suggested: one in which there is explicit control of how the data is processed, and one in which there is not. These are termed hierarchical and heterarchical control. As its name implies, hierarchical control suggests that the image is composed of a hierarchy of structures, as Marr suggested. The analysis of an image will therefore follow the hierarchy, either from the top or the bottom.

8.3.1 Top-down control

Figure 8.10 illustrates the nature of a top-down control strategy. The system is expected to hypothesise the identities of objects that it might encounter and then formulate a strategy for verifying their properties, identities, locations etc. While this might seem to be an ambitious aim, in reality the problem is simpler than this description suggests. Most vision systems are designed to solve specific problems and will therefore encounter a small number of objects. For example, a surveillance system would observe a number of static objects that are not critical, but it would also observe and be expected to recognise a number of different types of moving objects – people, cars, animals etc. – and make an appropriate response.

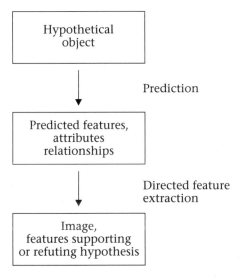

Figure 8.10   Top-down control.

Naturally, if the system makes the wrong hypothesis at the start of processing, it will be unable to recognise the object. The surveillance system
could not be expected to recognise a car as a dog, for example, but this may
not be a problem; an alternative hypothesis could be formulated and verified. The system will also, however, fail to recognise new objects.

8.3.2 Bottom-up control

Bottom-up control follows Marr's hierarchy in the manner in which processing is controlled: see Figure 8.11. Features, or tokens, are extracted from
the image and assembled into more complex objects by identifying the relationships between them. Objects are recognised from these structures.

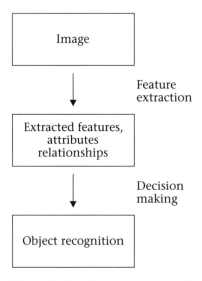

Figure 8.11   Bottom-up control.

This is the most commonly used method of controlling systems, possibly
because it follows an apparently logical progression: data is processed and
refined, and decisions made.

8.3.3 Critique

Hierarchical control methods are extremely inflexible in that once a
sequence of actions has been initiated it cannot be stopped: processing will
continue until a result is obtained, whether this is correct or not.

The approach is also vulnerable to errors in processing: if an incorrect decision is made at any stage of the processing, the consequences will propagate
to the conclusion, which will also then be in error. Hybrid methods of control have been suggested to overcome these problems.

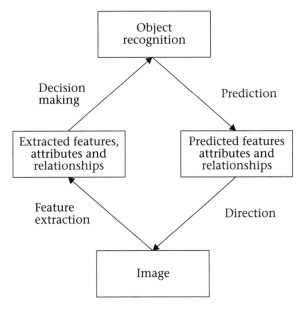

Figure 8.12 Hybrid control.

8.3.4 Hybrid control

Hybrid control methods do not enforce an order on the processing. Instead they allow a mixture of bottom-up and top-down control, as shown in Figure 8.12. Features are derived from the image in a bottom-up fashion. These might inform an object recognition process, which would hypothesise the identity of an object. Making predictions based on the suggested object can test the hypothesis in a top-down fashion: the system would predict the appearance of other image features that would be verified by investigating the image.

8.4 Heterarchical control

Heterarchically controlled systems have no control structure imposed on them, much like a forward chaining rule-based system. Instead, the system can be viewed as a community of experts who cooperate to solve a problem, shown in Figure 8.13. The experts, also known as knowledge sources (KS), each know how to solve a single specific problem and cannot solve each other's problems. They cannot therefore communicate directly with each other. Instead, communication is via a blackboard, which has all of the problem's data written on it. All experts will monitor the blackboard for some data that they recognise. When this occurs, the expert can process this piece

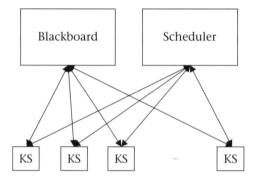

Figure 8.13 Blackboard architecture.

of data and post the results on the board. Gradually a solution to the problem will emerge. One further component of the architecture is the blackboard scheduler – this will arbitrate among the experts if more than one is attempting to process data simultaneously.

8.5 Information integration

So far in this chapter we have discussed how knowledge might be represented and how a system might be controlled. We discussed how goals might be achieved or hypotheses verified. Goals were either verified or not, i.e. a goal could take one of three logical values: true, false or unknown.

In actual fact, hypotheses should take real values to reflect the certainty of our belief in their truth. The truth value, or certainty factor (CF), of a hypothesis can be represented using a real value in the interval [0.0, 1.0] (some authors use [–1.0, +1.0]). A hypothesis that is known for definite to be true is given a truth value or CF of 1.0, and one that is known for definite to be false is given a CF of 0.0 or –1.0. Hypotheses that are not known to be true or false have this uncertainty reflected by an intermediate value.

Uncertainty in computer vision systems will be due ultimately to the uncertainties associated with pixel values: the value itself is an error-prone measurement of a brightness function and the location of the measurement is controlled by an error-prone clock in the system's analogue to digital converter.

These uncertainties will be propagated throughout the vision system's results and can cause confusion. Suppose, for example, we had three knowledge sources that attempted to identify cars in images of road junctions. They might produce evidence that a certain region of the image was a car with differing degree of certainty: one that identified cars using shape information might suggest that a region was a car with a certainty of 0.56, one using position might have certainty 0.66, and one using movement information 0.75. How can we combine these different pieces of evidence and different certainty factors?

$$CF\left(\bigwedge_i cf_i\right) = \min_i(cf_i) \tag{8.4}$$

$$CF\left(\bigvee_i cf_i\right) = \max_i(cf_i) \tag{8.5}$$

The approach taken in fuzzy logic when combining fuzzy truth values is defined by Equations (8.4) and (8.5) for conjunction (AND) and disjunction (OR) respectively: when combining facts using conjunction we take the minimum of the certainty factors, and when combining by disjunction we take the maximum. So the combined evidence to support the car would be given a certainty factor of 0.56. We may build a network of the facts that support a particular conclusion; Figure 8.14 illustrates the network describing the three simple rules above. Generally, the belief network would be much larger, reflecting a larger set of inferences. A segment spanning the arcs linking the supporting facts to the supported fact, as in Figure 8.14, would indicate conjunction of a set of facts. Disjunction is indicated by the absence of such a segment. Figure 8.15 illustrates an example network. In this network, the top-level fact, F1, is established by proving F1 AND F3. F1 is established by proving F4 OR F5, and F3 is established by proving F6 AND F7 OR F8. By applying the rules of Equations (8.4) and (8.5), it can be shown that the CF of F1 will be given by

$$CF(F1) = \min(\max(CF(F4), CF(F5)), \max(\min(CF(F6), CF(F7)), CF(F8))) \tag{8.6}$$

Once this certainty factor has been established, we must assess whether the evidence supporting the conclusion is sufficient to accept it as true, or whether it should be refuted. This will be achieved using a thresholding operation. Since the certainty values that propagate to the root of this type of

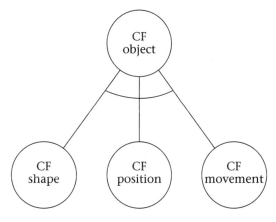

Figure 8.14 Bayesian belief network for a single inference.

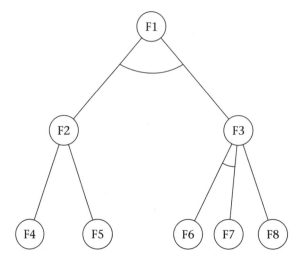

Figure 8.15 Sample belief network.

network are usually found to be rather small, the threshold is usually set to a low value.

This type of belief network provides numerical values for the confidence we have in a fact being true. It provides no support for evidence to the contrary, i.e. that the fact we are trying to establish is false, but only very weak support for the fact's truth. Dempster and Shafer suggested a mechanism for providing this information. They proposed that the certainty interval for each fact, [0, 1], be divided into three ranges. The lowest range [0, A] should be interpreted as a measure of disbelief and the highest range [B, 1] should be interpreted as a measure of belief. The intermediate range (A, B) reflects the uncertainty we have in this fact.

At the start of processing, the intervals (A, B) will be large, indicating that we have little or no evidence to support or deny each fact. As processing continues and evidence is gathered, the values of the As and Bs will alter: the As will be increased as evidence against a fact is found, and the Bs will be reduced as evidence supporting the various facts is obtained, and vice versa. Finally, we should reach a stable state when the evidence may be presented.

8.6 Summary

This chapter has been concerned with three topics:

- knowledge representation
- control of vision systems
- representing uncertainty

Knowledge representation is of fundamental importance in vision systems, as in all software. We are concerned to represent the information required in a manner that is efficient and allows comparisons with models to be made.

Several methods of controlling vision systems were examined. Each of them is appropriate for some tasks that a vision system will undertake; none are suited to the full range of tasks. For example, forwards chaining rule-based systems or procedurally coded knowledge might be appropriate for low-level vision tasks and backwards chaining rule bases would be suited to high-level tasks. A system integrating all levels ought to include multiple control strategies.

Finally, we examined how uncertainty in vision systems could be processed. All data that we can capture is uncertain due to the nature of the capture process. At present, system designers ignore this and proceed as if all the data was entirely reliable. In practice, given the amount of information and the mutual support provided by the data, this is not an unreasonable assumption. But it may be desirable to provide some measure of confidence in the conclusions drawn by a vision system. Mechanisms for providing this information were described.

8.7 Bibliography

Marr (1982) was influential in analysing visual systems. One of his contributions was to suggest that a visual algorithm should be analysed by asking *what* it does, *why* it does this and *how* it might be implemented.

Computational schemes for representing knowledge were reviewed by Binford (1982). Specific examples were first presented by Zahn and Roskies (1972) (pattern vectors), Lowe (1987) (relational structures), Ledley (1964) and Levine and Nazif (1985) (rules), Minsky (1975), Hanson and Riseman (1978) and Brookes (1981) (frames).

Erman *et al.* (1980) first presented the blackboard control scheme. Examples of other control schemes have been presented in references already cited.

Finally, integration of uncertainty was addressed in seminal publications by Rosenfeld *et al.* (1976), Shafer (1981) and Garvey *et al.* (1981).

8.8 Exercises

8.1   Build the relational graph that represents the plan view of a motorway junction.

8.2   It has been suggested that a rule-based system is capable of solving any vision problem. Is this true? Is a rule-based solution necessarily the best for all components of a vision system?

8.3 Design a rule-based system for recognising and tracing roads in an aerial photograph.

8.4 Build a frame representation of the room you are sitting in.

9

Motion tracking

It is the aim of motion tracking techniques to recover the movement of an object and perhaps also the movement of the camera through which the object is viewed. The object could be a guided missile, a car, a pedestrian, people in a shopping mall, a person's hands or lips; in fact, any moving object. The camera could be stationary, on a fixed mount free to rotate, or on a movable mounting. In all cases we shall be tracking the movement of an object in a sequence of images, and might also be interested in determining how the object moved through space and how the camera was moved.

9.1 Introduction

Tracking a moving object; that is, following the object's position as it moves in front of us, is an ability that we take for granted. It is, however, a difficult problem to solve, involving four significant subproblems:

- Separating moving objects from the static background.
- Identifying significant motion.
- Smoothly following an object.
- Solving the occlusion problem – which includes re-identifying a tracked object that was momentarily lost to view, a variation on the correspondence problem of Chapter 6.

Solutions to these problems will be discussed in this chapter. These solutions might give a list of the image coordinates occupied by a point on the object during the course of tracking, or we might translate these into world coordinates. In the latter case it is necessary to calibrate the camera, i.e. determine its location and orientation with respect to the world coordinate frame and determine how each pixel's coordinates translate into a vector in the world coordinate frame.

There are four combinations of moving and static object and camera.

- Static camera and static object (SCSO) is the typical problem that computer vision systems attempt to solve: how to interpret a still image.

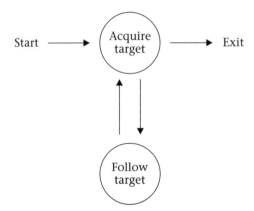

Figure 9.1   Phases of tracking.

- Static camera and moving object (SCMO) is typical of most observation tasks where we set up a camera and interpret the data that is captured. The data would represent any scene that contained moving objects: a road junction, the entrance hall of a building etc.
- Moving camera and static object (MCSO) might seem an unlikely problem to solve, but is in fact one of the less common inspection problems, the camera is moved around an object in order to gain information from all sides. A true three-dimensional view of the object can be created.
- Moving camera and moving object (MCMO) is the problem that is to be solved when the camera is free to move. In most cases the camera's movement is restricted to rotations about two axes, but it might also be capable of translation.

This chapter will restrict its attention to the SCMO and MCMO problems.

An object tracking system can be in one of two states; see Figure 9.1. In the first state the system will simply capture data and inspect it for changes. The changes could be due to many causes, among which is the appearance of a target. Having acquired a target, the system moves to the second state, in which the target is tracked. The system will return to the first state when the target is lost, either by it moving out of the field of view or simply being lost. The operations performed by a system in these two states are described. Firstly it is necessary to take another look a camera calibration.

9.2 Camera calibration revisited

9.2.1 Theory

Camera calibration is the process of defining the relationship between image coordinates, (x, y), and world coordinates, (X, Y, Z), measured in some

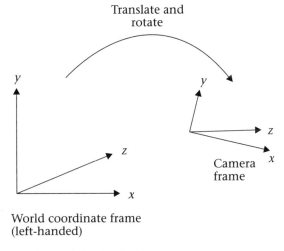

Figure 9.2 Extrinsic camera parameters.

reference frame. Note that we have two image coordinates but three world coordinates, making it impossible to determine the position of an object in the world uniquely from its position in an image. The relationship is defined as a two-step process. One relates the world coordinate frame to the camera coordinate frame by a translation and rotation and is specified by a set of extrinsic parameters. The second step relates the camera coordinate frame to the image coordinate frame and is defined by a set of intrinsic parameters.

Given that the extrinsic parameters are defined by a rotation and translation, we may simply write the relationship between a point in the world coordinate frame $\mathbf{P}_W$ and in the camera frame, $\mathbf{P}_C$ as:

$$\mathbf{P}_C = R(\mathbf{P}_W - \mathbf{T}) \qquad (9.1)$$

where R is a 3 × 3 element rotation matrix. Figure 9.2 defines the relationship.

The intrinsic parameters are the camera's focal length, f, the x and y scaling factors, s_x and s_y, the image's principal point (the intersection of the camera's optical axis and the image plane), (o_x, o_y), and the radial distortion coefficients k_x and k_y (which are often ignored). Equations (2.10) and (2.11) are repeated here for convenience:

$$\begin{aligned} x &= -(x_{im} - o_x)s_x \\ y &= -(y_{im} - o_y)s_y \end{aligned} \qquad (9.2)$$

$$\begin{aligned} x &= (1 + k_x(x^2 + y^2))x_d \\ y &= (1 + k_y(x^2 + y^2))y_d \end{aligned} \qquad (9.3)$$

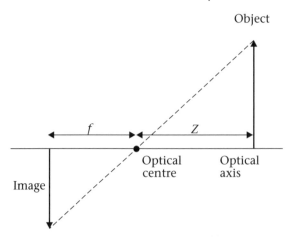

Figure 9.3 Pinhole camera model.

If we assume that we may ignore radial distortions for simplicity ($k_x = k_y = 0$), then Equation (9.3) reduces to an identity. This is not an unreasonable assumption, as the distortion introduced by an average quality lens of medium focal length will be about 1 part in 70 – in a 100 × 100 pixel image, the pixels in the corners will be displaced by about one position.

If we assume that the camera lens behaves as a pinhole, as in Figure 9.3, in which rays of light pass though one point in the lens without being deviated (the optical centre), then we may relate image and world coordinates using the similar triangles defined by the world X- or Y-coordinates and range, Z, and the image coordinates x or y and focal length, f:

$$\frac{x}{f} = \frac{X}{Z}$$

$$x = f\frac{X}{Z} \tag{9.4}$$

and

$$y = f\frac{Y}{Z} \tag{9.5}$$

If we substitute Equations (9.1) and (9.2) into these last two equations, we derive a relationship between image coordinates and the world coordinates:

$$-(x_{im} - o_x)s_x = f\frac{R_1^T(P_w - T)}{R_3^T(P_w - T)}$$

$$-(y_{im} - o_y)s_y = f\frac{R_2^T(P_w - T)}{R_3^T(P_w - T)} \tag{9.6}$$

where R_i is the ith row of the rotation matrix.

It is in fact possible to separate the intrinsic and extrinsic parameters in Equation (9.6) by using:

$$M_{int} = \begin{pmatrix} -f/s_x & 0 & o_x \\ 0 & -f/s_y & o_y \\ 0 & 0 & 1 \end{pmatrix} \tag{9.7}$$

and

$$M_{ext} = \begin{pmatrix} r_{11} & r_{12} & r_{13} & -R_1^T T \\ r_{21} & r_{22} & r_{23} & -R_2^T T \\ r_{31} & r_{32} & r_{33} & -R_3^T T \end{pmatrix} \tag{9.8}$$

where r_{ij} are the elements of the rotation matrix R, specified above. The relationship between the coordinates becomes:

$$\begin{pmatrix} p_1 \\ p_2 \\ p_3 \end{pmatrix} = M_{int} M_{ext} \begin{pmatrix} X_w \\ Y_w \\ Z_w \\ 1 \end{pmatrix} \tag{9.9}$$

and the image coordinates, x and y, are given by the two ratios p_1/p_3 and p_2/p_3.

9.2.2 Practice

The camera parameter matrices, M_{int} and M_{ext}, together have 11 independent parameters. These can be estimated if sufficient pairs of matching world and image points are available (at least six pairs). If more points are available, a least squares approach can be taken to solving the equations.

Writing the matrix Equation (9.9) explicitly and using the expressions for the x- and y-coordinates, we see:

$$\begin{aligned} x_i &= \frac{p_1^i}{p_3^i} = \frac{m_{11}X_w^i + m_{12}Y_w^i + m_{13}Z_w^i + m_{14}}{m_{31}X_w^i + m_{32}Y_w^i + m_{33}Z_w^i + m_{34}} \\ y_i &= \frac{p_2^i}{p_3^i} = \frac{m_{21}X_w^i + m_{22}Y_w^i + m_{23}Z_w^i + m_{24}}{m_{31}X_w^i + m_{32}Y_w^i + m_{33}Z_w^i + m_{34}} \end{aligned} \tag{9.10}$$

We therefore have an explicit (if involved) relationship between each world point and the corresponding image point that involves the elements of the combined camera parameter matrix m_{ij}. The m_{ij} can be found by solving the equation:

$$Am = 0 \qquad (9.11)$$

where

$$A = \begin{pmatrix} X_1 & Y_1 & Z_1 & 1 & 0 & 0 & 0 & 0 & -x_1X_1 & -x_1Y_1 & -x_1Z_1 & -x_1 \\ 0 & 0 & 0 & 0 & X_1 & Y_1 & Z_1 & 1 & -y_1X_1 & -y_1Y_1 & -y_1Z_1 & -y_1 \\ X_2 & Y_2 & Z_2 & 1 & 0 & 0 & 0 & 0 & -x_2X_2 & -x_2Y_2 & -x_2Z_2 & -x_2 \\ 0 & 0 & 0 & 0 & X_2 & Y_2 & Z_2 & 1 & -y_2X_2 & -y_2Y_2 & -y_2Z_2 & -y_2 \\ \vdots & \vdots & \vdots & \vdots & \vdots & \vdots & \vdots & \vdots & \vdots & \vdots & \vdots & \vdots \\ X_N & Y_N & Z_N & 1 & 0 & 0 & 0 & 0 & -x_NX_N & -x_NY_N & -x_NZ_N & -x_N \\ 0 & 0 & 0 & 0 & X_N & Y_N & Z_N & 1 & -y_NX_N & -y_NY_N & -y_NZ_N & -y_N \end{pmatrix}$$

$$(9.12)$$

and

$$m = \begin{pmatrix} m_{11} & m_{12} & \cdots & m_{33} & m_{34} \end{pmatrix}^{\mathrm{T}} \qquad (9.13)$$

Mathematical techniques exist to solve this system of equations. The individual parameters of the camera can be extracted from the parameter matrix if desired.

9.3 Target acquisition

As Figure 9.1 suggested, the first task to be performed by a tracking system is to identify an object to be tracked. This is usually done by comparison of the current image with either a background image or the previous one. The differences that are detected must then be assessed for their significance and classified. Two problems must be addressed:

- What changes can be observed?
- What is the image compared to?

9.3.1 Image differencing

Differences may be observed between a pair of images captured using the same camera but separated in time. These differences can be caused by:

- noise in the image data
- systematic variations in the image data
- movement of an object

As we saw in Chapter 2, image noise is due to thermal variations in the system's circuitry. It is usually of low amplitude. Therefore, when we subtract a pair of images that has been captured under these conditions (same camera location, separated in time) we would expect low-amplitude differences to be observed. Figure 9.4(a) shows the difference image computed from a typical pair of images. The data is offset: a mid-grey value indicates a difference of zero. Figure 9.4(b) is the histogram of the difference image, it can be shown that the variance of the histogram is   times the variance of the original

(a)

(b)

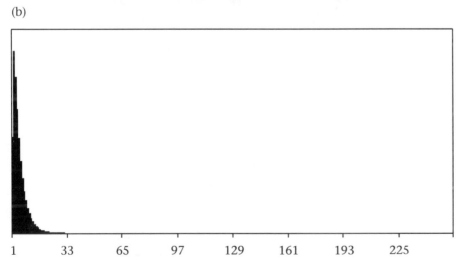

| 1 | 33 | 65 | 97 | 129 | 161 | 193 | 225 |

Figure 9.4 Temporal difference images. (a) Difference image derived from a pair of images taken at different times from a camera that was moved between captures; (b) histogram of the difference image.

image. We can therefore set a threshold value that will differentiate between noise and true differences.

It is also possible for a systematic change to have occurred in the time between the capture of the two images. This might be, for example, a global change in the illumination of the scene. Such a change would involve significant changes to a large number of the image's pixels, perhaps even all of them; see Figure 9.5. We might therefore set an upper limit on the number of pixels that are different if these pixels are to be acceptable as possible targets.

Figure 9.5   Change in scene illumination between capture of two images and the subsequent difference image.

Having identified pixels that have changed, we must now find the cause of the change. Initially, we consider the case of the static camera.

We may differentiate between different types of movement. At the simplest level we would have objects that can move but not rotate not deform. In this case, the causes of differences will include (Figure 9.6):

- One or more objects have changed their positions.
- One or more objects have left the scene.
- One or more new objects have entered the scene.

Figure 9.6 Simplest causes of image differences: objects may enter the scene, change their position in the scene or exit the scene.

If we now allow the objects to rotate in the image plane, we must have an additional cause of change:

- One or more objects have rotated in the image plane (Figure 9.7).

We may then also allow objects to rotate about axes parallel to the image plane or to deform (Figures 9.8 and 9.9), introducing two further causes of changes:

Figure 9.7   Rotation of an object in the image plane.

Figure 9.8 Rotation of an object about an axis parallel to the image plane.

- One or more objects have rotated about an axis parallel to the image plane.
- One or more objects have changed their shapes.

As each object moves, two further factors will affect the results of the subtraction (Figures 9.10 and 9.11):

- The object may move a small enough distance such that its final position overlaps its original location.

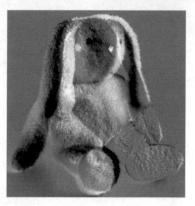

Figure 9.9 Deformation of an object.

- The object may be the same brightness or colour as the background it occludes, and is therefore invisible.

If we now include the case of the moving camera, we must realise that the camera's motion will cause the entire image to be different. Image differencing is not therefore an appropriate technique to be used for target acquisition.

Having detected the changes and decided that they are significant, they may be used to track objects. This is the subject of Section 9.4.

9.3.2 Background images

A background image is a version of the scene that is known to be void of any objects of interest. Any significant difference between a newly captured image and the background will be due to objects of interest.

Changes in an image sequence are detected by subtraction. Two methods were suggested: comparing each image with a background image, or comparing each image with the one immediately preceding it.

Figure 9.10 Small movement of an object. The initial and final positions overlap and there is cancellation of the object in the overlap region.

Two factors must be considered when selecting one or other of these methods. Firstly, the time interval between capturing images may not be large; therefore the distance moved by an object's projected image may not be large and there will be an increased probability that the final and initial positions of objects will overlap (Figure 9.10), which will increase the difficulty of tracking. Secondly, if we compare each image with a background, we must ensure that the background and the image are consistent; that is, no systematic changes have occurred since that background was acquired.

Figure 9.11   Matching of the object and background, a camouflage effect. Movement of such an object cannot be detected by image differences.

Provided that a consistent background image can be maintained, background subtraction is the preferred technique. The background may be updated using one of two methods. We may periodically replace the background with a fresh image, ensuring that there are no objects in the new image. Alternatively, we may incorporate the non-object portions of the current image into the background image. The second method is preferable.

When the image was originally compared against the background, any significant change was attributed to the appearance or disappearance of an object. The pixels that were not significantly different were assumed to be ones where no changes due to objects' motions had occurred: these were still background pixels. It is these pixels that will contribute to the updating of the background image: although they are not significantly different, there may be some small changes due to the evolution of the background. Therefore we absorb these into the background, $B(i, j)$, according to Equation (9.14):

$$B(i,j) = (1 - \alpha)B(i,j) + \alpha f(i,j) \qquad (9.14)$$

The constant α determines what proportion of the current image is absorbed into the background. A value of 0.1 would completely update the background within 10 images; much smaller values of α are generally used.

9.4 Target following

The second state of a tracking system is the one that performs the actual tracking, given the target or targets identified by the first state. The tracking state will report the locations of the targets derived from each image that is captured: either the image coordinates of a point on the objects or the objects' locations in a world coordinate system, if this is possible. Tracking may be performed offline using recorded data, but it is more usual (and useful) to perform it online using real-time data. This imposes some hard timing constraints: the images must be processed sufficiently fast for tracking to be performed.

Three types of algorithm will be described:

- Object matching, in which objects are found in an image and matched to the objects found in the previous image.
- Minimum path curvature, in which sensible trajectories are found.
- Model-based methods that attempt to reconcile the data derived from the images against a model of how the object or objects are moving.

9.4.1 Matching

Object matching is conceptually the simplest tracking technique, but also the least efficient. It relies on being able to derive a unique description of each object that will be used to identify the object in the following image.

The architecture of a simple tracking system is presented in Figure 9.12. The system maintains a database of the objects that are being tracked. Each entry will record the object's appearance (its description) and its location in the last processed image. The system will also maintain the background image. During the course of tracking, each image is processed in an identical manner. The image will first be compared to the background image to identify a set of objects from which a set of object descriptions is extracted. The

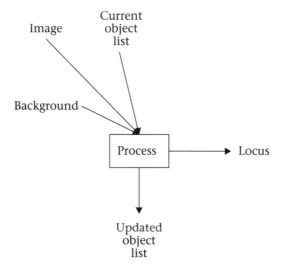

Figure 9.12 Object tracking state diagram.

object descriptions will be compared against those stored in the database. According to the analysis of Section 9.3.1, three cases must be dealt with.

- An object description matches a description in the database. The database is updated to reflect the object's new position and any changes in the description.
- An object description fails to match anything in the database. This is assumed to be a new object, which is inserted into the database.
- An entry in the database fails to match any description derived from the image. It is assumed that these descriptions relate to objects that have exited the field of view and can therefore be removed from the database.

Matching can be achieved using any of the techniques described in Chapter 6; any method can be used that derives a syntactic or, preferably, a numerical description of the object. One very effective description is the colour histogram. This is simple to compute and easily matched.

9.4.1.1 Colour histogram
The colour histogram of a set of pixels is derived by firstly normalising the colour values:

$$r = \frac{R}{R+G+B}$$
$$g = \frac{G}{R+G+B} \tag{9.15}$$

Some authors add 1 to the denominator to prevent divide by zero errors. Clearly only two independent components remain. These can be used to form a two-dimensional histogram using the pixel data from a region of the image. Since the region is likely to be small, and as there are normally 256 shades of each brightness value, the histogram entries will be small; in fact, they will be mostly zeros. To alleviate this problem, the number of bins in the histogram is reduced to a much smaller number: eight or sixteen shades of each colour is common.

The colour histograms of two regions are assessed for similarity according to

$$M_{ab} = \sum_r \sum_g \min(H_a(r,g), H_b(r,g)) \tag{9.16}$$

A large value is indicative of matching histograms. A value of the matching coefficient greater than some threshold would indicate that the histograms and therefore the regions from which they were computed are the same.

9.4.1.2 Affine tracking

A related technique is affine tracking. If we assume that an object, or part of an object, does not deform as it moves, then all the points on the object will undergo the same transformation. Affine tracking techniques use this and attempt to discover sets of points in the image that undergo the same affine transformation (combination of translation and rotation in the image plane).

It is impractical to use all of the points on an object, so we therefore select regions of interest, using one of the operators discussed in Chapter 6. Corner detectors are suitable.

9.4.2 Minimum path curvature

Minimum path curvature is a method that is suitable for determining the trajectories of a multitude of objects offline. The analysis must be performed offline, as all the data is required in the computation.

Newton's laws of motion describe how everyday objects move. In particular, the first law states that an object remains at rest or moves with constant velocity unless acted on by an external force. The external force would cause the object to accelerate in the direction of the force. In practice, this means that objects will move, and will be seen to move in straight lines, or will move following a circular trajectory, which will appear as an elliptical path.

Figure 9.13 illustrates this. The positions of two similar moving objects in three images are shown in part (a) of the figure. (The objects need not be similar, we might simply indicate the positions of dissimilar objects.) Parts (b)–(e) of the figure illustrate all of the alternative possibilities for the two objects' movements. Assuming that the objects do not collide, the alternative with the straightest paths is the one that is most consistent with the laws of motion.

The curvature of a path is computed by summing the local curvatures, which are in turn defined by the second differential along the path (Equation 9.17). The total curvature of a potential set of trajectories is therefore the sum of the curvatures of all of the paths being considered (Equation 9.18).

$$C_i = \cos\theta_i \tag{9.17}$$

$$C_{\text{tot}} = \sum_{\forall i} C_i \tag{9.18}$$

θ_i is the angle created by the vectors between points i to $i+1$ and $i-1$ to i. The solution having the minimum value of C_{tot} is accepted as being the one most likely to match the truth.

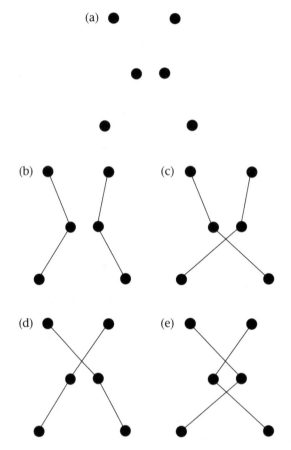

Figure 9.13 Minimum path curvature. (a) Positions of two tokens in three images; (b)–(e) alternative interpretations of the tokens' movements.

9.4.3 Model-based tracking

Model-based tracking systems are ideally suited to real-time applications. In general, a model-based tracking system will have the architecture of Figure 9.14. Central to the system is the motion model, which is simply a record of the motion parameters of each of the tracked objects, plus an object description. In contrast to the object matching techniques that process the image, find objects and then match them against a database, model-based tracking systems use the information in the database to predict a likely location for the tracked objects at some future time. At that time, an image is captured and the objects' locations are verified. If the predicted and actual locations match, then the model is correct; otherwise it must be updated somehow.

Again, we assume that objects move according to Newton's laws. Therefore, given the position, $r(t)$, and velocity, $v(t)$, of an object at time t, and possibly the object's acceleration, $a(t)$, we may predict its position and velocity at a time Δt later, assuming that the acceleration is constant:

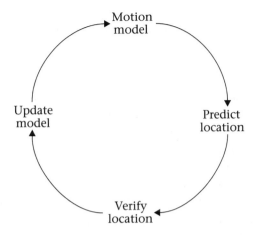

Figure 9.14 Architecture of a model-based tracker.

$$r(t + \Delta t) = r(t) + v(t)\Delta t + a(t)\frac{(\Delta t)^2}{2}$$

$$v(t + \Delta t) = v(t) + a(t)\Delta t \hspace{3cm} (9.19)$$

$$a(t + \Delta t) = a(t)$$

For simplicity, many authors assume zero acceleration.

We may therefore look for the object at this specified location. However, there is a certain degree of uncertainty associated with each of the components of the motion model, so the predicted location will therefore also be an uncertain estimate of the actual location. It can be shown that the uncertainty in velocity and acceleration contribute to the uncertainty in the position according to Equation (9.20):

$$\Delta r(\Delta t) = \Delta t \Delta v + \frac{(\Delta t)^2}{2}\Delta a \hspace{3cm} (9.20)$$

Not surprisingly, the magnitude of the uncertainty in position increases as the time interval over which the prediction is made becomes longer.

The consequence of this analysis is that we actually predict an area of the image that is likely to contain the object we are tracking. We then attempt to verify the location of the object using the other information in our database. This could be a colour histogram of derived from the object, or even a copy of the object's appearance – a bitmap abstracted from it. The matching techniques of previous chapters will be used. If the object is at the predicted location, then the model is accurate. If it is elsewhere, the model must be updated and the Kalman filter is often used for this purpose. The predictive nature of this operation is what makes it so efficient. Real-time operation is possible, and indeed this architecture has been used to guide autonomous vehicles on German motorways.

9.4.3.1 Kalman filter

The Kalman filter is a mathematically rigorous method of updating a model given uncertain measurements of the model's parameters and assuming certain properties of the noise introduced by the measurement process. The model is composed of the motion parameters of the objects being tracked: position and velocity (and occasionally acceleration) are used. A point fixed on the object can be used to represent the whole object, or two points defining the minimum bounding rectangle could also be used.

The Kalman filter requires the following quantities. k is a variable known as the epoch number; it is the ordinal value of the observation. It is a time-related measurement, but is definitely not the time.

- Measurements of the object being tracked: $\mathbf{y}(k)$. These will be the x- and y-coordinates of the points being followed. Therefore y will be an array of two or four elements.
- The state of the system, $\mathbf{x}(k)$. This is a record of our estimate of how the object is behaving. It will maintain a record of the motion parameters of the points being tracked.
- An observation matrix, $\mathbf{H}(k)$, that relates the system state to the measurements. That is, if the system is in a particular state, then the observation of that state will be defined by the product of $\mathbf{H}(k)$ and $\mathbf{x}(k)$. Although $\mathbf{H}$ is represented as being time-dependent, it is usually constant.
- An evolution matrix, $\mathbf{A}(k)$, that specifies how the system state changes between epochs. It too is usually a constant matrix.
- We also have two noise measures, $\mathbf{n}(k)$ and $\mathbf{v}(k)$, that record the measurement noise and the process noise: the uncertainties in the measurements and our estimate of the system state.

Given these quantities, we may relate the observations and the model by:

$$\mathbf{y}(k) = \mathbf{H}(k)\mathbf{x}(k) + \mathbf{n}(k) \tag{9.21}$$

The system's evolution is determined by

$$\hat{\mathbf{x}}(k+1 \mid k) = \mathbf{A}(k)\mathbf{x}(k \mid k) + \mathbf{v}(k) \tag{9.22}$$

By substitution, we may make a prediction of the observation at the $k + 1$th epoch:

$$\begin{aligned} \hat{\mathbf{y}}(k+1 \mid k) &= \mathbf{H}(k)\hat{\mathbf{x}}(k+1 \mid k) + \mathbf{n}(k) \\ &= \mathbf{H}(k)A(k)x(k \mid k) + \mathbf{n}(k) \end{aligned} \tag{9.23}$$

If we assume that we are tracking one point on the object and modelling just the position and velocity, we may state the form of each of the quantities. If the state vector, $\mathbf{x}$, is organised such that we have the x-coordinate of position, followed by the x component of velocity and then the y components, the observation matrix is:

$$H(k) = \begin{bmatrix} 1 & 0 & 0 & 0 \\ 0 & 0 & 1 & 0 \end{bmatrix} \tag{9.24}$$

The effect of this is to pick out the x- and y-coordinates, which are the observed quantities. The evolution matrix is:

$$A(k) = \begin{bmatrix} 1 & T & 0 & 0 \\ 0 & 1 & 0 & 0 \\ 0 & 0 & 1 & T \\ 0 & 0 & 0 & 1 \end{bmatrix} \tag{9.25}$$

where T is the time interval between epochs (assumed to be constant). The effect of this matrix is to maintain constant values of the velocity components and to increase the position components by the distance moved in the time T (the product of the velocity and T).

The filter may be used in the context of the tracking scheme presented above. Using the evolution matrix, we predict the state of the system and the observation that will be made at epoch $k + 1$ from the historical information. We then make a measurement. The difference between the predicted and actual measurements, $\Delta(k + 1 \mid k)$, is used to update the system state according to the Kalman gain functions:

$$\Delta y(k + 1 \mid k) = y(k + 1) - \hat{y}(k + 1 \mid k) \tag{9.26}$$
$$\hat{x}(k + 1 \mid k + 1) = \hat{x}(k + 1 \mid k) + G(k + 1)\Delta y(k + 1 \mid k)$$

$\mathbf{G}$ is the Kalman gain, which is derived from the process and measurement noise, the observation matrix and the evolution matrix:

$$\mathbf{G}(k + 1) = \mathbf{C}(k \mid k)\mathbf{H}^{\mathrm{T}} (\mathbf{H}\mathbf{C}(k \mid k)\mathbf{H}^{\mathrm{T}} + \mathbf{n})^{-1} \tag{9.27}$$
$$\mathbf{C}(k + 1 \mid k) = \mathbf{C}(k \mid k) - \mathbf{G}\mathbf{H}\mathbf{C}(k \mid k)$$

$\mathbf{C}$ is the system covariance.

The Kalman filter has been used extensively in tracking applications; even if the application has not quite matched the filter's requirements, the tracking has often been quite successful.

Figure 9.15   Sample results of a Kalman filter. The object is represented by the minimum bounding rectangle; the coordinates of two opposite vertices are tracked.

Figure 9.15 presents sample results from a Kalman filter designed to track people moving in a room. This problem presented particular difficulties when one person was occluded by another. The Kalman filter was able to overcome this. Each person was represented by the minimum-bounding rectangle that enclosed their region of the image. Person regions were described by the colour histogram. The Kalman filter tracked the position and velocity of two opposite corners of the bounding rectangles for each person region. Despite the volume of data to be processed, real-time operation is achievable.

The major weaknesses of the Kalman filter are due to its dependency on the assumed motion model and the noise distributions. Whilst the noise distributions are not overly critical, the tracker will lose contact with the tracked object if the motion model changes. This is not an unusual occurrence; for example, a pedestrian may change direction to avoid an obstacle in the pavement, creating a change in her motion and causing the filter's motion model to become outdated. The condensation tracker was proposed to avoid these shortcomings.

9.4.4 Condensation tracking

A moving object can be in any one of a continuum of states. Each state will describe the object's relevant properties, such as position and velocity, and shape for a non-rigid object. Any measurements derived from an image of the moving object will be more or less consistent with all of the possible

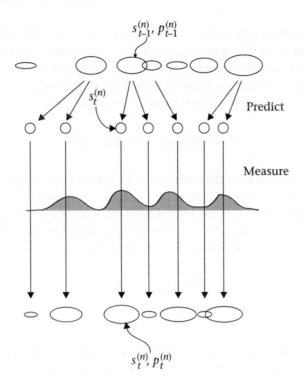

Figure 9.16 Condensation tracking: distribution of motion states and their approximation (after Isard and Blake (1996)).

object states: some measurements will be completely inconsistent, and therefore the probability of the object being in that state will be minute; other measurements will be more consistent and the probability that the object is in those states will be larger.

It is not possible to represent the continuum of states due to the finite resources available to any computer system. We therefore represent the distribution by taking a number of samples from it. This number is selected according to the available computing power and desired performance. Figure 9.16 illustrates the case of a one-dimensional state, which will not usually be encountered; rather, the state vector will be multidimensional, recording position (two dimensions for the two coordinates) and velocity (another two dimensions) of at least one point. Extending the analysis to multiple dimensions is straightforward. The continuous curve in the figure represents the probability distribution, $p(x)$, of the states that could be occupied by the object. This distribution is sampled at N points and each sample is represented by a sample value, $s^{(i)}$, and a weight, $\pi^{(i)}$. The weight is proportional to the conditional state density function at this state (i.e. the probability of this state being observed):

$$\pi_i \propto p(z \mid x = s^{(i)}) \qquad (9.28)$$

The condensation algorithm will maintain the sample set and weights, adjusting them as each image is captured to maintain consistency between the samples and measurements. The best estimate of the current state of the object being tracked can be derived from this sample set.

At time step $t - 1$, the tracker will have a sample set:

$$\{s_{t-1}^{(n)}, \pi_{t-1}^{(n)}, c_{t-1}^{(n)}, \quad n = 1, \ldots, N\} \tag{9.29}$$

where $s_{t-1}^{(n)}$ are the vectors that describe the state of the object being tracked (which could be position and velocity measurements etc.); $\pi_{t-1}^{(n)}$ are the weights associated with each state (collectively these approximate the conditional state density); and $c_{t-1}^{(n)}$ are cumulative weights used to improve the efficiency of the sampling process, described below:

$$c_t^{(k)} = c_t^{(k-1)} + \pi_t^{(k)}$$
$$0 \leq c_t^{(k)} \leq 1 \tag{9.30}$$

The tracker iteratively modifies the sample set and ensures that it is consistent with the image data. This is done in three stages: selection, prediction and measurement.

The selection stage will choose N samples from the sample set. Ones with large values of π are more likely to be selected. This selection is achieved by generating a random number, r, from a uniform unit distribution: $0 \leq r \leq 1$. We identify the smallest value of j satisfying:

$$c_{t-1}^{(j)} \geq r \tag{9.31}$$

and the new sample will be:

$$s'_{t}^{(n)} = s_{t-1}^{(j)} \tag{9.32}$$

It is possible, and indeed likely, that samples having large values of π will appear more than once in the set of new samples. This is a strength of this tracking scheme.

The prediction stage will apply the underlying motion model to each new sample and predict the state of the object at time t. If the object is behaving in a predictable fashion (that is, it has a well-defined motion model), we could write

$$s_t^{(n)} = As'_t^{(n)} + Bw_t^{(n)} \tag{9.33}$$

where $\mathbf{A}$ is the matrix describing the motion model, much like the evolution matrix in the Kalman filter; $\mathbf{B}$ is the system covariance; and $w_t^{(n)}$ is a set of random variates which perturb the prediction slightly. If the object's motion were completely unpredictable (that is, the object is moving at random), which is the model that is assumed in many tracking applications, we would write:

$$s_t^{(n)} = s'_t^{(n)} + Bw_t^{(n)} \tag{9.34}$$

The final stage of the cycle is to make measurements from the image and update the weights using them. Measurements are denoted by z_t, and we attempt to measure the compatibility between the estimated states and the measurements. Thus the weights are given by the probability that the measurement is a sample derived from the population defined by the predicted state:

$$\pi_t^{(n)} = p(z_t \mid x_t = s_t^{(n)}) \tag{9.35}$$

Finally, the new weights are normalised to sum to unity and the new cumulative probabilities are computed.

Once the N samples have been constructed, the 'true' state of the object can be estimated by computing the weighted sum of the state vectors, $\mathbf{s}^{(n)}$, using the weights $\pi^{(n)}$. A function must be derived to extract the required data from the weight vectors. Compare the Kalman filter's observation matrix, $\mathbf{H}$:

$$\langle f(x_t) \rangle = \sum_{j=1}^{N} \pi_t^{(j)} f(s_t^{(j)}) \tag{9.36}$$

How well does the filter perform? Figure 9.17 is a set of images abstracted from a sequence that included a person wandering around a well-lit area. Since we could not define how the person moved, no motion model was used; instead, Equation (9.34) was used in the prediction stage. It is apparent that the person's location is determined accurately in all frames. Other authors have applied the condensation algorithm to tracking objects against cluttered backgrounds and other difficult motions.

9.4.5 Hidden Markov models

A Hidden Markov Model is a graphical representation of the states that a system can occupy, the allowed transitions between states and the relative probabilities of those transitions occurring. For example, the system in

Figure 9.17 Sample results of the condensation filter used to track a person wandering. The cloud of points indicates the states being tracked by the algorithm, and the X indicates the point that most closely matches the model of the object being tracked.

Figure 9.18 may be in any of the three states indicated, but it may only move between the states that are connected by the directed arcs. The arcs are labelled by the probability of their being selected: the sum of the probabilities of all the arcs leaving a node must be 1, because a transition must occur. Therefore, we can say that the probability of the transition from state one to state two is p and the probability of the transition from state one back to state one will be $1 - p$, as only two arcs leave state one.

The model is hidden, as we cannot directly determine what state the system is in. We can only make observations that enable us to estimate the system's state.

For example, a system designed to read American Sign Language from a video sequence of a signer must infer a state for each sign. The state is internal to the signer and cannot be determined directly; rather, we guess it

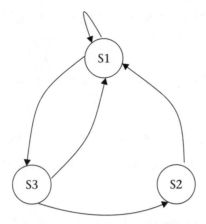

Figure 9.18   Sample Hidden Markov Model.

from observations of the signer's hands. The signer's internal state will change quite rapidly as he speaks, and so too will the hand positions. The allowed changes are dictated by the grammar of the language that will be known to the observer (this is not to say that ungrammatical transitions do not occur; rather, they are contradictory to the model). We therefore have two pieces of information that can be used to help translate the sign language:

- observations of the hand gesture
- probabilities of the occurrences of different sequences of observations

Formally, a sequence of measurements is said to form a Markov chain if the probability distribution of one measurement is dependent only on the distribution of the preceding measurement. Further, the chain is homogeneous if the probability distributions do not change. So the sign language can be represented by a set of probabilities, p_{ij}, that are the probabilities of transitions between pairs of states – collectively they form the state transition matrix, **P**.

Observation will also yield the probability of making measurements that are consistent with each state; that is, the probability of observing each state, π_i.

Given these two measurements, it is possible, using the Trellis Model, to compute the probability of generating a given sequence of symbols using a given Markov model. Assuming the Markov model of Figure 9.18, and taking a four-symbol sequence, we can build the trellis diagram (Figure 9.19) by taking four copies of the state space (the nodes of Figure 9.18) and drawing them in four columns. A node, i, in column n is linked to a node, j, of column $n + 1$ if p_{ij} is non-zero. Note that the weights associated with the nodes and arcs have been omitted for clarity. The paths through the trellis, starting from the leftmost column, indicate all possible sets of four states that may be

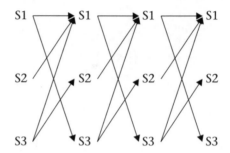

Figure 9.19   Trellis diagram derived from the HMM of Figure 9.18.

generated by the Markov model. The probability of observing each path is simply the product of the nodes' probabilities and the transition probabilities along each path.

It is also possible to compute the sequence of states that is most consistent with a sequence of measurements. This is achieved using the Viterbi algorithm. If the number of non-zero elements in $\mathbf{P}$ is small, then there will be $O(k^n)$, paths of length n selected from k states. It is not feasible to search these exhaustively. Fortunately, the problem may be solved inductively. Assuming that we know the best $(n-1)$-step path ending in each state, then it is a simple matter to determine the best n-step path terminating at each state – we need only inspect a single step.

There also exist techniques for creating a hidden Markov model from various data sets using expectation–maximisation methods.

9.5 Optic flow

Optic flow is the generic name given to many techniques that aim to derive dense estimates of motion within an image sequence. In this context, dense implies an estimate at the pixel level rather than the object level. The estimation of pixel movement may be performed by matching features, small regions or even individual pixels.

Feature matching is performed using the techniques of earlier chapters. Features are extracted from each image in the sequence and matched between successive images. It is important that the features are easily separable, to avoid combinatorial explosion of matches. Various measures of interest have been suggested for identifying suitable features. Corners have also been used widely.

Matching at the region level is achieved using correlation. A region is selected in image i. The matching region is sought in image $i + 1$. The match between the regions in the two images is assessed by measuring the squared difference between the two regions:

$$E_{ij}(u,v) = \sum_{u=i-w}^{i+w} \sum_{v=j=w}^{j+w} (I(x,y,t_i) - I(x+u,y+v,t_{i+1}))^2 \qquad (9.37)$$

The displacement, (u, v), for which this is a minimum is the motion at this location, (x, y). Whilst this technique is a recognised part of the MPEG family of video coding standards, it is not often used for determining motion flow where further analysis is to be performed. This is due to the limited accuracy and the sparseness of the motion estimates.

Optic flow at the pixel level was first formulated by Horn and Schunk (1981). Although many modifications to their algorithm have been proposed, theirs still yields the most accurate results.

The algorithm assumes that a pixel's intensity does not change over time. Therefore we may write

$$I(x,y,t) = I(x+\Delta x, y+\Delta y, t+\Delta t) \qquad (9.38)$$

Several methods can be used to derive the optic flow equation. One may either expand the right-hand side of Equation (9.38) as a Taylor series, truncating at the second-order terms, or one may simply set the differential of the image function to zero. In either case, the derivation yields the optic flow equation:

$$\frac{\partial I}{\partial x} v_x + \frac{\partial I}{\partial y} v_y + \frac{\partial I}{\partial t} = 0 \qquad (9.39)$$

where v_x and v_y are the components of the pixel's velocity in the x and y directions, and the partial derivatives are the image gradients in the x and y directions and with respect to time.

Given just this equation, the magnitude of the pixel's motion (its speed) can be estimated, but not the direction of its motion. An additional constraint is required for this; the so-called smoothness constraint is usually invoked. This assumes that adjacent pixels will have similar velocities. It is not an unreasonable assumption for large regions of the image: pixels within the bulk of the same object will move together and hence have the same velocities. The assumption breaks down when the neighbouring pixels span the boundary between differently moving regions. In this case, the estimated velocity will change smoothly from the velocity of one to the other's; we will not compute the correct abrupt change.

The smoothness constraint minimises the total sum of squared velocity gradients:

$$\sum_{\text{image}} \left(\left(\frac{\partial v_x}{\partial x}\right)^2 + \left(\frac{\partial v_x}{\partial y}\right)^2 + \left(\frac{\partial v_y}{\partial x}\right)^2 + \left(\frac{\partial v_y}{\partial y}\right)^2 \right) \qquad (9.40)$$

Using the optic flow equation and the smoothness constraint an iterative solution to the problem is obtained in which the two components of the velocity are estimated as:

$$v_x = \bar{v}_x - E_x \frac{P}{D} \tag{9.41}$$

and

$$v_y = \bar{v}_y - E_y \frac{P}{D} \tag{9.42}$$

where

$$\begin{aligned} P &= E_x \bar{v}_x + E_y \bar{v}_y + E_t \\ D &= \lambda^2 + E_x^2 + E_y^2 \end{aligned} \tag{9.43}$$

E_x, E_y and E_t are the differentials of the image data with respected to the subscripted index. λ is a constant.

The algorithm can produce accurate results, provided that:

- there is sufficient image detail to produce finite values when the image is differentiated
- the smoothness constraint is satisfied.

If either of these provisos fails, then the results that are generated will be in error. For example, the smoothness constraint is violated at the boundary between differently moving regions, and the detail constraint is violated in totally smooth areas of the image. We could argue that it is impossible to determine the motion of an object that has no distinguishing features, so the fact that this property causes the algorithm to fail ought not to be considered a disadvantage.

9.6 Summary

This chapter has examined methods of determining the motion of objects in an image. The moving objects might be rigid or non-rigid. We have restricted the discussion to rigid objects for simplicity.

Tracking may use calibrated or uncalibrated systems, the difference being that a calibrated system is able to determine the world coordinates of objects that are found. Uncalibrated systems can only track in image coordinates. Both systems find applications.

Tracking is usually performed online; that is, in real time. Although there are applications in which offline tracking is useful, they will often use the same techniques, the difference being that the processing time is not critical. Online systems have two hard processing constraints:

- Processing time must be consistent with the object's motion in the image plane. That is, the movement of the object in the time taken to process each image must be insignificant.
- Tthe latency of the system must also be consistent with the object's motion in the image plane. That is, the movement of the object in the time taken to process an image must be insignificant.

If these constraints are not kept, then the tracking system will be more error-prone.

Tracking may be performed using a range of image features: objects, regions or individual pixels may be tracked. At present, most high-performance systems utilise some form of model-based object tracking algorithm.

9.7 Bibliography

Calibration is discussed by Trucco and Verri (1998) and other authors. Image differencing algorithms and the effects that can be observed are analysed by Jain *et al.* (1995). A probabilistic method of detecting targets, as well as the background updating method, was presented by Wren *et al.* (1997).

Colour indexing was suggested by Swain and Ballard (1991) and has proved to be very effective. Affine tracking has been used by many authors, including Gee and Cipolla (1996).

Predictive tracking was suggested in a report edited by Swain and Strickland (1991), and used, for example, by Dickmans and Mysliwetz (1992).

The Kalman filter (Kalman, 1960), despite its shortcomings, has been and continues to be widely used. The major contender is the condensation filter (Isard and Blake, 1998). Hidden Markov Models may become popular as a solution to the motion tracking problem, provided that they can be determined accurately from the available data. There is also the problem of the number of models that must be processed when analysing an image sequence – one model is required per motion model. Nevertheless, it has been demonstrated that HMMs are capable of decoding a small subset of American Sign Language (Starner and Pentland, 1995).

Horn and Schunk (1981) presented the original solution to the optic flow problem. Although it has been researched ever since, no solution has been found that gives more accurate results.

9.8 Exercises

9.1   Capture two images of a scene containing moving objects and subtract
      one from the other. What differences do you observe and to what can
      you attribute these differences? Design an algorithm to classify the dif-
      ferences and hence, if possible, track the moving objects.

9.2   Assume that you are tracking an object using Kalman filtering. The
      object's motion changes suddenly. What are the consequences of this
      for the tracker?

9.3   Build the Kalman filter matrices for a motion model that includes the
      object's acceleration.

9.4   How would you use object-following techniques to estimate the cam-
      era's movement if the camera was moving and the objects in a scene
      were stationary? What use would this have?

10
Image and video coding

Digital imagery requires efficient methods for its storage and transmission. This is becoming of greater importance as more images are originated digitally and the amount of digital data being transmitted is increasing rapidly. Image coding methods aim to improve the efficiency with which the data is stored. This is done by identifying portions of the data that may be discarded without losing the information contained in the original signal. The data that is discarded may or may not make a contribution to the reconstructed signal; that is, the coding algorithm might give an exact reproduction of the original, or it might give an approximate reproduction. These two broad categories of compression methods are termed lossless and lossy algorithms.

The chapter starts by justifying the need for image compression. It then examines the general principles underpinning coding algorithms. The bulk of the chapter is devoted to an explanation of image coding algorithms, culminating in the JPEG standard, and video coding algorithms, especially MPEG.

10.1 Why is coding necessary?

Digitised visual data can occupy enormous amounts of storage volume, as illustrated in Tables 10.1 and 10.2. These show the amounts of storage required for uncompressed images of varying spatial resolutions and for ten second clips of colour video data of varying spatial and temporal resolutions. But what are the practical consequences of these storage requirements? To digitise a photograph for everyday use we would usually require high spatial resolution and great colour depth to give perceptually high-quality images. The table indicates that in excess of 5 Mbyte is required per image. To store a feature film of 90 minutes duration would require in excess of 115 Gbyte if it were stored at the highest resolution listed without any form of compression.

Therefore there is an acute need to compress this data to more manageable sizes. Two reasons are apparent:

Table 10.1 Storage volumes required for still images.

Image dimensions (pixels)	Colour depth (bits)	Volume of data (bytes)
128 × 128	8	16,384
760 × 580	8	440,800
760 × 580	16	1,322,400
1600 × 1200	16	5,760,000

Table 10.2 Storage volumes required for ten second colour video clips.

Image dimensions (pixels)	Frame rate (fps)	Volume of data (Mbyte)
160 × 120	10	5.5
320 × 240	10	21.9
320 × 240	25	54.9
640 × 480	10	87.9
640 × 480	25	219.7

- Compression is necessary for image and video storage if we are not to be overwhelmed by storage media.
- Compression is necessary if we are to be able to transmit data through a communications channel of finite capacity either in real time or without using the whole channel to the exclusion of all other users.

10.2 General principles underlying coding algorithms

When coding images we must make the distinction between information and data. Data is the pattern of bits that is stored on disk and will make up the image or sequence of images. Information is the meaningful content of the image. The same information might be represented in many formats, using different data. The letter 'A' might be represented as a bitmap image or as an ASCII code word, as in Figure 10.1. Clearly, the two representations have the same information, but the data is very different. Or we might have two newspaper articles of different lengths relating the same story; the story

(a)

(b) "A"

Figure 10.1   (a) Bitmap image of letter 'A', 9216 bytes; (b) ASCII code of letter 'A', 1 byte.

(information) is the same in both cases, but the lengths (the data) differ. Coding algorithms are designed to identify the minimum amount of data that is consistent with retaining all or a significant amount of the information present in the image. The data that is not required can be discarded; it is usually termed 'redundant'.

Image data is highly redundant. That is, images usually contain much less data than the information content would justify. This is a direct consequence of the sampling requirements discussed in the previous chapter. Nyquist's theorem was used to justify a minimum sampling rate in order that an object is seen in an image. Naturally, this sampling rate is well below that which is required to recognise or identify the object. Sampling rates of ten to twenty times greater are required for these purposes. The consequence of these higher sampling rates is that adjacent pixels usually have very similar values. Thus, if we have information about a pixel (its grey or colour values), than we have some information about the neighbouring pixels, since they are likely to have similar values. Therefore there exists some redundancy in the image data by virtue of the fact that the data is well sampled. Four types of redundancy can be identified and are described below.

One of the redundancies is due to the various properties of the human visual system. These may be exploited to identify data that may be discarded with no apparent loss of information. Thus, image coding algorithms may be described as lossless and lossy. These terms are defined in this section.

Finally, we will examine the methods used to describe the efficiency of image coding algorithms.

10.2.1 Spatial redundancy

As described above, a well-sampled image implies a degree of similarity between adjacent pixels. This can be exploited, by, for example, predicting the value of a pixel from its neighbours' values. Then we might store one value plus a sequence of small difference values. Compression will result if we can assign a smaller storage unit to the difference value than to the original. Figure 10.2 illustrates a monochrome image and the horizontal difference image, i.e. the image of the differences between horizontally adjacent pixels. In the difference image, a mid-grey value indicates a zero difference, brighter pixels a positive difference and darker ones a negative difference. It should be noted that the difference image is extremely uniform. This is confirmed by inspecting the difference image's histogram: values are tightly grouped around the zero amplitude bin.

10.2.2 Chromatic redundancy

In a colour image, there is correlation between colour channels. Figure 10.3 shows a colour image's colour histogram. The graph plots the relative frequencies

(a)

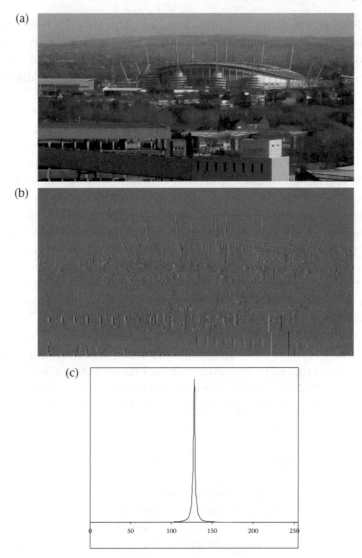

(b)

(c)

Figure 10.2 Spatial redundancy. (a) Monochrome image; (b) image of the differences between horizontally adjacent pixels; (c) histogram of the differences.

of occurrence of each unique RGB triplet value. The high degree of correlation is apparent: the value of any component of a pixel is strongly related to the other values. This correlation can be exploited by, for example, alternative colour representations.

10.2.3 Temporal redundancy

In Chapter 2, Nyquist's theorem was used to justify a temporal sampling rate for video data, such that the fastest motion in the sequence could be

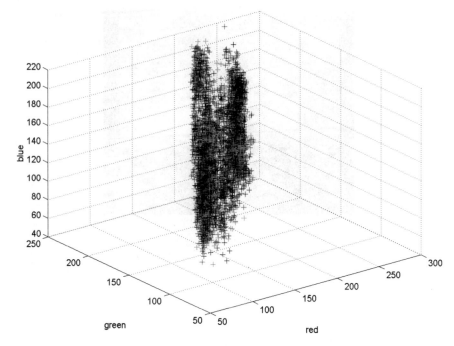

Figure 10.3 Colour histogram of an arbitrary image. The histogram indicates the large correlation between pixels' colour values.

represented unambiguously. However, it is apparent that in any video sequence only small areas of the image change between frames. Much of the image data is, in fact, static. For example, consider a video clip of a newsreader: only the areas of the image corresponding to the newsreader's head will contain any motion, and much of this area will also be static. Thus, if we were to code the sequence by storing only the changes between frames, we would require much less data than for the original clip. This is illustrated in Figure 10.4, showing one frame from a sequence, and the difference between that frame and the previous one.

10.2.4 Perceptual redundancy

The human visual system's properties can be exploited to determine what portions of an image can be discarded without the observer noticing. In particular, the human visual system is relatively insensitive to high-frequency components (a property that leads to the phenomenon of Mach bands, whereby false edges are seen adjacent to a real step change in brightness). Thus we might discard high-frequency components in the data without apparent loss of information. There is also a limit to the number of brightness levels that can be distinguished at any one time; having more than this in the image might be inefficient.

Figure 10.4   Temporal redundancy. One frame from an image sequence and the differences between it and the succeeding frame.

10.2.5 Lossless and lossy coding methods

Coding algorithms can be defined that are able to reconstruct the original data exactly. Such methods are known as lossless coding algorithms, since they imply no loss of data and consequently no loss of information.

Coding algorithms may also be defined that discard some of the image data. The reconstructed image will be an approximation to the original image. The closeness of the approximation will be a function of the amount of data that is lost and of how the discarded data was selected. It is sensible to choose the data with regard to our understanding of the human visual system; therefore we could choose to restrict the number of brightness levels, or to discard high-frequency components in the image. With a careful choice of discarded data, the differences between the original and reconstructed images will be perceptually negligible, as Figure 10.5 suggests. This figure shows an image, its reconstruction from a lossy coded version and the

(a) (b)

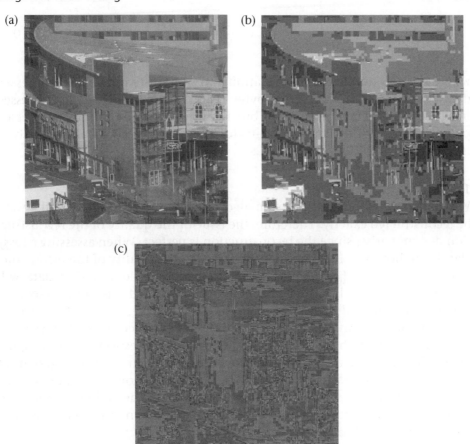

(c)

Figure 10.5 JPEG compression. (a) An original image, uncompressed; (b) a JPEG compressed and reconstructed image; (c) the difference image, scaled in brightness to exaggerate differences.

differences between these two images. It is apparent that the coded version of the image appears very similar to the original, but it is also obvious that the differences between these two images are significant.

10.2.6 Assessment of coding methods

An image coding algorithm is assessed primarily by how effective it is in compressing the data. The quality of the reconstructed image is also important for lossy compression techniques (lossless images reconstruct the original image exactly). In some cases, the time taken to compress the data is also important.

10.2.6.1 Compression ratio
The compression ratio, C, is defined as:

$$C = \frac{n}{n_c} \qquad (10.1)$$

where n is the number of information-carrying units in the uncompressed dataset (that is, the number of bytes required to store the uncompressed image, or the average number of bits required to store each uncompressed pixel), and n_c is the same quantity for the compressed data. Naturally, a higher value of C is more desirable.

10.2.6.2 Quality

When using a lossless compression algorithm, the original image will always be reconstructed exactly. Therefore, the issue of the quality of the reconstruction does not arise, since the reconstruction is perfect. When assessing a lossy algorithm, however, it is important to consider the quality of the reconstruction. The quality of the image reconstructed from lossy coded data will depend on what and how much data has been discarded. Discarding excessive amounts of data will have a detrimental effect on the quality of the reconstruction. But how should the quality of the reconstruction be assessed?

The coded data should always be assessed with respect to the original image. In effect, we are attempting to measure the amount of degradation introduced by the coding process, and this cannot be done without reference to the input data. A simplistic method of assessing the coding is simply to measure the differences between the original and reconstructed images. The root mean squared differences are often computed:

$$\varepsilon = \left[\frac{1}{MN} \sum_{i=0}^{M-1} \sum_{j=0}^{N-1} (\hat{f}(i,j) - f(i,j))^2 \right]^{1/2} \qquad (10.2)$$

In this expression M and N are the image dimensions, and f and $\hat{f}$ are the original and reconstructed images. Small values of this error indicate that the original and reconstructed images resemble each other. This measure is imperfect in that it takes no account of the magnitude of the image value. It might be preferable to measure a variant of the signal to noise ratio – that is, the ratio of the difference between the original and reconstructed images to the original image:

$$\varepsilon = \sum_{i=0}^{M-1} \sum_{j=0}^{N-1} \frac{\hat{f}(i,j) - f(i,j)}{f(i,j)} \qquad (10.3)$$

The improvement introduced is that this measure increases the weight accorded to an error in inverse proportion to the image magnitude at that location. Thus an error is more significant if the image magnitude is small than the same error at a location with greater original brightness.

Table 10.3 Subjective Picture Quality Scale (PQS).

Quality value	Quality rating	Image characteristics
0	Unusable	An image of too poor quality to be watchable.
1	Inferior	A poor quality but watchable image. Objectionable interference.
2	Marginal	Poor quality image, interference is present.
3	Acceptable	Acceptable quality, interference is not objectionable.
4	Good	High-quality image, some interference.
5	Excellent	Extremely high-quality image, as good as could be desired.

However, neither of these error measures can give an assessment of quality that is readily comprehended, since we do not normally correlate an error value with the perceived quality of the image. It is therefore more appropriate to use a subjective quality scale such as the sample one in Table 10.3, which is defined for the assessment of video sequences.

Using this human-centred method, the image quality can be measured in a way that conveys practical meaning to the reader. However, automatically computing the quality rating is not as simple as the difference measures. Methods of doing so are the subject of ongoing research.

10.2.6.3 Compression time

A less obvious assessment criterion of compression algorithms is the time required to compress or decompress the data. In some coding applications, the time available to compress the data may be limited (for example in originating live digital broadcast material). In other applications the time required to code the data is not critical, but the time allowed for decoding is limited, and the required compression might be great; in such cases, much time could be devoted to achieving highly compressed images, provided that decompression is rapid.

The symmetry of a compression method is the balance between the times required for compression and decompression. Thus a symmetric algorithm will require similar amounts of time for the two operations, whilst an asymmetric one has very different compression and decompression times. Typically a symmetric algorithm would be selected for applications where the data is compressed as frequently as it is decompressed.

10.3 Lossless image coding methods

Lossless image coding algorithms are designed to exploit spatial and chromatic redundancy. They will identify the redundant data and discard it. On decompression, the coded data is used to reconstitute the redundant data; thus no data is lost, no information is lost and the decoded image matches the original one exactly.

In this section we shall examine three algorithms that exploit spatial redundancy and two that use variable length code words. The algorithms are presented for monochrome images. They are equally applicable to colour images. In that case, the three colour planes would normally be treated as three separate monochrome images.

10.3.1 Difference coding

The difference between horizontally adjacent pixels was shown above in a specific case to be small (Figure 10.2). In fact, this is generally true for well-sampled images. Figure 10.6 is the histogram of intra-image differences derived from the images of a short sequence.

Compression would result if the original value of one pixel were stored, followed by a sequence of difference values, each packed into a smaller storage unit than the original value. For example, in a monochrome image of 256 shades, each pixel would normally be stored as a byte: an 8 bit storage unit. Using difference coding, the difference values could, for example, be stored as 4 bit numbers.

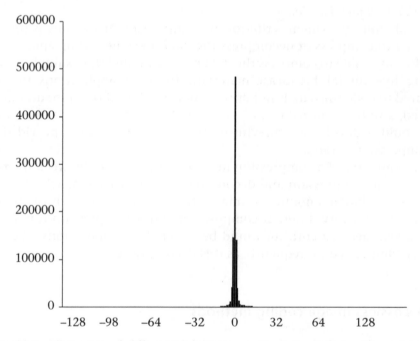

Figure 10.6 Histogram of differences between equivalent pixels in adjacent images summed over all image pairs in a short sequence.

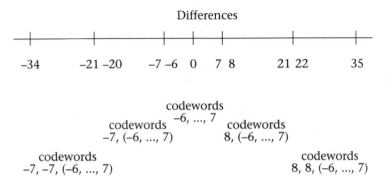

Figure 10.7 Difference coding codewords.

In this regime, we have 16 difference values, which could be used to represent the 16 differences in the range –7 to +8, provided of course that no differences fall outside of this range. Inspection of the histogram reveals that a small number of difference values do fall outside of the range. The solution to this problem is to reserve the codewords for –7 and +8 to indicate a more negative or a more positive difference. The remaining 14 codewords will indicate differences in the range –6 to +7. Therefore, a difference value of –8 is represented by the codewords –7 to indicate underflow followed by the codeword +6: the underflow and overflow codewords indicate that the range of codes is shifted *en bloc* downwards or upwards. Differences lying further outside of the range can be represented by repeated application of the under- and overflow codes. This is illustrated in Figure 10.7.

In practice, difference coding is usually applied to each line of the image separately. This is to reduce the effect of transmission errors: only the remainder of a line will be corrupted following the error; and logically, can we expect the first pixel of a line to be related in any way to the last pixel of the previous line?

The compression achievable by this algorithm is not large. C will typically be between 1.5 and 2.5.

10.3.2 Predictive coding

Difference coding exploits the correlation between adjacent pixels to code the image by suggesting that they have the same values and by coding the difference. An alternative statement of this is that we are making a naïve prediction of the value of one pixel by saying it is the same as the previous value. However, we can improve the accuracy of this prediction if we have some knowledge of the image statistics.

We may set up a prediction model that estimates the value of a pixel as a linear function of the preceding pixel:

$$\hat{f}(i,j) = \alpha f(i-1,j) + \beta \tag{10.4}$$

Optimal values of α and β may be computed using least squares minimisation, and can be shown to be the image's correlation coefficient and mean grey value.

It is also possible to extend the range of image values that are input into the predictor, such that the predicted value is a linear combination of the previous n pixels:

$$\hat{f}(i) = \sum_{k=i-1}^{k=i-1-n} \alpha_k f(k) \tag{10.5}$$

The benefit is that the predictor becomes slightly more accurate, thereby improving the compression. The cost is the increased time required to compute the coefficients and the increased time in performing the prediction for each pixels being coded.

10.3.3 Runlength coding

Runlength coding is an algorithm that is really only applicable to images with a very small number of grey values or extremely large areas of uniform shading. In other cases, the compressed image might actually be larger than the uncompressed one!

In the context of runlength coding, a run is defined as a sequence of one or more consecutive pixels on the same line of the image having the same grey value. Images having a wide range of grey or colour values are less likely to have runs of any significant length; hence the poor compression given by this algorithm with this type of image.

The algorithm would take a sequence of pixels with grey values:

$$2 \quad 2 \quad 3 \quad 3 \quad 4 \quad 4 \quad 4 \quad 5 \quad 5$$

and replace them with the sequence of duples of (run length, grey value):

$$(2, 2) \quad (2, 3) \quad (3, 4) \quad (2, 5)$$

Therefore a set of nine grey values is coded as eight units. Obviously, the degree of compression will increase as the average run length increases, which occurs as the image becomes smoother (less variation in grey value) or the number of grey values is reduced. In the extreme case, where the image is binary and only has two grey values, further compression may be achieved, since we may dispense with the grey value information for all runs except the first. Therefore a binary image is coded by storing the value of the first run and its length, followed by the length of the second run, which by implication has the other brightness, followed by the length of the third run (having the same brightness as the first run), and so on.

Runlength coding has a niche application in the transmission of fax images, since these are inherently binary.

10.3.4 Huffman coding

Huffman coding works on a different principle to the previous algorithms, which exploit redundancies in the actual data. Huffman coding replaces each grey value in the image with a codeword of variable length: shorter codewords are assigned to the more frequently occurring grey values. Since each grey value must have a unique codeword, this results in the less frequently occurring grey values having longer codewords. Compression will occur if there are a greater number of grey values having shorter codewords.

The workings of the algorithm are best explained with reference to an example. Consider an image that has eight grey values occurring with the frequencies listed in Table 10.4. The algorithm will combine the two least frequently occurring grey values, assigning one a 0 and the other a 1 (which symbol is given to the more or less frequently occurring value is not important, provided that the assignation is performed consistently). The combined probabilities are inserted into the correct place in the reduced histogram. The two least frequently occurring symbols are selected and a 0 and a 1 are appended to the codeword before the symbols are combined and reinserted into the histogram. The process repeats until two histogram entries remain and the tree structure of Figure 10.8 has been produced. At this point the codewords to be assigned each grey value can be read from the leaf nodes.

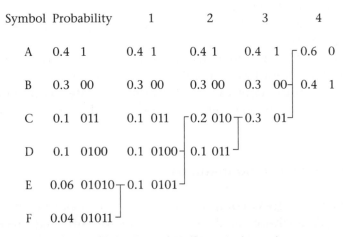

Figure 10.8   Tree of Huffman codewords.

Table 10.4 Histogram of grey values of an arbitrary image.

Grey value	Probability	Codeword	Length	$L \times P$
0	0.35	11	2	0.70
1	0.25	10	2	0.50
2	0.10	010	3	0.30
3	0.10	001	3	0.30
4	0.07	000	3	0.21
5	0.06	0110	4	0.24
6	0.04	01111	5	0.20
7	0.03	01110	5	0.15

The codewords are also listed in Table 10.4, as are the length of each codeword and the product of the length and probability of each codeword appearing. The sum of the entries in this last column gives the average length in bits of the units required to store this image: 2.6 bits. The non-compressed image requires three bits per pixel. In this case, the Huffman algorithm yields a modest amount of compression; it would be much greater if the probability distribution was less uniform.

10.3.5 GIF

Huffman coding replaced each symbol in the image with a variable length codeword. A family of compression algorithms, originally developed by Lempel and Ziv, exist that have fixed length code words representing variable amounts of data. In these algorithms a dictionary is built that translates codewords into a sequence of image values. When coding the image, strings of data are compared with entries in the dictionary. If a match is found, then the dictionary index replaces the string. The coded data will consist of, amongst other pieces of information, the dictionary and the codewords that have been generated.

Since GIF-coded images are constrained to be no more than 256 shades of grey or colour, a colour look-up table is also included in the file. The coded image data, each unit being an eight-bit value, is treated as an index into the look-up table. The decoded pixel is therefore the value indexed in the table.

10.4 Lossy image coding methods

As described above, lossy compression algorithms seek to compress images by discarding data whose loss does not degrade the information content to a serious extent. The success or otherwise of these methods relies on their being able to identify the information that can be discarded. Two algorithms have been adopted into the various JPEG standards:

- the discrete cosine transform
- the wavelet transform

10.4.1 Wavelet coders

Transform coders are based on the idea that the coefficients of a transform that decorrelate the image data can be coded more efficiently than the data itself. Further, if any of the transform's coefficients are small or zero, then they can be discarded with little impact on the quality of the reconstructed image. The wavelet transform provides a very efficient means of reorganising the image data in this fashion.

The wavelet transform was described in Chapter 3. The example image and transform from that chapter are reproduced here (Figure 10.9). The

Figure 10.9 Sample image and wavelet transform.

usefulness of the transform for coding is immediately apparent: most of the coefficients are extremely small or even zero; they could therefore be discarded with little change in the quality of the reconstruction.

Three factors must be considered when designing a wavelet-based image coder:

- the wavelet basis to use
- how the sub-bands should be treated
- how the data should be coded

Numerous wavelet basis functions exist. When selecting any one for use in compression, two criteria must be considered: the computational complexity and the quality of the reconstruction. They cannot be satisfied simultaneously, since a simpler basis function will not give as good a reconstruction as a more complex one. This is illustrated qualitatively in Figure 10.10, which shows the same image (a still from a video clip of a game of American football) transformed, compressed and reconstituted using the Haar, Bi-Coiflet, Brislawn and FBI basis functions. It is apparent that the Haar wavelet, which has four coefficients and is therefore the simplest, performs worst in reorganising the data: much information remains spread over the whole of the transform. Conversely, the FBI wavelet, which has a much larger number of coefficients, organises the data much more efficiently and results in a smoother, more detailed image.

Figure 10.9 also indicates that there is a wide variation in the quantity of information represented in each sub-band. This suggests that each sub-band could be treated differently. Some might be discarded entirely, while others

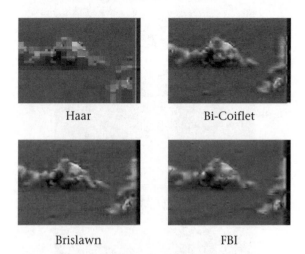

Haar   Bi-Coiflet

Brislawn   FBI

Figure 10.10 An image coded using four wavelet basis functions. The diagram illustrates the trade-offs between short basis functions (rapid but low-quality coding) and basis functions having more coefficients.

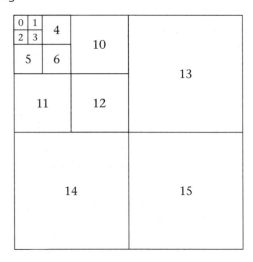

Figure 10.11   Treatment of sub-bands by a wavelet coder.

Table 10.5 Reconstruction levels.

Component	Sub-bands 0–3	Sub-bands 4–12
Y	512	128
Cb/Cr	128	32

might be represented at different resolutions. Experimentation using a range of test images suggests that a useful compromise between compression ratio and reconstruction quality may be achieved by deleting sub-bands 13–15, coding sub-bands 4–12 with a certain number of reconstruction levels, and coding sub-bands 0–3 with twice as many reconstructions levels, as indicated in Figure 10.11 and Table 10.5.

Coding of the resultant coefficients can be performed using the equivalent methods, as used in the JPEG algorithms described below. However, more efficient methods have been suggested, notably the tri-zero tree.

10.4.2 JPEG standards

The JPEG image compression standard was drawn up by the Joint Photographic Experts Group (essentially a subcommittee of the International Organization for Standardization) and was adopted as an international standard in 1991. Its aim was to derive a method by which continuous-tone grey scale or colour images could be compressed without loss of visual quality. Since publication, the standard has been adopted worldwide as an image compression and storage method.

The JPEG method uses a number of data compression algorithms in sequence, each exploiting data redundancy in a different way. The various parameters required of the algorithms have been set to be optimal for as wide a range of image types as possible. Overall, the algorithms specified by the standard aim to identify the perceptually important information in the image being coded and discard the less important data. Compression is therefore achieved at the cost of a loss of information, and the amount of compression directly influences the quality of the reconstructed image. A schematic diagram of the JPEG encoder's architecture is shown in Figure 10.12.

The JPEG standard states that an image may have up to 255 components. These could be from different spectral bands, but are most usually just the three different colour bands (the other 252 components remain unused). The components need not all be of the same size, provided that the ratio of their dimensions is 1, 2, 3 or 4. Each component is coded independently of the others.

The standard dictates that the image should first be divided into blocks of 8×8 pixels whose values are shifted from the range $[0, n)$ to $[-n/2, n/2)$. The blocks are passed through a discrete cosine transform (DCT) whose purpose is to determine the frequency make-up of the data. Low-frequency information (slowly changing grey values) will be revealed as high values in the low-order transform coefficients. Since most of the image information is low frequency, it will be found that the low-order coefficients have much larger

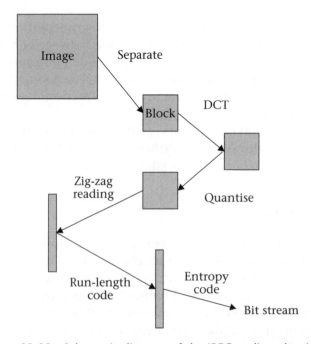

Figure 10.12   Schematic diagram of the JPEG coding algorithm.

values than the remaining coefficients. In fact, a large proportion of the coefficients will be negligibly small.

The DCT generates real-valued outputs, these are quantised into integer values lying in the range 0 to 255. The threshold values that separate the steps of the quantiser should be determined specifically for each image, display and viewing situation. In practice this is too labour-intensive and a set of threshold values have been suggested by the JPEG that are adequate for most cases. Quantisation is a significant source of lossiness in DCT-based coders.

The first coefficient in the transform is known as the DC coefficient, as it represents the average grey value of this data block. Since these values change slowly across an image, they are treated differently from the other coefficients (the AC coefficients). The DC coefficient is differentially coded with respect to the DC coefficient in the preceding block. Since this value is always the largest, compression is thereby improved.

The quantised DCT data is then reordered. Rather than represent the data as a two-dimensional array having significant values in the low-order entries, the data is read in a zigzag fashion into a one-dimensional array in which the significant values are clustered at one end and less significant ones at the other. The less significant coefficients are set to zero, and the array is runlength coded by retaining the finite values plus the number of zero valued entries (rather than the entries themselves). The threshold separating 'significant' and 'non-significant' coefficients may be altered; this is the major source of lossiness in the algorithm and the major influence on the quality of the reconstructed image. The data is finally encoded using Huffman coding, which achieves additional compression without loss of data.

It has been observed that compressing the input data by a factor of 4 to 5 results in no visible loss of quality. In fact, the coded image is usually indistinguishable from the original. Compressing the data by a factor of 16 results in good quality data that is sufficient for many applications. Data may be compressed by up to 32× before its quality is degraded to an extent that the data is unusable.

Decoding of the data is simply the reverse of the coding process. All of the coding steps are exactly reversible, except for quantisation. Quantisation is a process by which a range of input values map to a single output value. It is therefore impossible to dequantise correctly. Instead the dequantisation step gives the central value from the range that was input.

Figure 10.13 illustrates the transform of a 4 × 4 block of pixels. The original pixels are shown, together with the transformed data and the differences between the two. It is apparent that the differences are finite, but small in comparison to the original values. Figure 10.14 illustrates the same information for an image. The difference image has been scaled by a factor of 16 and the values offset to allow display. Thus a difference of zero corresponds to a

(a) 139 144 149 153   144 146 149 152
     144 151 153 156   148 150 152 154
     150 155 160 163   155 156 157 158
     159 161 162 160   160 161 161 162

(b) −5 −2 0 1
     −4 1 1 2
     −5 −1 3 5
     −1 0 1 −2

Figure 10.13   An arbitrary block of data processed by the JPEG algorithm. (a) The data coded and decoded using the JPEG algorithms; (b) the difference values.

Figure 10.14   Quality of the JPEG codec. (a) An uncompressed image; (b) the image coded and subsequently decoded; (c) the difference image. Differences have been scaled by a factor of 4 and the brightness values offset. Thus a mid-grey brightness corresponds to zero difference.

midgrey tone, and brighter values to positive differences. Whilst there is apparently little difference between the two images, the difference image reveals that this is not so, but the differences that exist are not discernible.

A significant update to the JPEG standard, JPEG 2000, has been published and is becoming available. It provides increased flexibility in the compression of data and access to the compressed information. It is based on the wavelet transform using one of two wavelet bases dependent on whether lossless or lossy compression is to be used.

10.5 Video coding

Many video coding standards are in use, most of which are proprietary. In this section we shall describe the MPEG series of standards, which are the internationally accepted standard family of algorithms for video and audio coding and transmission. We shall also briefly examine some of the proprietary standards.

10.5.1 MPEG standards

MPEG (Moving Pictures Experts Group) is also a committee organised under the International Organization for Standardization umbrella. Its activities concern the compression of video and the associated audio data, and the control of their interaction. Since 1989 they have proposed a series of standards dealing with the representation and transport of audio-visual data.

The first standard, which became known as MPEG-1, was concerned with the specification of digital video for storage on and reading from CD-ROM. It specified a maximum transmission rate of 1.5 Mbyte/s, which implies a significant compression rate (recalling that full screen video requires a data rate of 33 Mbyte/s for the images alone). MPEG-1 was to deliver VHS quality data (that is, the same quality as is obtained from a domestic video recorder). If the playback of a video tape is frozen, the extremely poor quality of the images will be revealed, but the human visual system is able to interpolate between the poor quality images and derive a reasonably good quality moving image. The coded data was to include the video, audio and control streams: 1.150 Mbyte/s was to be assigned to the video data, 0.256 Mbyte/s to the audio and the remaining 0.094 Mbyte/s to the system.

The compression algorithm was also required to allow random access to the individual frames, to allow fast forward/reverse searches, reverse playback, audio-visual synchronisation, and several other minor features.

The solution MPEG proposed included predictive and interpolative coding and relied on a variation of the JPEG coding scheme. The video stream was first divided into three types of frame, arranged as shown in Figure 10.15:

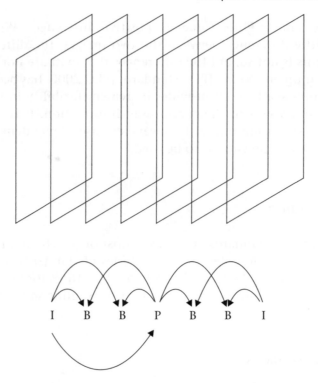

Figure 10.15   Organisation of frames under the MPEG coding scheme.

- Intraframes (I)
- Predicted frames (P)
- Bidirectionally interpolated frames (B)

The intraframes are coded using an algorithm similar to the JPEG scheme. They provide a means of randomly accessing the data, even if there are a limited number of random access points. They also provide a reference frame for the P- and B-frames.

Predicted frames are the compressed difference between the current frame and a predicted version of it based on the previous Intra or Predicted frame. The prediction is based on motion compensation. This assumes that blocks in the input image do not change their appearance significantly over a period of time, but can change their locations. The predicted frame therefore comprises the displacements to be applied to each block of the input frame. In practice, the blocks do change appearance; therefore the difference values must be computed. The data in the Predicted frame is therefore the difference values for each motion compensated block and the displacement. A block size of 16 × 16 pixels is used.

B-frames are derived from the closest pair of I- and P- frames. Again motion prediction is used, but rather than look for an exact match between a pair of blocks in an I-frame and the one being coded, the closest match is found between blocks in the previous or following or both I- and/or P-frame. All of the blocks in the intervening B-frames are then interpolated and the errors between the true and interpolated frames are recorded.

The first MPEG standard was released in 1992, and has since been joined by three others. MPEG-2 (1994) was intended to specify coding techniques for digital television and asynchronous transmission networks. It therefore had a higher data rate (15 Mbyte/s) that enabled higher quality images and sound to be transmitted. The standard included specifications for incorporating interlaced video (necessary for television signals), for scalable coding (to enable the systems to function when the available bandwidth altered) and for graceful degradation as errors appeared in the data.

MPEG-4 was released in 2000. Rather that being concerned with how digital video and television should be represented and transmitted, this standard takes a somewhat more abstract viewpoint and is concerned with how multimedia objects ought to be coded and how their interactions can be specified. It will also allow the users to interact more fully with the data, rather than simply stop and start the sequence.

10.5.2 Other video coding standards

Both Microsoft and Apple have developed standards for representing video data. Due to the overwhelming presence of these organisations, their standards have become widely adopted. Neither standard implements a novel coding architecture; both rely on well-publicised methods.

10.6 Summary

The chapter has examined the theory underpinning image and video compression and a range of compression algorithms, culminating in a description of the ISO standards from image coding (commonly called JPEG) and video coding (commonly called MPEG).

10.7 Bibliography

Image and video coding are discussed in many of the introductory texts cited in Chapter 1. Gonzalez and Woods (2002) is a particularly good source. Fidelity criteria were discussed by Frendendall and Behrend (1960); although the reference is dated, the methods proposed have not changed.

Huffman (1952) suggested the coding scheme in a paper written while he was a graduate student.

LZW coding, as used in the GIF format, is based on coding strategies proposed by Ziv and Lempel (1977, 1978).

The various ISO standards are available from national standards bodies. JPEG documents are also available at `http://www.jpeg.org/` and MPEG from `http://mpeg.telecomitalialab.com/`.

10.8 Exercises

10.1 Assuming that pixel values are randomly distributed with a mean of m and a standard deviation of s, compute the mean and standard deviation of the distribution of pixel difference values, taking the forward differences between horizontally adjacent pixels.

10.2 One image has a grey level distribution that is broad and flat. Another has a distribution that shows a sharp peak concentrated around a single grey value. Which image is compressed most using the Huffman coding strategy?

10.3 The JPEG standard specifies a compromise of block size and quantisation levels that is good for a range of image types. Suggest the consequences of changing the block size (making the blocks bigger and smaller) and altering the quantisation levels on the compression ratio.

11
Conclusions

This text has attempted to present a selection of image processing and computer vision topics in a systematic fashion. Naturally, in a book of this length it has been necessary to omit a vast amount of information, but what is here is hopefully sufficient to provide the grounding for an understanding of more advanced topics.

In the Preface it was stated that computer vision is a mature topic. Some authors believe that this implies that all of the discoveries that are to be made have been made. All that remains now is to apply known techniques to new problems. However, a glance at the contents of any of the many journals devoted to this topic, or at the list of papers presented at any of the many relevant conferences will reveal that while there are many novel applications being developed and there is much incremental development, there are also significant new discoveries being reported.

What are the active research topics at present?

Compression has always an active research topic, but is becoming more critical for two reasons. Firstly, a large number of images are being generated per day; for example, the latest Earth observation satellites generate terabytes of data daily. Storing this data and making it readily accessible is an acute problem. Secondly, home entertainment is now distributed digitally, and there is a wish to distribute content on demand, rather than at fixed times. How can a feature film be distributed to a number of consumers starting at different times?

Biometrics is becoming an active research area. As applied to computer vision, this is the problem of identifying individuals from visible physical characteristics, such as fingerprints, iris patterns, gait or handprints. It is suggested that for security applications, such as accessing banking services or controlling access to buildings, a biometric property is preferable to the current security methods of PIN codes or swipe cards. To be effective, any biometrically based security system must have an extremely low error rate, as it would be problematical if, for example, the wrong people were allowed access to a building, or the right people were prevented from entering it.

Computer vision systems are already prevalent on the factory floor, replacing human quality control inspectors and releasing them for more productive tasks. A vision system is able to perform to a higher standard than the human, being able to make measurements more rapidly, more reliably and for longer periods of time without interruption. Current research is aiming to further improve these systems, making them more reliable, more flexible, easier to program and able to make more complex measurements. Not long ago, inspection systems were able to inspect blister packs of tablets for incorrectly formed packs. Now, systems are able to make complex measurements on machine-assembled parts, such as the wheels and axles of cars.

Factory-based systems, while they are able to analyse images of complex structures, have the advantage of having a well-controlled input: the scene's illumination is controlled and the object being inspected can be accurately positioned. These factors enable the vision system to be greatly simplified. Contrast this with the scenario of attempting to process outdoor images: the lighting cannot be controlled, and neither can the position and orientation of any of the objects in the scene. Naturally this adds to the complexity of any system, but if these problems can be addressed, then the systems will be more useful.

The *performance* of a vision system will always be an issue for real-time systems. Methods of simplifying systems in order to improve throughput are always being researched. The predictive tracking systems of Chapter 9 are an example: the naïve approach to tracking an object would involve identifying the object in each image that was captured; the more intelligent method uses all of the information to hand to improve performance – in this case by predicting an object's future location and then verifying it. System performance can also be improved by designing application-specific hardware, although this topic is beyond the scope of this book.

Currently, most vision systems are purpose-built, designed for one task and reusing few components from other applications. This situation is slowly changing as general purpose vision libraries are becoming available, notably Intel's OpenCV. However, the problem remains that an image processing or computer vision expert is required to design and implement the software. It might be preferable if tools could be provided that would allow domain experts to build their own vision systems. Such tools are also being actively researched.

It is apparent, even from this very brief survey, that computer vision is a thriving research area whose results are increasingly being applied in real-world applications.

Appendix A
The Fourier transform

The Fourier transform was suggested by Jean Baptiste Joseph Fourier and first appeared in English translation in 1878 (Fourier, 1878). The theorem stated that any periodic signal could be represented as a sum of sines and cosines of different frequencies. The series of coefficients is known as a Fourier series.

A non-periodic signal can also be represented by an integral of a weighted set of sine and cosine functions, provided that the sum of the function is finite. The Fourier transform is used to compute the weighting function. Both transforms are reversible; that is, the original function can be reconstructed by applying a reverse transformation.

Initially, the Fourier transform was computed graphically. Inefficient software implementations were developed that computed the transform as defined in Chapter 3. In 1965, an efficient algorithm, the Fast Fourier Transform (FFT), was published (Cooley and Tukey, 1965), which is the version of the transform that is now used exclusively.

This appendix will present some of the more useful properties of the transform and some also investigate some Fourier transform pairs.

A.1 Properties of the 2D Fourier transform

As stated in Chapter 3, the Fourier transform, $F(u)$, of a one-dimensional function, $f(x)$, is defined as:

$$F(u) = \int_{-\infty}^{\infty} f(x)e^{-2\pi i x u}\,dx \qquad (A.1)$$

where $i = \sqrt{-1}$. Conversely, $f(x)$ may be computed from $F(u)$ using the inverse Fourier transform:

$$f(x) = \int_{-\infty}^{\infty} F(u)e^{2\pi i x u}\,du \qquad (A.2)$$

The extension of the equations to two dimensions is straightforward.

Substituting Euler's formula ($e^{-i\theta} = \cos\theta - i\sin\theta$), we see that Equation (A.1) becomes:

$$F(u) = \int_{-\infty}^{\infty} f(x)[\cos 2\pi ux - i\sin 2\pi ux]\,dx \tag{A.3}$$

Therefore each term of the Fourier transform is made up of a weighted sum of all of the values of the signal. The weighting factors are sines and cosines of various frequencies. The domain (the values of u) is therefore called the frequency domain. The elements of $F(u)$ are called the frequency components. Since we are interested in the transformations of images, the x values will be spatial coordinates; we therefore sometimes talk of spatial frequency.

Equations (A.1) and (A.2) may be translated to their discrete forms:

$$F(u) = \frac{1}{N}\sum_{x=0}^{N-1} f(x)e^{-2\pi ikx/N} \tag{A.4}$$

and

$$f(x) = \sum_{u=0}^{N-1} F(u)e^{2\pi ixu/N} \tag{A.5}$$

If we set $u = 0$ in Equation (A.4), we observe that $F(0)$ is equal to the average of the function being transformed. $F(0)$ is known as the DC component, as it is at the zero frequency.

The Fourier transform is a complex function, having real and imaginary parts. It is often more useful to express the data in polar coordinates:

$$F(u) = |F(u)|e^{-i\phi(u)} \tag{A.6}$$

where

$$|F(u)| = (\mathrm{Re}^2(u) + \mathrm{Im}^2(u))^{1/2} \tag{A.7}$$

is the magnitude or spectrum of the transform, and

$$\phi(u) = \tan^{-1}\left(\frac{\mathrm{Im}(u)}{\mathrm{Re}(u)}\right) \tag{A.8}$$

is the phase angle or phase spectrum.

Appendix A

It can be shown that the Fourier transform of a real function, such as an image, is conjugate symmetric, that is:

$$F(u) = F'(-u) \qquad \text{(A.9)}$$

The ' indicates the complex conjugation $(x + iy \rightarrow x - iy)$. It is therefore apparent that the spectrum is symmetric.

The discrete signal that is transformed in Equation (A.4) is indexed by a zero-based value. The transform has a zero frequency component and positive and negative frequency components. If the signal is transformed using the FFT as it is, the zero frequency component appears at $F(0)$, positive frequency components appear in $F(1)$, $F(2)$, ..., and negative frequency components appear in $F(N-1)$, $F(N-2)$, ..., as indicated in Figure A.1. The result of the transform would be clearer if the zero frequency was at the centre, with negative frequencies to the left and positive ones to the right, as in Figure A.2.

This effect can be easily achieved. We may interchange the two halves of the transform or opposing quadrants in the transform of an image. The same effect can be achieved by multiplying each data point in the signal by $(-1)^x$, or each point in the image by $(-1)^{x+y}$ prior to transforming. If this is done, the result of the inverse transform must be multiplied by the same factor to obtain the correct result.

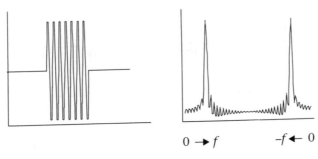

$$0 \rightarrow f \qquad\qquad -f \leftarrow 0$$

Figure A.1   The Fourier transform of an arbitrary signal.

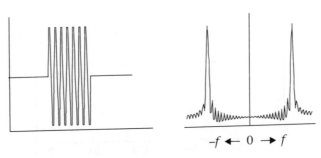

$$-f \leftarrow 0 \rightarrow f$$

Figure A.2   The transform reorganised to aid understanding.

Further useful properties of the Fourier transform are given by Bracewell (2000).

A.2 Fourier transform pairs

An intuitive appreciation of a signal's frequency composition can be gained by studying the Fourier transforms of particular signals.

Figure A.3 presents the Fourier transform of an impulse function; that is, a function defined according to Equation (A.10):

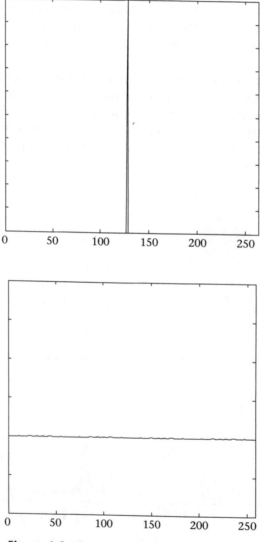

Figure A.3   Fourier transform of an impulse.

$$\delta(a) = \begin{cases} 1 & \text{at } x = a \\ 0 & \text{elsewhere} \end{cases} \qquad (A.10)$$

The figure illustrates a general property of signals: signals of a short duration are composed of a large range of frequency components. In the limit of an infinitesimally short pulse, an infinite number of frequency components are required.

Figure A.4 presents the Fourier transform of a square pulse and Figure A.5 (overleaf) the transform of a Gaussian.

These three transform pairs may be derived analytically.

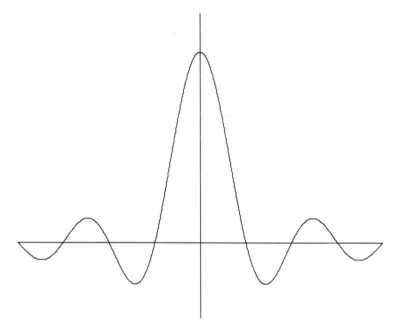

Figure A.4   Fourier transform of a square pulse.

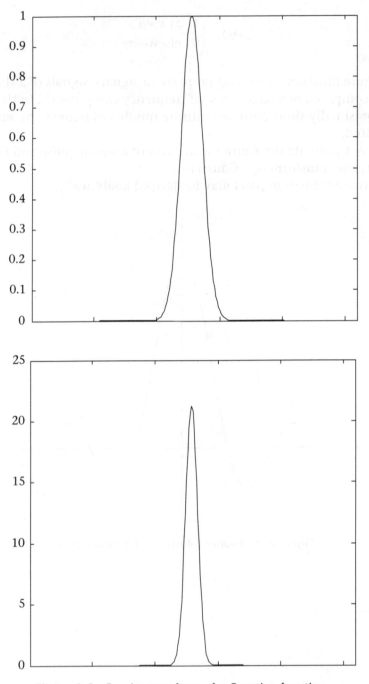

Figure A.5   Fourier transform of a Gaussian function.

Appendix B
The wavelet transform

The fundamentally useful property of the wavelet transform is that it analyses data according to scale. This was one of Marr's (1982) foremost claims regarding the human visual system: we process visual data according to the scale of the objects we see. Thus we can consciously choose to view large objects or small objects. Contrast this property with the behaviour of most image processing functions, which analyse data at the scale of individual pixels, i.e. the smallest possible scale.

The wavelet transform represents a signal as a linear combination of a number of basis functions. This is not an unusual method of representing data. Consider a vector in a Cartesian space: the basis functions are the unit vectors along the x-, y- and z-axes; any point is specified as a linear combination of these vectors. The Fourier transform uses sine and cosine functions as its basis functions, and in this case there is a large number of basis functions (effectively an infinite number for the continuous transform). The wavelet transform uses a more complex set of basis functions that are less intuitive that the Fourier transform's but not less meaningful.

The wavelet transform's basis functions are localised in space and frequency, unlike the Fourier transform's, which are localised in frequency only. Consequently, the transformed data informs us about the localised spatial frequency properties of the signal. Any transformed signal is therefore 'sparse', i.e. contains many zeros; see Figure B.1, which illustrates an input image, its wavelet transform and the histogram of the transform. The sparseness of the transform makes it useful for image coding, feature extraction and some other applications, notably noise reduction.

Although many wavelet bases have been defined, and methods of generating them have proliferated, as discussed in Chapter 3, deciding which basis function to use for a given application remains an art rather than a science. The size of a basis function has an influence on the smoothness of the decomposition and the time required to perform the decomposition: the larger the basis function, the smoother the decomposition, but the longer to compute it. It has also been suggested that matching the shape of the basis function to the shape of the feature being sought will improve the feature detection process.

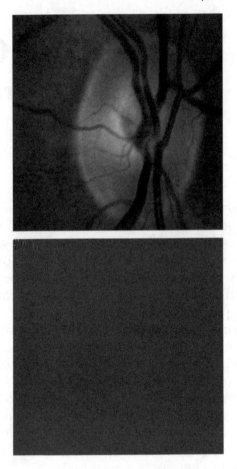

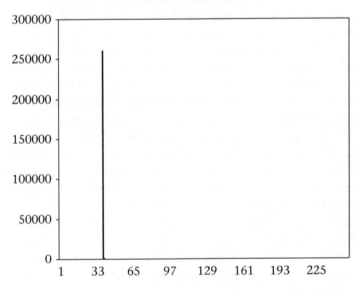

Figure B.1   Sample wavelet transform of an image and its histogram.

Appendix C
Linear mathematics

This appendix presents a selection of topics from linear mathematics that are relevant to this text. We present a discussion of vectors and matrices including methods of manipulating them and an overview of sufficient topics from statistics to enable the material of the text to be understood.

C.1 Matrices and vectors

A *scalar quantity* is represented as a single value. The mass of an object and its length are scalar quantities.

A *vector* is a one-dimensional array of quantities, usually represented as a column:

$$v = \begin{bmatrix} a_1 \\ a_2 \\ \vdots \\ a_n \end{bmatrix} \tag{C.1}$$

A *matrix* is a multi-dimensional array of quantities. It may have, one, two or more dimensions. Images are represented as two-dimensional matrices. Alternatively, the columns of an image could be stacked to form a vector representation.

$$m = \begin{bmatrix} a_{11} & a_{12} & \cdots & a_{1n} \\ a_{21} & a_{22} & \cdots & a_{2n} \\ \vdots & \vdots & \ddots & \vdots \\ a_{m1} & a_{m2} & \cdots & a_{mn} \end{bmatrix} \tag{C.2}$$

The matrix's dimensions are the numbers of rows and columns. The matrix of Equation (C.2) is of dimension $m \times n$.

Two matrices may be added or subtracted, provided they are of the same dimensions. The elements of the combined matrix are the combinations of the equivalent matrix elements.

Two matrices **A** and **B** may be multiplied provided that **B** has the same number of columns as **A** has rows. Elements of the product matrix, $C[i, j]$ are given by:

$$C[i,j] = \sum_k A[i,k]\,B[k,j] \tag{C.3}$$

Matrix multiplication is not associative: $\mathbf{AB} \neq \mathbf{BA}$.

A superscripted T after the matrix indicates that the matrix is transposed: its rows and columns are interchanged:

$$\mathbf{C}^T[i,j] = C[i,j] \tag{C.4}$$

The identity matrix, **I**, is defined as being square (its dimensions are equal) and having all the elements on its leading diagonal equal to one and all other elements equal to zero.

$$\mathbf{I}[i,j] = \begin{bmatrix} 1 & 0 & \cdots & 0 \\ 0 & 1 & \cdots & 0 \\ \vdots & \vdots & \ddots & \vdots \\ 0 & 0 & \cdots & 1 \end{bmatrix} \tag{C.5}$$

A symmetrical matrix has equal elements on either side of the leading diagonal. It is its own transpose.

The inverse of a matrix, $\mathbf{M}^{-1}$ is defined by:

$$\mathbf{M}^{-1}\mathbf{M} = \mathbf{I} \tag{C.6}$$

The eigenvalues, λ, and eigenvectors, v_i, of a matrix, **A**, are defined by the solutions of:

$$|\mathbf{A} - \mathbf{I}\lambda| = 0 \tag{C.7}$$

where $|\cdot|$ signifies the determinant operator. The matrix must be square and the number of eigenvalues/vectors it has is equal to the dimension.

Libraries of functions for computing these quantities are available in the public domain, e.g. Press *et al.* (2002).

C.2 Statistics

C.2.1 Measures of central tendency and spread

Many excellent statistics texts are available, e.g. Spiegel *et al.* (2000). This appendix cannot be a substitute; all it does it to summarise the more important statistical methods used in this text.

The *mean* is defined as the average value of a set of samples:

$$\mu = \frac{1}{N} \sum_{i=1}^{N} x_i \tag{C.8}$$

The *standard deviation* is a measure of the dispersion of a set of values:

$$\sigma^2 = \frac{1}{N} \sum_{i=1}^{N} (x_i - \mu)^2 \tag{C.9}$$

The *histogram* is defined as the frequency that each value is observed in a population of samples, as shown in Figure C.1. The *mode* is the most frequently observed value. The *median* is the value that splits the population into two equal portions: those less than the median and those greater than it. Similarly, centiles are defined that divide the population into 100 equally occupied ranges.

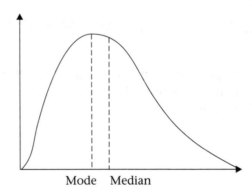

Mode   Median

Figure C.1   Histogram showing mode and median.

C.2.2 Least squares minimisation

This is a technique often used in determining optimal estimators. For example, it was used to design the predictive coder. In use, the estimator is designed to have one or more parameters. A measure of the difference between the value being estimated and the actual value is created. The squared error is computed, since this will always be a positive quantity. An expression for the total squared error is found. This will be minimised with respect to the estimator's parameters. This results in a system of simultaneous equations that are easily solved.

For example, the predictive coder was defined with two parameters:

$$\hat{x}_{i+1} = \alpha x_i + \beta \tag{C.10}$$

The error between the actual pixel value, x_{i+1} and this estimate can be found:

$$\varepsilon_i = \hat{x}_{i+1} - x_{i+1} \tag{C.11}$$

and squared:

$$
\begin{aligned}
\varepsilon_i^2 &= (\hat{x}_{i+1} - x_{i+1})^2 \\
&= (\alpha x_i + \beta - x_{i+1})^2 \\
&= \alpha^2 x_i^2 + \beta^2 + x_{i+1}^2 + 2\alpha\beta x_i - 2\alpha x_i x_{i+1} - 2\beta x_{i+1}
\end{aligned} \tag{C.12}
$$

and summed to give the total squared error:

$$
\begin{aligned}
E &= \sum_i \varepsilon_i^2 \\
&= \sum_i (\alpha^2 x_i^2 + \beta^2 + x_{i+1}^2 + 2\alpha\beta x_i - 2\alpha x_i x_{i+1} - 2\beta x_{i+1})
\end{aligned} \tag{C.13}
$$

The minimisation is performed by differentiating this expression with respect to α and β, equating the result to zero and solving the pair of simultaneous equations that result.

References

Ballard, D. H. and Brown, C. M. (1982). *Computer Vision*. Prentice Hall, Englewood Cliffs, NJ.

Beucher, S. and Meyer, F. (1992). The morphological approach to segmentation: the watershed transformation. In *Mathematical Morphology in Image Processing* (ed. E. Dougherty). Marcel Decker, New York.

Binford, T. C. (1982). Survey of model-based image analysis systems. *Int. J. Robotics Research*, 1, 18–64.

Bracewell, R. N. (2000). *The Fourier Transform and its Applications*. McGraw-Hill, New York.

Burt, P. J. and Adelson, E. H. (1983). The Laplacian pyramid as a compact image code. *IEEE Trans. Communications*, pp. 532–540.

Brooks, R. A. (1981). Symbolic reasoning among 3-D Models and 2-D Images. *Artificial Intelligence*, 17, 285–348.

Canny, J. (1986). A computational approach to edge detection. *IEEE Trans. Pattern Analysis and Machine Intelligence*, 8(6), 679–698.

Castleman, K. R. (1996). *Digital Image Processing*. Prentice Hall, Upper Saddle River, NJ.

Cooley, J. W. and Tukey, J. W. (1965). An algorithm for the machine calculation of complex Fourier Series. *Math. of Comput.*, 19, 297–301.

Cootes, T. F., Cooper, D. H., Taylor, C. J. and Graham, J. (1992). Trainable method of parametric shape description. *Image and Vision Computing*, 10(5), 289–294.

Cootes, T. F., Taylor, C. J., Cooper, D. H. and Graham, J. (1995). Active shape models – their training and application. *Computer Vision and Image Understanding*, 61(1), 38–59.

Dickmans, E. D. and Mysliwetz, B. D. (1992). Recursive 3-D road and relative ego-state recognition. *IEEE Trans. Pattern Analysis and Machine Intelligence*, 14(2), 199–213.

Dougherty, E. (1992). *An Introduction to Morphological Image Processing*. SPIE Press, Bellingham, WA.

Duda, R. O. and Hatt, P. E. (1973). *Pattern Classification and Scene Analysis*. John Wiley & Sons, New York.

Duda, R. O., Hatt, P. E. and Stork, D. G. (2001). *Pattern Classification*. John Wiley & Sons, New York.

Erman, L. D., Hayes-Roth, F., Lesser, V. R. and Reddy, R. (1980). The Hearsay-II speech-understanding system: integrating knowledge to resolve uncertainty. *Computing Surveys*, 12, 213–253.

Fishler, M. A. and Elschlager, R. A. (1973) The representation and matching of pictorial structures. *IEEE Trans Computers*, 22, 67–77.

Forsyth, D. A. and Ponce, J. (2003) *Computer Vision*. Prentice Hall, Upper Saddle River, NJ.

Fourier, J. (1878). *The Analytical Theory of Heat* (transl. A. Freeman). Cambridge University Press, Cambridge.

Freeman, H. (1961). On the encoding of arbitrary geometric configurations. *IEEE Trans. Elec. Computers*, **10**, 260–268.

Freeman, H. (1974). Computer processing of line drawings. *Comput. Surveys*, **6**, 57–97.

Frendendall, G. L. and Behrend, W. L. (1960). Picture quality – procedures for evaluating subjective effects of interference. *Proc. IRE*, **48**, 1030–1034.

Frisby, J. P. (1979). *Seeing: Illusion, Brain and Mind*. Oxford University Press, Oxford.

Fukunaga, K. (1972). *Introduction to Statistical Pattern Recognition*. Academic Press, New York.

Garvey, T. D., Lowrance, J. D. and Fischler, M. A. (1981). An intelligence technique for integrating knowledge from disparate sources. *Proc. Int. Joint Conf. on Artificial Intelligence*, Vancouver, pp. 319–325.

Gee, A. and Cipolla, R. (1996). Fast visual tracking by temporal consensus. *Image and Vision Computing*, **14**(2), 105–114.

Gonzalez, R. C. and Thomason, M. G. (1978). *Syntactic Pattern Recognition: An Introduction*. Addison-Wesley, Reading, MA.

Gonzalez, R. and Woods, R. (2002). *Digital Image Processing*, 2nd edn. Prentice Hall, Upper Saddle River, NJ.

Gregory, R. L. (1997). *Eye and Brain*. Oxford University Press, Oxford.

Hanson, A. R. and Riseman, E. M. (1978). VISIONS: a computer system for interpreting scenes. In *Computer Vision Systems* (eds. A. R. Hanson and E. M. Riseman). Academic Press, New York.

Haralick, R. and Shapiro, L. (1992). *Computer and Robot Vision*, Vols I and II. Addison-Wesley, Reading, MA.

Haralick, R. M., Shanmuhan, S. R. and Dinstein, I. (1973). Textural features for image classification. *IEEE Trans. Syst. Man Cyb.*, **6**(3), 610–621.

Hecht, E. (1998). *Optics*. Addison-Wesley, Reading, MA.

Helmholtz, H. von (1881). *Popular Lectures on Scientific Subjects*. Longmans, London.

Hotelling, H. (1933). Analysis of a complex of statistical variables into principal components. *J. Educ. Psychol.*, **24**, 417–441, 498–520.

Horn, B. K. P. and Schunk, B. G. (1981). Determining optical flow. *Artificial Intelligence*, **17**, 185–203.

Hubel, D. H. (1988). *Eye, Brain and Vision*. Scientific American Library, W.H. Freeman, New York.

Huffman, D. A. (1952). A method for the construction of minimum redundancy codes. *Proc. IRE*, **40**(10), 1098–1101.

Isard, M. A. and Blake, A. (1996). Visual tracking by stochastic propagation of conditional density. *Proc. 4th European Conf. Computer Vision*, pp. 343–356.

Isard, M. and Blake, A. (1998). Condensation – conditional density propagation for visual tracking. *Int. J. Computer Vision*, **29**(1), 5–28.

Jain, R., Kasturi, R. and Schunk, B. (1995) *Machine Vision*. McGraw-Hill, New York.

Kalles, D. and Morris, D. T. (1993). An efficient image skeletonisation algorithm. *Image and Vision Computing*, **11**(9), 588–603.

Kalman, R. E. (1960). A new approach to linear filtering and prediction problems. *Trans. ASME – Journal of Basic Engineering*, **82**(D), 35–45.

Kass, M., Witkin, A. and Terzopoulos, D. (1987). Snakes: active contour models. *Proc. First Int. Conf. Comput. Vision*, London, pp. 259–269.

Kittler, J., Illingworth, J. and Paler, K. (1983). The magnitude accuracy of the template edge detector. *Pattern Recognition*, **16**, 607–613.

Ledley, R. S. (1964). High speed automatic analysis of biomedical pictures. *Science*, **146**, 216–223.

Levine, M. D. and Nazif, A. M. (1985). Rule-based image segmentation: a dynamic control strategy approach. *Computer Vision, Graphics and Image Processing*, **32**, 104–126.

Lindberg, T. (1994). Scale space theory: a basic tool for analysing structures at different scales. *J. Applied Statistics*, **21**(2), 224–270.

Lowe, D. G. (1987). Three dimensional object recognition from single two-dimensional images. *Artificial Intelligence*, **31**, 355–395.

Marr, D. (1982). *Vision*. Freeman, San Francisco.

Marr, D. and Hildreth, E. (1980). Theory of edge detection. *Proc. R. Soc. Lond.*, **B207**, 187–217.

Marr, D. and Poggio, T. (1979). A Computational theory of human stereo vision. *Proc. R. Soc. Lond.*, **B204**, 301–328.

Minsky, M. (1975). A framework for representing knowledge. In *The Psychology of Computer Vision* (ed. P. H. Winston). McGraw-Hill, New York.

Moravec, H. P. (1977). Towards automatic visual obstacle avoidance. In *Proc. Int. Joint Conference on Artificial Intelligence*, Cambridge, MA, p. 584.

Myler, H. R. and Weeks, A. R. (1993). *The Pocket Handbook of Image Processing Algorithms in C*. Prentice Hall, Upper Saddle River, NJ.

Newton, I. (1931). *Optiks, or a Treatise of the Reflections Refractions Inflections and Colour*. Bell, New York.

Parker, J. R. (1997). *Algorithms for Image Processing and Computer Vision*. John Wiley & Sons, New York.

Press, W., Flannery, B. P., Teukolsky, S. A. and Vetterling, W. T. (2002). *Numerical Recipes in C++: The Art of Scientific Computing*. Cambridge University Press, Cambridge.

Rosenfeld, A., Hummel, R. A. and Zucker, S. W. (1976). Scene labelling by relaxation operations. *IEEE Trans. Syst. Man and Cybern*, **6**, 420–433.

Rosin, P. L. (1997). Techniques for assessing polygonal approximations of curves. *IEEE Trans. Pattern Analysis and Machine Intelligence*, **19**(6), 659–666.

Schalkoff, R. J. (1989). *Digital Image Processing and Computer Vision*. John Wiley & Sons, New York.

Serra, J. (1982). *Image Analysis and Mathematical Morphology*. Academic Press, New York.

Serra, J. (ed.) (1988). *Image Analysis and Mathematical Morphology*, Vol. 2. Academic Press, New York.

Shafer, G. (1981). Constructive probability. *Synthesise*, **48**, 1–60.

Shapiro, L. S. and Stockman, G. C. (2001). *Computer Vision*. Prentice Hall, Upper Saddle River, NJ.

Smith, S. M. (1996). Flexible filter neighbourhood designation. In *Proc. 13th Int. Conf. on Pattern Recognition*, Vienna, 25–29 August, pp. 206–212.

Sonka, M., Hlavac, V. and Boyle, R. (1999). *Image Processing, Analysis and Machine Vision*. PWS Publishing, New York.

Spiegel, M. R. *et al.* (2000). *Schaum's Outline of Probability and Statistics*. McGraw-Hill, New York.

Starner, T. and Pentland, A. (1995). Real-time American Sign Language recognition from video using Hidden Markov Models. In *Proc. Int. Symp. Computer Vision*, Coral Gables, USA. IEEE Computer Society Press.

Stroud, J. M. (1956). The fine structure of psychological time. In *Information Theory in Psychology* (ed. H. Quastler). Free Press, Glencoe, Ill.

Swain, M. J. and Ballard, D. H. (1991). Colour indexing. *Int. J. Computer Vision*, **7**(1), 11–32.

Swain, M. J. and Strickland, M. (eds.) (1991). Promising directions in active vision. University of Chicago *Technical Report CS 91–27*.

Trucco, E. and Verri, A. (1998). *Introductory Techniques for 3-D Computer Vision*. Prentice Hall, Upper Saddle River, NJ.

Umbaugh, S. E. (1998). *Computer Vision and Image Processing: a Practical Approach Using CVIP Tools*. Prentice Hall, Upper Saddle River, NJ.

Voss, K. and Suesse, H. (1997). Invariant fitting of planar objects by primitives. *IEEE Trans. Pattern Analysis and Machine Intelligence*, **19**(1), 80–84.

Wren, C., Azerbayejani, A., Darrell, T. and Pentland, A. (1997). pFinder: real-time tracking of the human body. *IEEE Trans. Pattern Analysis and Machine Intelligence*, **19**, 780–785.

Young, T. (1807). *Lectures on Natural Philosophy*, Vol II. Johnson, London.

Yuille, A., Cohen, D. S. and Halliman, P. W. (1986). Feature extraction from faces using deformable templates. *IEEE Proc. CVPR*, San Diego, pp. 104–109.

Zahn, C. T. and Roskies, R. Z. (1972). Fourier descriptors for plane closed curves. *IEEE Trans. Comput.*, **C21**(3), 269–281.

Ziv, J. and Lempel, A. (1977). A Universal algorithm for sequential data compression. *IEEE Trans. Info. Theory*, **23**(3), 337–343.

Ziv, J. and Lempel, A. (1978). Compression of individual sequences via variable rate coding. *IEEE Trans. Info. Theory*, **24**(5), 530–536.

Index